Liveness in Modern Music

This study investigates the idea and practice of liveness in modern music. Understanding what makes music live in an ever-changing musical and technological terrain is one of the more complex and timely challenges facing scholars of current music, where liveness is typically understood to represent performance and to stand in opposition to recording, amplification, and other methods of electronically mediating music. The book argues that liveness itself emerges from dynamic tensions inherent in mediated musical contexts—tensions between music as an acoustic human utterance, and musical sound as something produced or altered by machines. Sanden analyzes liveness in mediatized music (music for which electronic mediation plays an intrinsically defining role), exploring the role this concept plays in defining musical meaning. In discussions of music from both popular and classical traditions, Sanden demonstrates how liveness is performed by acts of human expression in productive tension with the electronic machines involved in making this music, whether on stage or on recording. Liveness is not a fixed ontological state that exists in the absence of electronic mediation, but rather a dynamically performed assertion of human presence within a technological network of communication. This book provides new insights into how the ideas of performance and liveness continue to permeate the perception and reception of even highly mediatized music within a society so deeply invested, on every level, with the use of electronic technologies.

Paul Sanden teaches in the Department ~~~~~ at the University of Lethbridge, Canad

D1145730

Routledge Research in Music

Liveness in Modern Music
Musicians, Technology, and the Perception of Performance

Paul Sanden

Routledge
Taylor & Francis Group
NEW YORK   LONDON

First published 2013
by Routledge
711 Third Avenue, New York, NY 10017

Simultaneously published in the UK
by Routledge
2 Park Square, Milton Park, Abingdon, Oxon OX14 4RN

First issued in paperback 2017

Routledge is an imprint of the Taylor & Francis Group,
an informa business

© 2013 Taylor & Francis

Library of Congress Cataloging-in-Publication Data
Sanden, Paul.
   Liveness in modern music : musicians, technology, and the perception
of performance / Paul Sanden. — 1st ed.
      p. cm. — (Routledge research in music)
   Includes bibliographical references and index.
   1.   Music—Performance—History.   2.   Musical perception.
   3.   Music—Psychological aspects.   I. Title.
   ML457.S23 2012
   781.1'1—dc23
   2012031561

ISBN 13: 978-1-138-10797-7 (pbk)
ISBN 13: 978-0-415-89540-8 (hbk)

Typeset in Sabon
by IBT Global.

For Evan, who never lacks liveness

Contents

Musical Examples, Figures, and Tables

Acknowledgments and Notes on the Text

As countless authors before me have recognized, and as countless authors after me will undoubtedly repeat, undertaking a project such as this requires immense amounts of commitment, sacrifice, and patience not only from the author but also from those around him or her in the home, the workplace, and the broader community. I owe debts of gratitude, and return favors, to far more people than are listed here, but these are the people to whom I am most indebted.

My thanks go first and foremost to the co-supervisors of my PhD dissertation at the University of Western Ontario, from which this book arose: Jonathan Burston, for giving tirelessly of so much of his own time and energies (even long after his "contractual obligations" to do so had expired) and for introducing me to so many useful ideas and theories (and clarifying them for me when I missed the point); Sandra Mangsen, for keeping me on task and ensuring that I found a way to make these ideas work in a musicological study and for making me think often and hard about what performance is all about. I also wish to thank Richard Parks for his helpful comments on the final draft of the dissertation and for his sage advice throughout my entire degree program. Special thanks go to Omar Daniel, who consulted with me about this project from the early stages and also shared freely his time and materials during my research into his own work; to Gordon Mumma, who generously provided me with several documents pertaining to his piece *Hornpipe*; and to Paul Théberge, for sharing with me some of his (then) unpublished work on Glenn Gould.

I also benefited greatly from sharing my developing ideas with friends, colleagues, and other mentors throughout this long process, and I wish to thank them for their helpful questions and comments. During my time at the University of Western Ontario as a student and as a professor, Norma Coates, Anthony Cushing, Anita Hardeman, Bryn Hughes, Mathieu Langlois, Keir Keightley, Makoto Mikawa, Catherine Nolan, John Pippen, and Richard Semmens (in addition to those mentioned above) were warm and generous not only in general but also in their support of and interest in my work. Lisa Philpott, the immensely clever and talented reference librarian for the University of Western Ontario's music library, has more than earned her own entire sentence here in recognition of my immense gratitude for her generosity, her professional support, and her friendship.

In my new home at the University of Lethbridge, I have been welcomed and encouraged by all my colleagues (and a great many students as well), but I feel particularly indebted already, for their support and for helping me get through the first year in a new place, to Brian Black, Ed Jurkowski, Deanna Oye, Arlan Schultz, Peter Visentin, and Janet Youngdahl. Mark Richards and Andrew Stewart, who were also newcomers in 2011, have helped me settle in with them and have graciously found time to take an interest in my project even as they, too, work to adjust to their new environment.

Many of the people already listed have read through earlier versions of the work represented in these pages; I would also like to thank Ananay Aguilar, Garreth Broesche, and Nicholas Cook for their generosity in offering me the same favor. This book is much better for all your efforts, and a great many of its strong points are a reflection of your immensely helpful suggestions. Murray Dineen, William Echard, David Gramit, Sherry Lee, and Alan Stanbridge offered similarly helpful insights at various conferences and colloquia. In addition, because this is largely a book about listening to music, I must express my immense appreciation for those friends and family members with whom I first learned to listen. Many hours of my life have been spent sharing sound-space with Trevor Borycki; Jason Caslor; my brothers, Joel and Adam Sanden; Jonas Thompson; and Regan Woytowich. Each of you has opened my ears in new ways, and for that you will always have my gratitude.

Finally, I wish to express how grateful I am to my family for all they have done not only during the years that I have dedicated to this project but in all the years before then. To my parents, Rick and Janet, for helping me learn about the beauty and power of the written word, for their unwavering support, and for understanding why I couldn't visit as often as I would have liked; and to Ross and Dale, for giving up time with their daughter so that I could finish and for demonstrating more pride and belief in me than any son-in-law has a right to ask: I offer my most humble appreciation. To my brothers, Joel and Adam, thank you for your words of encouragement. To my wife, Carolyn, especially, thank you for being here with me every step of the way and for making me better in everything that I do. This could never have happened without you. And finally, to our beautiful and marvelous son, Evan: What can I say? You light me up.

Most of Chapter 3 and a small portion of Chapter 1 appeared in "Hearing Glenn Gould's Body: Corporeal Liveness in Recorded Music," in *Current Musicology* 88 (Fall 2009). Chapter 6, with very few differences, was published in "Virtual Liveness and Sounding Cyborgs: John Oswald's 'Vane,'" in *Popular Music* 31, no. 1 (2011). I would like to thank the editors and publishers of these journals for their assistance in making these chapters better and for granting permission to use these materials in this book. I would also like to thank Liz Levine and the editorial team at Routledge/

Taylor & Francis for taking on this project, and for so patiently and seam-lessly walking a first-time author through the whole process.

TO THE READER

I offer here a few notes that will help clarify some of the details in the fol-lowing pages:

Pitch nomenclature: Throughout the book, I adopt the Helmholtz system of octave designation, with C beginning the octave below middle C, *c'* the octave at middle C, *c''* the octave above that, and so forth. See Lloyd and Rastall ("Pitch Nomenclature") for further explanation.

Date of composition, publication, recording: In many of my discussions of the compositions, recordings, and publications under scrutiny in this book, it has been worthwhile to recognize multiple "dates of completion," as we are often dealing with different dates for the composition of a work, the publication of its score, its recording, the reissue of that recording, and so forth. My standard practice is to provide a date immediately before or after the name of a piece to indicate its accepted date of completion or date of first recording (if dealing with music first released in a recorded format rather than in a published score, for instance). Any further reference (for example, to a subsequently published score or reissued recording) follows standard author-date format and directs you to that particular resource in the reference list at the end of the book. Thus, for example, the score for Stockhausen's *Mikrophonie II* (1965) can be consulted in Stockhausen (1974), and the piece can be heard on Stockhausen (1995a). Carly Simon's 1972 hit "You're So Vain" is found on Simon (1990).

SUPPLEMENTARY MATERIALS

I would also like to direct the reader to my website, www.paulsanden. com, to access many supplementary materials for this book. In many cases, the reader will benefit greatly if he or she is able to consult the audio and visual materials cited in the analyses I undertake. Some of these, such as the recordings of Glenn Gould and The White Stripes, are very easy to track down. Others, however, are more obscure or, in a couple of rare instances, unavailable through the usual channels. Web links and embedded media files are therefore provided to assist in the task of locating and/or access-ing these materials. I have also provided many other Web links to augment my discussions of various composers, artworks, musical genres, subcul-tures, and so forth. If, as you are reading, you can think of other materials that would add to this resource, I invite you to suggest them through my website's contact page. Finally, I have included a glossary to provide further definitions and explanations of many of the terms introduced in the book. The very broad field of "Modern Music" encompasses an immense variety of musical genres and styles, many of which are addressed in these pages. I therefore expect that my readers will come from a broad range of backgrounds and may not always be familiar with some of the language that I use. I hope that this glossary helps mitigate this particular hurdle.

1 Introduction

The performance had already started (performance is no better than show, but most of these words just don't work properly anymore).

David Toop, *Haunted Weather*

WHY *LIVENESS*? (AND WHAT IS IT?)

Consider the following hypothetical (although highly plausible) scenario: A well-known hip-hop act appears on a live television show as that evening's musical guest, performing its latest top-selling single. The identity of the show does not much matter for our purposes—late-night talk shows and other live entertainment programs have featured musical guests for decades as part of their standard formats. Nor does the identity of the hip-hop act much matter, as the scenario I describe could apply to recent televised performances by a number of artists. The performance itself involves several identifiable "categories" of musical utterance, and it is to the diversity of, and relationships between, these categories that I wish to draw my readers' attention.

A DJ, hunched over a table at center stage, establishes a rhythmic background layer (a *beat*) using a variety of prerecorded and synthesized materials: A basic repetitive beat of recognizably (though synthetic) drumlike sounds is set in motion with the push of a button or click of a mouse and will continue to loop for the remainder of the performance. This beat is punctuated and embellished periodically by the DJ's live manipulations of recorded sound, as he drags (*scratches*) a couple of vinyl records back and forth with incredibly dextrous skill beneath the tone arms of twin turntables. The precise motions of his hands are difficult to track, as fingers not in contact with the records at any one moment are moving quickly from one switch, dial, or fader to another, all these movements breathing new life and new identities into musical recordings once considered fixed in their aural properties (this type of performance is often referred to as *turntablism*).

Standing farther upstage and off to one side are four horn players—the musical and racial lineage from hip-hop back through funk, soul, early R&B, and jazz is foregrounded by repeated trumpet and saxophone riffs during the tune's chorus, or *hook*. On the other side of the stage stands a group of back-up singers, who also contribute to the hook with harmonized vocals that contrast with the rapped verses. And over all this activity reigns the MC, the rapper, standing in front of the rest of the group and delivering her lyrics with appropriate attitude and posturing. The arm holding the microphone is bent sharply, the elbow raised parallel to the MC's face, with the microphone itself in almost direct contact with her lips so it catches all the pops and sibilants of her vocal apparatus at extremely close range. Moreover, the microphone clearly feeds these vocals through a signal processor: The voice that emanates from the loudspeakers has been made to sound as though it is coming from a megaphone that cannot quite handle the full frequency and dynamic ranges of the vocalist. The MC paces deliberately back and forth across the front of the stage as she raps, gesticulating at appropriate moments not just with her free arm and hand but with her entire body. As the spoken verses give way to the sung hooks, her physical demeanor changes to emphasize the musical contrasts achieved within the song's overall structure.

At the end of the performance, the studio audience applauds wildly, many of its members suitably satisfied to have witnessed in a live performance the track they had been listening to on a daily basis via the earbuds attached to their portable MP3 players. Some have no idea that the DJ's turntable performance, presented in a seemingly improvisatory manner on stage, was captured on the "original" recording in multiple takes and pieced together for maximum effectiveness; or that the four horn players they just saw and heard were replicating the studio performance of one adept musician, who recorded each of the four parts in turn so the producer could layer them together in the final mix. Other, more informed fans are aware of these distinctions in general practice between studio recording and live performance and are impressed with how successfully the spirit and overall sound of the recording were replicated in this live setting.[1]

The following day, a digital copy of the television broadcast of this performance is uploaded to the Internet, and over the following weeks and months multiple links to this data file and its copies are circulated in e-mails and, even more frequently, on social networking sites. Online viewers share their impressions of the performance, praising or condemning it for various reasons: the physical intensity and effectiveness of the MC's overall delivery, the apparent skill of the DJ at the turntables, the obvious mistake made by one of the saxophonists as she fumbled one of the riffs, the similarly unexpected lyrical changes (when compared to the studio recording) made to a single phrase in the song's second verse, and so forth. Some even compare this live performance to one that they saw on a different television program a few weeks earlier or to live performances in various arenas throughout North America they were lucky enough to attend. Several contributors also draw comparisons between these live performances and the song's studio-produced music video, which depicts much of the same physical choreography enacted by the MC in her live performance. Throughout the majority of this discussion, and also in the individual experiences of most others who have seen this performance but have not participated in the discussion, one significant common element of perception remains consistent, despite the unique inflections of each interpretation: As I have attempted to convey in the language of my description, most witnesses to this musical event experience it as *some type* of *live performance* (whether they see it in person, on television at the initial time of broadcast, or on the Internet in the following months).

I emphasize the qualifying words *some type*: As has been repeatedly argued in recent years, most extensively by Philip Auslander (2002, 2005, 2008), *liveness* is a rather fluid concept, contingent upon historical context, cultural tradition, implicated technologies, and various other factors for its exact articulation. Whereas live music was once understood simply as musical performance that was experienced in person—what I call *traditional liveness*—rather than on a recording, the current state of performance can no longer be suitably served by such a simple binary reduction (live/recorded), because many other musical contexts exist, seemingly between these poles, in which liveness plays an important defining role.[2] Whereas many elements of this particular musical event can be singled out as evidence *against* defining it conventionally as a live performance— the most obvious of which might be its existence as a televised event, its reliance on prerecorded materials, and its continued circulation as a recording long after the moment of its initial utterance—nevertheless, the existence of a temporally continuous performance before a group of in-studio audience members would be sufficient reason for most viewers to maintain that "live" classification. If questioned further, many would undoubtedly allow that this performance was not *fully* live or was not live in the purest sense (because of the factors just listed). They would still wish to use the word *live*, however, to distinguish this unique recorded event from a typical studio recording, which most people, particularly among hip-hop's fan base, understand to be the product of many hours of work in one or several recording studios.

My task in this book, simply stated, is to address why and how the word *live* is still used in such modern musical contexts, despite its apparent ontological inappropriateness in many of those situations; to offer an account of the current state not of live performance itself but of its attendant *concept* of liveness. More specifically, I propose here a theoretical framework for understanding how the concept of liveness is active in the creation of music's meaning, especially (although not exclusively) at an aesthetic level. As is apparent already from the description with which I begin this chapter, the overall terrain of modern musical performances and their recorded representations is a highly complex one in which to map the meaning of such a concept as liveness. As suggested above, this concept's early history demonstrates a more straightforward social and musical context, which is important to consider more fully if we are to make any sense of the current meanings of liveness.

With the widespread proliferation of recorded music in the first half of the twentieth century, for the first time in history, the adjective *live* was required to distinguish between different types of musical experiences. What was once referred to simply as *music* or *performance* now became identified as *live music* or *live performance*. Recorded music, on the other hand, often picked up identifying (and derogatory) adjectives, such as *canned* and *mechanical*.[3] Although musical recordings had many advocates, the use of the word *live* usually carried with it a particular value judgment, even if only implicitly: Despite whatever benefits that recording technologies may have offered, live music was typically considered more real, more authentic, and in the final balance, more desirable. As Sarah Thornton argues:

> Liveness became the truth of music, the seeds of genuine culture. Records, by contrast, were false prophets of pseudo-culture.
> . . . The expression "live music" soaked up the aesthetic and ethical connotations of life-versus-death, human-versus-mechanical, creative-versus-imitative. (1995, 42)

Despite the considerable increase in the frequency and complexity of the use of electronic technologies in modern music since the early twentieth century, much of the ideology originally implicated in the concept of liveness has remained constant. The term *live* still carries with it a defining connection to unmediated musical performance along with the aesthetic and ideological values associated with that performance. What have changed are the diversity of contexts in which the concept of musical liveness is now invoked and the ontological makeup of those musical contexts (i.e., their essential categories of existence as strictly performed acoustic sound, as prerecorded and replayed sound, etc.). As the ontologically complex televised performance described above partially demonstrates, the range of musical experiences in the early twenty-first century includes (and often combines), among other categories, live performances, live broadcasts, live recordings, live performances *of* recordings, and live performances of electronically synthesized sound. In all these situations, a concept of liveness plays a central part in the creation of musical meaning. The fact that liveness still exists for many musickers even in situations that are not live (according to traditional definition) is a testament to its power as a concept through which meaning is interpreted.[4] That is, if liveness were still strictly understood only as representing an ontological category in firm opposition to recorded music, even the idea of a live televised performance would be incomprehensible.

As a concept, however, liveness can inform one's perception of a given musical experience, despite its ontological makeup; it can provide a perspective from which musical meaning is gleaned,[5] even when audiences are faced simultaneously with the supposedly oppositional categories of live and recorded sound. Further consideration of our hypothetical hip-hop performance demonstrates some of the different ways in which the concept of liveness is invoked while also highlighting the extremely complex relationships established between the categories *performance* and *recording/*

mediation in the construction of this concept. Perhaps the most obvious reason for our turn to the idea of liveness in this instance is, as noted above, the performance's initial occurrence before a live audience in the television studio. That is, witnesses were present at the same time and in the same space as the initial performance, a condition that lies at the heart of the liveness concept for most musickers. Many of those watching the initial broadcast of this performance on their televisions would also understand the performance as live in a temporal sense, even though they are not present in the same physical space as the performers. They are, after all, witnessing this performance in the moment of its initial utterance.[6]

My description of this entire scenario also mentions some potential public (online) responses, including the singling out of individual elements of the live performance for praise or condemnation. I cite the demonstrations of physical skill and energy by the DJ and MC and the unexpected variances from the known musical text (i.e., the recording) in this particular performance, whether intentional (the MC's lyrical changes) or unintentional (the saxophonist's mistake). Recognition of these elements of the performance reflects common observations about the corporeal grounding of live performance in the actions of performers' bodies, on one hand, and the spontaneous and unexpected nature of live performance—its "non-take-two-ness"[7]—on the other. Further appeal to common perceptions of liveness can be found in the group's incorporation of traditional acoustic instrumentalists (the horn section) and vocalists within an environment that otherwise features a high level of mediation (the DJ's wholesale reliance on recorded and synthesized sound and the signal processing applied to the MC's vocal performance).

If these elements all add to the perception of liveness in the context of this performance, many seemingly contrasting elements may work against such a perception. Most obviously, this live performance is only live in the most traditional sense for the few hundred members of the studio audience. Everyone else sees and hears a recording (albeit a *live* recording). Whereas the initial television audience may experience this performance as a live broadcast, the subsequent Internet audience can claim no such temporal proximity to the initial event. The performances of the two central musicians also trouble traditional understandings of musical liveness. Unlike the members of the horn section and the vocalists, the DJ himself does not physically produce musical sound, despite the physicality of his performance; he recalls it from prerecorded and preprogrammed sources and arranges it anew. For her part, the MC produces new sound as a direct result of (some of) her body's movements, but this acoustic sound is immediately lost to the amplification and modifications that begin with her microphone and end with the loudspeakers.

At a more complex level, the reception of this performance in constant reference to a recorded original and the seeming evaluative equality of live performance, televised performance, recording, and Internet video for most fans reflect Auslander's observations about the wholesale confluence of live and mediated events within modern culture (2008, esp. 10–72). Ontological distinctions that were once fiercely defended between live and recorded modes of musical reception seem to mean little any more, particularly for many fans of popular music, with respect to their ability to glean aesthetic appreciation from the musical event. The recorded seems live, and the live is heard as (or at least in reference to) the recorded.

Two significant factors are already apparent in this preliminary discussion about the complexities of modern musical liveness. First, the concept of liveness persists for many musickers, even when the musical event in which they participate is not strictly live in a traditional sense. Second, this concept acts in constant reference to the opposing implications of electronic mediation (primarily recording). On an ontological level, liveness first emerged from the distinctions between recorded and unrecorded music, distinctions that, as we have already established, have lost much of their significance in recent years. On a conceptual level, these historic distinctions still exist, or the idea of liveness itself would have long since lost all cultural currency.[8] If such a concept as *the live* still exists, such a concept as *the not-live* must also exist. Complications arise, however, when one attempts to draw a clear defining line between the two, because modern musickers regularly allow for significant amounts of mediation even *within* their conceptualizations of liveness. From this perspective, then, I argue that the perception of liveness depends not necessarily on the total eschewal of electronic mediation but on the persistent perception of *characteristics* of music's live performance within the context of—and often with the help of—various levels of such mediation. Liveness represents a perceived *trace* of that which *could be live* in the face of the threat of further or complete electronic mediation and modification.

Defining more precisely what this concept represents, and its different manifestations, constitutes a significant part of my work in all the chapters that follow. Indeed, I argue throughout this book that the most useful way to understand liveness is as a flexible concept, with different shades of meaning for different musickers in different times and places and in different musical contexts. From the outset, however, I clarify some basic premises (to be further developed in Chapter 2) that summarize my discussion to this point and that underlie all my forthcoming discussions:

- The concept of liveness derives from the concept of music as performed.
- The perception of liveness in a particular musical experience, then, amounts to the perception of performance—not necessarily *actual* performance, but some characteristic that resonates with a particular musicker's concept of performance.[9] As Simon Emmerson (2007, 93) argues, the conceptualization of liveness rests on *perception*, not *actuality*.
- Finally, liveness emerges not just from this perception of performance but from the dialectical tensions inherent between this perception and

the perceived encroachment of electronic technologies into the terrain of fully human performance. In this sense, the concept of liveness usually represents authenticity and other musical values that are associated with performance to protect against claims of inauthenticity that are often associated with the musical use of electronic technologies. Put another way: Values of traditional performance + Threat of technological encroachment on these values = Liveness concept.

Various examples in this book also demonstrate that the use of electronic technologies themselves in many contexts acts to *enhance* the perception of liveness, not just in a reactionary sense but in the ability of those technologies to simulate or augment some recognizable characteristic of live performance. In such cases, the dialectical tensions between performance and recording, natural and artificial, human and machine, and similar discursive pairings are deeply implicated.

SOME TERMINOLOGY: *MUSICKING* AND *MEDIATIZATION*

It is important to emphasize that I understand liveness to be a concept working at all levels of musical experience. This broad approach to the topic has emerged from the recognition of two important factors during the course of my research, both of which are worth addressing at this point. First, it is apparent that liveness matters to people engaged in all different aspects of musical activity: Composers, performers, recordists, concertgoers, record buyers, and other musickers not so easily classified have all contributed to the broad discourse on this topic. For this reason, Christopher Small's earnest reminder (1998) that all participants in a musical experience—a social experience that involves much more than the presentation of a composer's work for a passive audience—share in the creation of identity, meaning, and significance attached to that experience informs the arguments that I put forward here; I have been and will continue using his term *musickers* to signify this broad category of people when appropriate. In an effort to reflect the importance of the diversity of perspectives present within any group of musickers, I have attempted to develop a theory of liveness with as much applicability to these diverse perspectives as possible. In other words, I move quite freely from consideration of the composer's perspective, to the performer's, to the record producer's, to the listener's, stopping at many points in between (indeed, it is very often apparent that different musickers may share a similar experience of liveness, regardless of their precise roles; moreover, many musickers occupy multiple roles simultaneously, many of which are not so easily defined as those of composer, performer, producer, and audience).

The second factor that informs my approach to liveness is that this concept applies with equal significance to many different genres and subgenres of musical practice. Rock musicians, symphony attendees, hip-hop turntablists, connoisseurs of classical piano recordings, composers of live electronic art music, not to mention musickers in fields of musical activity not addressed in this book, such as non-Western musical styles and traditions—all have opportunity to encounter the concept of liveness in their musicking. Just as it cannot be confined to considerations of only one type of musical activity, the concept of liveness cannot be confined to considerations of only one musical genre or tradition.[10] The primary reason for this is rather obvious but no less worth stating for its apparentness: Very little (if any) musical activity of the late twentieth and early twenty-first centuries has entirely escaped the profound influence of electronic mediation.

Because the concept of liveness itself derives from dialectical tensions between one's understanding and perception of performance on the one hand and electronic mediation on the other, a musical experience of any kind in which electronic mediation plays a part—that is, the vast majority of modern musical experiences—may provide fertile ground for a discussion of this concept. The musicking I address in this book, therefore, spans several genres and traditions. Recordings by Glenn Gould and the White Stripes, live electronic art music from the 1960s and from the early twenty-first century, and sample-based plunderphonics and turntablism provide my primary case-study material, and numerous other examples are featured in these discussions less prominently where appropriate. I hope that all these examples provide a clear demonstration of the broad area of practice and discourse that I call *mediatized performance*, in which liveness constitutes a central signifying aesthetic element.

The term *mediatization* has been employed usefully in the study of mass-mediated culture, particularly by Jean Baudrillard (1981) and, following him, Auslander (2008), to indicate the extent to which those media have influenced and shaped cultural activity. Auslander's use of this term is especially germane to my own study, due to his strong focus on theatrical and musical performance. For Auslander, mediatized performance is, first, "performance that is circulated on television, as audio or video recordings, and in other forms based in technologies of reproduction" (2008, 4).[11] The greater significance of this characterization lies primarily in how Auslander expands on these "other forms" and in his observation that mediatization has come to dominate what he calls "the cultural economy": He argues repeatedly that the vast majority of performance, even (or especially) live performance, exists in constant reference to models presented by the mass media. Thus, theater productions imitate the televisual, live performances of pop songs invoke their recorded "originals," and so forth. Mediatized performance, then, is not just performance that is mediated (via recordings, television, and other technologies), but, more importantly, it is performance that "depends on mediation for its significance" (Auslander 2008, 34), even if only by indirect reference to that mediation.

Auslander's concerns with the relationship between liveness and mediatization are primarily ontological and epistemological. Ontologically speaking, live performance in its purest sense no longer exists in the vast majority of cases: It has become mediatized. Epistemologically speaking (i.e., on the level at which we *understand* or *know* its identity), live performance has absorbed much of its identity, characterization, and meaning from mediatized forms of culture. These ontological and epistemological conditions of mediatization have resulted from the dominance of mass-mediated forms of culture *over* live performance within the cultural economy, with very real implications for the fiscal economy. Auslander repeatedly demonstrates the extent to which ubiquitous mediatized performance ultimately serves the economic ends of mass-mediated culture (and of the corporations that stand to profit from the circulation of that culture), basing many of these demonstrations on his thesis that "whatever distinction we may have supposed there to be between live and mediatized events is collapsing because live events are increasingly either made to be reproduced or are becoming ever more identical with mediatized ones" (2008, 35).

Although he argues that liveness is best understood as a flexible concept, which is especially contingent in its formation on different historical, social, economic, and other cultural factors, Auslander's focus on proving the ubiquitous mediatization of live performance in modern Western culture (an ontological, epistemological, and ultimately economic concern) allows little room for realizing the theoretical potential of understanding just *how* the concept of liveness itself is formed in all its flexibility and diversity. Moreover, shortly after stating that "the emerging definition of liveness may be built primarily around the audience's affective experience" (Auslander 2008, 62) of mediatized performance, he discounts several of "the audience's" common understandings of liveness (such as communal interaction, spontaneity, and presence) as invalid on ontological grounds, arguing instead that the definitions of liveness and mediatized performance really derive from their relationships to the cultural economy (2008, 63–72). Rather than recognizing the still-vital conceptual differences apparent in comparisons of live performance and electronically mediated culture, Auslander remains fixated on the ontological encroachment of the latter into the domain of the former.[12]

I wish to recognize more fully the role of the *perceiver* of liveness in my discussion, whether this be a member of "the audience" of mass-mediated culture, a performer, a composer, a critic, or any other musicker involved in the musical event in question. In other words, common understandings of liveness, such as those cited and discounted by Auslander, obviously constitute important aspects of a collective liveness concept, regardless of their ontological veracity. Ultimately, I argue that a liveness concept shared by everyone in exactly the same way does not exist. What I refer to here is an understanding of this concept that allows for a maximum diversity of experiences rather than one that disqualifies many of those experiences as invalid and misinformed. The significant factor here is that the concept of liveness persists even where (as Auslander rightly demonstrates) traditional live performance does not. One way to investigate different formations of this concept is to turn to the musical artifact/event itself, not just in its socioeconomic context but as an aesthetic experience. Auslander's own explanations of mediatization point to an additional potential use of this term, which features relatively little in his discussions but allows for the type of theory I am proposing here. Performance—or the mediated representation of performance—very often "depends on mediation for its significance" not just at broader social or economic levels (as Auslander intends) but also at an aesthetic level. In other words, the significance and meaning of a mediatized aesthetic artefact (a musical performance or a pop record, for instance) very often emerge from the ways in which electronic media are employed in its creation.

I therefore employ the term *mediatization* when I wish to emphasize, at the musical level, the extent to which electronic *mediation* (a comparatively neutral term) factors in the creation of aesthetic meaning. Of course, as my discussions demonstrate, the impact of mediatization very often goes beyond the purely aesthetic, as when the musical impact of a particular technology entwines with cultural ideologies surrounding its use and signification (such as gender-coded performances of the electric guitar in rock music, for instance). But in theorizing the aesthetic significance of processes of mediatization, one also places the discussion of liveness in the aesthetic realm, which is the primary goal of this study. If we accept that modern concepts of liveness emerge from dialectical tensions between the conceptual categories of performance and electronic mediation, with both categories remaining equally and vitally "in the mix," then we may arrive at a better understanding of how this concept contributes so significantly to our reception and aesthetic appreciation of mediatized performance. For Auslander, the live is perceived in reference to the mediatized (it *is* mediatized). I propose here, and argue throughout this book, that the mediatized is also perceived in reference to the live (despite its reliance on electronic mediation, it is to many musickers still imbued with liveness).

That debates over liveness still flourish, even within the increasingly mediatized performance environment that Auslander identifies, is a testament to the central importance of this concept in navigating such an environment. *Traditional* liveness may have succumbed to mediatization over the past half century, but this very development has made *new* concepts of liveness an increasingly essential and vital element of many musickers' relationships with modern musical performance. The desire for recognizably human elements in an increasingly mediatized culture maintains a great deal of significance with respect to our understanding and appreciation of the music made within this culture. This truth becomes especially apparent if we approach liveness as an element of musical and aesthetic significance, adding it to the musicologist's toolbox of musical parameters worthy of study and analysis. Just as careful attention to elements of pitch, rhythm, texture, and structure yield for the musicologist valuable insights into a given musical artifact's potential meanings and significances, so too does attention to its communicative context (i.e., its presentation and reception), of which liveness has become a central element in the late twentieth and early twenty-first centuries. Because liveness has so much to do with how individual sights and sounds are perceived, its study allows a unique opportunity to link these sights and sounds—as aesthetic elements—directly to the socially situated communicative process and to the diversity of individual subjectivities found within this social context.[13]

PRACTICING A THEORY OF LIVENESS: APPROACHES AND METHODOLOGIES

In Chapter 2, I elaborate further on the primary theoretical ideas underlying this study. The remaining five chapters then put these theories into practice in individual readings/hearings of liveness in different examples of mediatized music. The central governing principle of these theories is that the concept of liveness is perceived and articulated from a number of different perspectives, each corresponding to an identifiable characteristic of traditional performance. Drawing heavily from discourses on performance from a number of disciplines and musical traditions, I have identified seven "categories" of liveness and explain and contextualize each of them with respect to the discourses from which it has emerged. Some of these categories have already been invoked in this introduction, such as the temporal sense in which television and radio broadcasts may be live. In another vein, my description of the televised hip-hop performance, like many descriptions of liveness, focuses on the corporeality of the performers. The full list of categories is as follows:

- *Temporal Liveness:* Music is *live* during the time of its initial utterance.
- *Spatial Liveness:* Music is *live* in the physical space of its initial utterance.
- *Liveness of Fidelity:* Music is *live* when it is perceived as faithful to its initial utterance, its unmediated (or *less* mediated) origins, or an imagined unmediated ideal.
- *Liveness of Spontaneity:* Music is *live* when, in its utterance, it demonstrates the spontaneity and unpredictability of human performance.
- *Corporeal Liveness:* Music is *live* when it demonstrates a perceptible connection to an acoustic sounding body.
- *Interactive Liveness:* Music is *live* when it emerges from various interactions between performing partners and/or between performers and listeners/viewers.
- *Virtual Liveness:* In some cases, music can be *live* in a virtual sense even when the conditions for its liveness (be they corporeal, interactive, etc.) do not *actually* exist. Virtual liveness, then, depends on the perception of a liveness that is largely created *through* mediatization.

I propose that each of these categories be observed in mediatized music as elements or areas of a dynamic network of relationships rather than as absolute values. Corporeal liveness, for example, may be invoked in many different registers in different pieces/performances (or even at different times within the same piece/performance). And although corporeality remains central to many perceptions of liveness, it is sometimes enhanced by one or more of these other conditions of liveness. In other cases, issues of corporeality may be made all the more apparent by their *absence* from a musical experience, even if alternate perceptions of liveness exist. What often result, then, are what might usefully be called *networks of liveness*: various combinations of perceptual and conceptual relationships, not only between performance and mediatization (or more broadly, between human and machine) but also between different characteristics of performance, such as interactivity, corporeality, and temporality.[14]

I also wish to clarify at the outset that my aim here is to provide *explanations* for different categories of liveness rather than finite definitions. I believe these categories to be useful because they provide general descriptions of different ways in which people experience liveness. I do not presume to capture with this list of categories, nor with the descriptions of these categories themselves, the diversity of nuance to be found in these collected experiences. I do hope that, particularly in light of the discussions found in the following chapters, this list provides a sufficient range of examples to act as models for the recognition of further categories and/or for the theoretical development and refinement of the categories already proposed.

Chapters 3 through 7 each introduce a different case study—an example (or small collection of examples) of mediatized music that allows for a specific and unique discussion about liveness and its implications. Some of these chapters focus primarily on one of the seven categories outlined above, and others demonstrate examples of the networks of liveness just described. In each case, conclusions are drawn not only about the construction of the liveness concept as it may relate to the musical context in question but also about what an analysis of liveness may reveal more broadly about the place of mediatized music in modern culture. In Chapter 3, I embark on a discussion of corporeal liveness and its prominence in the recordings of the pianist Glenn Gould and, to a lesser extent, of pop singer Sondre Lerche. I begin with corporeal liveness for two reasons. First, issues of technology and corporeality are already an important part of discourses on musical liveness; thus I begin my case-study discussions in somewhat familiar territory, adding my own voice to the debate on embodiment and music technologies. Second, this chapter allows me to confront the live/recorded binary construction directly and immediately; indeed, my arguments about liveness in Gould's recordings rely wholly on the negation of this construction at the experiential level. Within my discussions, I also confront another, similar construction—a mind/body binary—prevalent in Western musical practice. Ultimately, this chapter uses the mind/body binary and corporeal liveness as central tropes with which to counter, first, Gould's reputation as a "cerebral" musician and, second, an abiding understanding in musical discourse that electronic mediation—particularly recording—leads to disembodied representations of musical practice.

Chapter 4 addresses another body of recorded work—the recordings of the White Stripes—with reference to a liveness of fidelity that is invoked in much of the material written about the band and its singer/guitarist/songwriter/producer Jack White (press materials, interviews, other rock journalism, etc.), and evident in the production values of these recordings. The resulting analysis involves a discussion of the role played by the concept of liveness in the discourse of rock authenticity; in particular, the concept of liveness is deeply implicated in a framing of the White Stripes' musical values (including especially White's production values) within a discourse of authenticating historicism. That is, the band's work is presented and received as representing a particular type of rock authenticity, which itself is validated through the celebration (even fetishization) of "old-fashioned," predigital recording technologies and their associated musical values. A liveness of fidelity—particularly in a perceived representation of a more "performable" and less "overly produced" overall recording aesthetic—is found to play a central role in the descriptions and discursive celebrations of these "historically authentic" rock values. Ultimately, my framing of a liveness of fidelity as a deliberately sought-after characteristic of the White Stripes' music demonstrates a very important characteristic of the liveness concept's evolution and development: that it now exists as a self-reflexively subversive (and at least partially controllable) construction within a highly mediatized musical environment. In comparison with the slick, highly (and digitally) produced pop-music soundscape of the early twenty-first century, the White Stripes seek to present a more "authentic" alternative—one partially defined by, and valued for, its liveness.

In Chapter 5, I frame a discussion of interactive liveness within a historical account of the emergence of live electronic art music in the late 1950s and 1960s. In this discussion, I contrast a Modernist understanding of technology as a tool of systematic control, which permeated most electronic art music before and immediately after World War II, with an alternative paradigm of musician/technology relations that emerged in some early live electronic music practice. This new paradigm was characterized by an understanding of electronic technologies as facilitators for social models of performance; the resulting technologically enhanced interaction between performers has continued to inform many mediatized music performances into the twenty-first century.

In Chapter 6, I venture beyond categories of liveness that are already well established in the discourse (reliant as they are on familiar ideas, such as corporeality, fidelity, and interactivity) and propose the concept of *virtual liveness*. Through analysis of John Oswald's plunderphonic work, "Vane," I demonstrate that even when encountering a piece of music that lacks a physically co-present audience, largely unmediated acoustic sound, and a live performer, the term *performance* may still be usefully applied. In these cases, however, the perceived liveness connected to this idea of performance is often more *virtual* than *actual*. "Vane" sounds not just like a combination of Oswald's two source recordings (Carly Simon's and Faster Pussycat's versions of "You're So Vain") but like a new technological entity: Oswald's manipulations of his source material result in sounds that are decidedly "of the machine," even as they invite us to sing along with Simon's and Faster Pussycat's performances. We enter into a complex network of references between performance as represented in the original recordings and this new, virtual performance—the performance, ultimately, of a sounding cyborg.

Chapter 7 moves this figuration of the sounding cyborg into the realm of live performance as it is more conventionally understood (i.e., musician(s) performing in real time before a co-present audience). This chapter also demonstrates how different categories of liveness, as I have presented them here, may interact in specific contexts to form complex networks of liveness, where relationships among performers, spectators, and technologies are formed in ways that were not possible sixty or seventy years ago when the concept of liveness first began to emerge. These very modern performance contexts provide excellent frameworks within which to recognize the important ways that the concept of liveness has evolved from its origins as a simple signifier of nonmediation.

This chapter focuses on two different instances of performing cyborgs, who perform *human* and *machine* simultaneously. First, the very theatrical presentation of Omar Daniel's live electronic work, *The Flaying of Marsyas*, frames instances of corporeal liveness, interactive liveness, and virtual liveness in a network of complex relationships and significations. Much tension is produced around the competing ideas of human and machine, as an audience is confronted with overt themes of corporeality, acoustic sound, and conventional musicianship (the performance of a violinist) on the one hand and "disembodied" recorded samples, synthesized sound, and a modern "wired" musicianship (the performance of a suspended musician attached to multiple electronic sensors) on the other. A performance of this work, then, can be read as being very much *about* the complexities of modern liveness at the same time that it is about presenting a modern interpretation of an ancient myth (the musical duel between Marsyas and Apollo). Second, I address the central dialectic (as far as liveness is concerned) of turntablism: that such a performative (i.e., live) practice relies so heavily—exclusively, with regards to sound production—on material that would be considered completely nonlive under an older understanding of the concept of liveness. Like the suspended musician in Daniel's work, the turntablist as performing cyborg presents us with a liveness *founded* in large part on mediatization. Furthermore, the performance in question presents the audience/analyst with a rich network of liveness to sort through: Issues of corporeality, spontaneity, interaction, temporality, and spatial proximity all contribute to the experience of liveness associated with a turntablist's performance, bringing us once again to a discussion of virtual liveness and the performing cyborg.

This chapter ultimately serves two broad purposes. First, it acts as a culmination of my rather broad discussion of liveness in modern music, bringing together various threads of discussion (particularly as those threads focus on individual categories of liveness) in focused analyses of specific musical contexts. Second, it demonstrates the broad and diverse potential of a theoretically flexible approach to liveness, such as the one I present throughout this book, to help elucidate some of the significances and meanings communicated in encounters with modern mediatized music. I deliberately use here a phrase greatly lacking in specificity (*encounters with modern mediatized music*) rather than a more carefully confined (and less awkward) phrase (*modern performance*) to reflect some of the "stakes" of the overall discussion on which I am about to embark. *Performance*— as a conceptual category, as an activity, as a way in which we encounter music—is currently in the midst of incredibly significant changes, in which the concept of liveness emerges as an extremely vital and equally dynamic element. The vast majority of these changes find much of their impetus in the increasing role of electronic technologies within the musical practices of the developed world. Understanding what liveness means, and how that meaning is constructed, with respect to the mediatization of modern music will greatly aid in our efforts to understand this music's broader meanings in a modern mediatized culture.

These case studies, and any analyses of liveness therein, should therefore be read with this ultimate goal in mind and not as attempts to define the experience of any specific works invoked. These chapters present *my* interpretations of liveness in a variety of musical contexts. These interpretations are based on extensive research and on my own experience and training as a musicologist and performing musician; but they are also based in part on my own musical values and interests, because those values and interests greatly inform how I experience liveness myself. My case studies, then, are intended primarily as *examples* of how a theory of liveness might work in practice. This practice, as I demonstrate in each chapter, helps us reveal deeper significances about particular works, artists, musical ideologies, and the like but does not—at least in my view—reveal any single "correct" readings of these acts of musicking.

In bringing together the diverse threads of discussion in this book, I employ something like what Joseph Kerman calls "methodological eclecticism" (1994, xii), drawing as appropriate from a number of academic disciplines and discursive traditions. My primary reason for this approach is simply that the topic of liveness, dependent as it is on broad cultural understandings of such categories as human and machine, natural and artificial, stretches far beyond the specific realm of musical activity.

Accordingly, I rely throughout this book on ideas and theories not only from the disciplines of musicology and popular-music studies (disciplines that already encompass a multitude of different fundamental ideologies and methodologies) but also from media studies, cultural studies, philosophy, and theatrically based performance studies. In most cases, I turn to these other disciplines because they offer further useful perspectives on performance and on the use of electronic technologies in cultural production to those found in music scholarship; I also hope to demonstrate the utility of bridging the existing gaps between these supposedly disparate areas of critical inquiry.

In consideration more specifically of the musicological discipline(s), I must also address another fluidity of perspective that my readers will encounter in the pages to come: my periodic avoidance of identifying or addressing clear distinctions between musical works, performances, scores, recordings, hearings, and any number of other ontological and experiential categories into which the discussion of music can be divided. The broad field of mediatized performance and its resulting concept of liveness, as I have emphasized, invoke nearly all elements of modern musical activity, not just the presentation of composers' works by performers for audiences (to invoke a traditional—and limited—discursive framework). To methodically practice a consistent approach to this material (such as focusing only on scores, recordings, live performances, or even limited combinations of these categories) would present an unnecessarily restricted view of the topic. Again, although I cannot pretend to achieve a complete account of modern musical liveness, I do aspire to present a large framework within which a much more thorough account may potentially be constructed, one study at a time.

To this end, I consider each of my case studies in an individual *performance context* within which liveness acts to realize important elements of communicative meaning. By *performance context*, I mean the particular conditions for performance and for the consideration of performance occasioned by a specific composition, performer, performance, technician, technology, musical genre, or combination of any two or more of these elements. I believe that this phrase accurately reflects how I approach the gray areas, so to speak, between works, performances, scores, recordings, and other instantiations of musical processes and products. These gray areas are made apparent when we recognize the extent to which the concept of performance insinuates itself into various understandings of *each* of these ontological and epistemological states of musical practice and discourse. Scores, works, recordings, performances, performers, instruments, or other technologies used in performance, and even discussions of performances, all present *contexts* in which one may usefully perceive, engage with, and/or theorize aspects of music performance and, by extension, liveness.[15]

My primary sources of study have then accordingly been the elements that make up or reflect on these individual performance contexts: notated works, audio and video recordings, and written discourse by musickers of all types, be they composers, performers, record producers, spectators, or mixtures of these categories. In each of the case-study chapters, and especially in the theoretical chapter that precedes them, I also rely heavily on academic discourse that deals with liveness and related topics. The theory of liveness I present here draws together collective experiences of liveness, categorizes them, and proposes strategies for applying this concept to the interpretation of other mediatized music—strategies that reflect the profound changes musical performance has undergone in the past several decades.

2 A Theory of Liveness in Mediatized Music

> But in a studio the unexpected can be tamed and contained. To be live is to *have to* respond because there are people listening. . . . We are observing a kind of "live studio" composition where mistakes—perhaps there are no such thing, just consequences—cannot be "corrected."
>
> Simon Emmerson, *Living Electronic Music*

> The "live" has become little more than a "sound" produced and consumed in private. The domestic space has become one of the primary sites of these new technological practices—a private and increasingly isolated site of musical production and consumption.
>
> Paul Théberge, *Any Sound You Can Imagine*

> The importance of live performance lies precisely in the fact that it is only here that one can see the actual production of the sound, and the emotional work carried in the voice. The demand for live performance has always expressed the desire for the visual mark (and proof) of authenticity.
>
> Lawrence Grossberg, *We Gotta Get Out of This Place*

WHENCE LIVENESS?

Philip Auslander (2002, 16–17) argues that the concept of live music emerged in the mid-1930s in response to a crisis, brought on by radio broadcasts of recorded music, in listeners' ability to distinguish between live performances and recorded performances. Whereas recorded performances had existed in opposition to live performances since the advent of recording technology at the turn of the century, radio threatened to obscure this clear opposition by removing the physical sources of musical sounds—performers and records—from the listener's view. Thus arose the necessity of distinguishing by name between live music and recorded music, because radio listeners often could not tell which they were hearing just by listening—was a broadcast conveying a live performance or canned music? As Auslander explains, "The word 'live' was pressed into service as part of a vocabulary designed to contain this crisis by describing it and reinstating the former distinction discursively even if it could no longer be sustained experientially" (2002, 17).

Sarah Thornton describes a similar emergence of the discursive concept of liveness, although she places this emergence in the 1950s, when recorded music began threatening to usurp live performance as the primary mode of musical consumption. As she argues, "Records became synonymous with music itself. It was only music's marginalised other—performance—which had to speak its difference with a qualifying adjective" (1995, 41). That adjective, of course, was *live*. In Auslander's and Thornton's accounts, liveness is framed as "a historically and ideologically determined concept" (Auslander 2005, 8) that has been invoked repeatedly since its emergence to connote a sense of human production that is different from that found in mediated music or that is, at the very least, resistant to the transformative powers of mediatization.[1]

It is also important to recognize that anxieties about electronic technologies in music were not confined only to the perceived threat of these technologies to the identity of performance; nor was a general technophobia confined to the field of music. As much as the beginning of the twentieth century ushered in what was referred to by many as the Machine Age, with its Modernist enthusiasm—often bordering on fetishization—for all that new technologies could contribute to the growth and prosperity of civilization,[2] strong warnings against these technologies were also heard from many who were uncomfortable with their perceived impersonal and dehumanizing nature. Fritz Lang's 1927 silent film *Metropolis* (Lang 2002) is perhaps the best-known and most overtly technophobic cultural example of such anxious warnings, with its themes of humans enslaved by machines, corruption sown by power over technology (on the part of Rotwang, the inventor, and Joh Fredersen, the master of the city), and technology as a tool of destruction (Rotwang's robot impostor sent to spread dissent like a cancer throughout the city).

In the realm of music, in 1933, George Gershwin expressed related anxieties over the potential threat of modern technologies to the composer's role as creator, even as he actually expressed enthusiasm for the dissemination of the composer's work on recordings. Prefiguring concerns that would circulate about two decades later when the first studios for the electronic composition of music emerged, Gershwin locates the identity of the entire art of music in the *human* act of composition and worries about music's fate if machines were to take over that task. He writes:

> The radio and the phonograph are harmful to the extent that they bastardize music and give currency to a lot of cheap things. They are not harmful to the composer. The more people listen to music, the more they will be able to criticize it and know when it is good. When we speak of machine-made music, however [i.e., music *composed* by machines], we are not speaking of music in the highest sense, because, no matter how much the world becomes a Machine Age, music will have to be created in the same old way. The Machine Age can affect

music only in its distribution. Composers must compose in the same way the old composers did. . . . The composer has to do every bit of his work himself. Hand work can never be replaced in the composition of music. If music ever became machine-made in that sense, it would cease to be an art. (2004, 389)

The discursive distinction Auslander sees emerging between live performance and recorded music in the 1930s, then, does so within the context of a human/machine binary already firmly entrenched in Western thought. More broadly, one might also think of common references in Western culture to distinctions between the categories *natural* and *artificial*. No matter the specificity of the discursive categories involved (i.e., whether the actual discussion is about nature, humans, or live performance), it is clear that wider societal concerns about the relationships between humans and their technological creations are deeply implicated in the construction of these commonly observed binary pairs.

The oppositional construction of difference between these various categories reflects a broader Western predilection for oppositional thought. Such structures of thought, Jacques Derrida reminds us, are "conflictual and subordinating" and far from neutral and objective. For within these oppositional structures, "one of the two terms governs the other (axiologically, logically, etc.), or has the upper hand." There is no "peaceful coexistence" between categories, in other words, "but rather . . . a violent hierarchy" (1981, 41). Within these oppositional binaries, according to Derrida, it is not possible to value *both* of the opposing halves equally.[3] By this logic, furthermore, it is not possible to attribute both opposing qualities to a single entity: Music is either live or mediated. It emanates from either a human or a machine. It is either a product of natural means or artificial means. According to conventional Western values, the former half of each of these particular binaries is usually favored, while the latter half, in these instances, is viewed as the degraded "other."

As might be expected within this context, then, recording, sound synthesis, electronically programmed music, and various other forms of "machine music" have historically been understood as music performance's electronic others—others, because the use of electronic technology in music to record, modify, and reproduce these sounds threatens to disrupt music's traditional performance paradigm: human performers producing acoustic sound kinetically (by blowing, striking, scraping, etc.) before a co-present audience. Electronic technologies threaten this paradigm in part because they can be used to cause various disjunctions between sounds and their sources. For instance, recordings remove musical sounds from the physical site of their production so listeners can no longer see the bodily gestures responsible for that sound (such as the movements of a pianist's hands or a drummer's arms). Even subtle electronic manipulations of an acoustic sound in performance (for example, digital reverberation or simple amplification) can also challenge the perceptible connections one usually makes between physical performance gestures and the sounds resulting from those gestures.

A general technophobia is still clearly present in much musical discourse—particularly that concerned with art music's relationships with modern technologies[4]—and this technophobia informs the perseverance of traditional understandings of liveness in a great deal of this discourse. This type of anxiety is evident—even acknowledged—in R. Murray Schafer's use of the term *schizophonia* to indicate the "split between an original sound and its electroacoustical transmission or reproduction" (1994, 90). He further explains:

> I coined the term schizophonia . . . intending it to be a nervous word. Related to schizophrenia, I wanted it to convey the same sense of aberration and drama. Indeed, the overkill of hi-fi gadgetry . . . creates a synthetic soundscape in which natural sounds are becoming increasingly unnatural while machine-made substitutes are providing the operative signals directing modern life. (1994, 91)

Schafer's arguments about the sonic effects of what he calls "the Electric Revolution" clearly depict the telephone, the radio, and the phonograph (the "three most revolutionary sound mechanisms of the Electric Revolution" [1994, 89]) as technologies that ushered in unnatural and troublesome conditions for hearing sound (particularly musical sound where the radio and phonograph are concerned). Thus the binary constructions of natural/unnatural, human/machine, and by extension live/recorded, are upheld.

However, as discussed in Chapter 1, an ontology of music and its performance based solely on distinctions between the live and the recorded is no longer capable (if it ever was) of addressing all the nuances of modern mediatized music nor all of its various invocations of liveness. Particularly when considering most popular-music practices (and also several art-music practices), one must recognize the extent to which recordings and other forms of mediatization have been allowed inside common constructions of liveness. As music/technology relationships have changed, so too have the different articulations of the ontology of performance and the concept of liveness. A brief consideration of these changing relationships, then, allows for a more viable theory of liveness to emerge.

TECHNOLOGIES OF LIVENESS

Whereas the conceptual emergence of liveness in the 1930s depended on developments in the use of older technologies (i.e., radio and phonograph, both turn-of-the-century inventions), significant challenges to the simple live/recorded construction were made possible by further developments in audio technologies and techniques in the late 1940s—namely, vast improvements to, and the subsequent spread of, magnetic tape recording. Prior to these developments, most musicians used sound-recording technology only to capture and then reproduce acoustic sound as faithfully as possible. Creative use of electronically mediated sound was considered the domain of electronic musical instruments, such as the theremin and ondes martenot. There were, of course, exceptions to the norm, which provided early examples of the types of developments that would become widespread in the 1950s and would then effect a substantial blurring of the previously established lines between sound production and sound reproduction.

As early as the 1920s, pioneering artists, such as Paul Hindemith and Darius Milhaud, and more famously Pierre Schaeffer and Les Paul in the 1940s, were experimenting with the manipulation of phonograph recordings, using these sound-reproduction technologies as creative musical instruments. Recorded sound thus became raw material for musical composition. The commercial adoption of magnetic tape in the 1950s allowed for much easier manipulation of recorded sound, and the phonograph techniques developed by these artists—such as recording at different speeds to effect a change in recorded pitch and speed upon playback, layering multiple recorded events simultaneously, and editing segments of a recording or multiple recordings into newly ordered sequences—were adopted in the use of this new tape technology, whereby they became foundational elements of recording-based musical genres through the 1950s, 1960s, and beyond. Electronically produced tape music, such as that created by the composers at the studio for *elektronische Musik* in Cologne, Germany, was especially notable not only for its creative/compositional use of sound-reproduction technologies (i.e., magnetic tape) but also for its reliance on electronically *produced* (i.e., synthesized) sound. The machine was thus implicated at every level of this music's production, dissemination, and reception, throwing any possible understanding of its liveness severely into question.[5]

Whereas the above-mentioned artists confined most of their work to the studio, others also began to use electronic sound technologies in performance, challenging in the process a traditional understanding of live performance as a primarily acoustic event. In the late 1930s, for instance, crooners began transferring a microphone-based singing style honed over the previous decade in the radio studio to the dance hall. This style of singing, which featured a softer, more intimate delivery, relied on the electric microphone (first adopted by the music industry in 1925) to make even subtle vocal expressions fully audible to an audience, even when sung to the accompaniment of a full-size big band. Significantly, crooning—singing that relied wholly on electronic amplification for its effectiveness—was often considered a more "natural" singing style than European operatic singing.[6]

The phonograph was also introduced as an instrument for real-time performance, first by John Cage in 1939 with his *Imaginary Landscape No. 1*. As the performance of electronically mediated music developed, various mixtures of live and recorded sounds, produced acoustically and synthetically, were introduced. Karlheinz Stockhausen's *Mikrophonie II* (1965), for instance, one of the many examples of the rapidly developing field of live electronic music in the mid-1960s, presents a highly complex mixture of all these elements.[7] Developments in the performance practice of the electric guitar (feedback, distortion, effects pedals, etc.) in late-1960s rock music and the introduction of portable synthesizers in the early 1970s (seen most commonly in the performance of progressive rock acts, such as Yes and Emerson, Lake & Palmer) constituted the most significant elements in popular music's continued reconfiguration of the permissible elements of live performance. As digital sound technology began to supplement and then supplant analog sound technology from the late 1970s onward, the layers of liveness and nonliveness within given works and performances became even more intricately woven. In our current state of highly compact, extremely powerful digital microtechnology, the production, manipulation, and reproduction of sound often all originate from the same source (for example, a laptop computer).

As many have observed, these technological developments have challenged our previous performance paradigms, in large part due to the ways they have reconfigured the role of human performing bodies in music (Corbett 1990; Emmerson 2007; Frith 1996; Toop 2004). As suggested above, the idea that performance contains live, unmediated sound stems in part from a shared historical understanding that music performance emanates directly from exertions of human bodies. Singing is the most obvious example of this type of performance, but performance on pianos and other acoustic instruments also involves deliberate bodily actions that relate directly and kinetically to the sounds produced by those actions. The use of sound-reproduction technologies and other electronic instruments, however, allows for performances in which bodies no longer remain the privileged sites of performance. Recordings seem to present disembodied music, because listeners can no longer see the people responsible for the music they hear. Even in scenarios where performers sing or play acoustic instruments to the accompaniment of prerecorded fixed media (such as in Mario Davidovsky's series of *Synchronisms* [1964–1992]),[8] sound emanates not only from those human performers but also from loudspeakers. The distinctions made manifest in such performances between human flesh and its electronic/technological other seem too great for the collective Western imagination to ignore.

In various examples of mediatized music, these perceived distinctions (human/machine, natural/artificial, live/recorded) have often been exploited in efforts either to reinforce them or to subvert them. For instance, many critics and artists alike, consistent with the typical deployment of such evaluative binary constructions, have reacted to the apparent "coldness" of highly mediatized music, leading in some cases to attempts at "humanizing" musical uses of electronic technology (Mauceri 1997, 189). Similarly, many see the obvious intervention of the recording technology in recordings of traditional, acoustic art music as incompatible with the more "human" aspects of music performance (such as spontaneity and physical displays of virtuosity).[9] Not all musical framings of the human/machine binary observe this typical evaluative quality, however. In *Déserts* (1954),[10] one of the first compositions for acoustic instruments and magnetic tape, Edgard Varèse emphasizes differences between acoustic sounds and electronically processed recorded sounds, clearly establishing an oppositional relationship between human and machine without valorizing one over the other. He says of the piece, "It contrasts the sounds of man-powered instruments with electronically treated sounds, alternating but never combining" (1998b, 206). In other cases, such as with many early composers of acousmatic music,[11] sound synthesis and recording technologies were favored for their seemingly limitless sonic resources over the limitations of human performers. Speaking in 1939, for instance (before such technologies had been invented), Varèse explains his desire for electronic technologies with which he could compose rather than just record and reproduce sound: "If you are curious to know what such a machine could do that the orchestra with its man-powered instruments cannot do, I shall try briefly to tell you: whatever I write, whatever my message, it will reach the listener unadulterated by 'interpretation'" (1998b, 200). In much modern popular music that features extensive use of Auto-Tune and vocoder technologies (Cher's "Believe" [on Cher 1998] and Kanye West's album *808s & Heartbreak* [2008] are well-known examples), voices are electronically manipulated to the extent that they might easily be heard as celebrations of the modern ability to trouble their human identities by technological means. It can be said that in such cases, the typical human/machine binary is reversed (machine/human).

Furthermore, as technology has developed, it has become easier to close the distance and challenge the boundaries between human and machine in very concrete ways. Digital microcircuitry has enabled the invention of many different sound-control devices whose articulations are so carefully mapped onto bodily gestures that they confuse distinctions between performer and instrument. This merger is achieved, for instance, by Laetitia Sonami's Lady's Glove, a specialized electronic music instrument. The glove, wired with several electronic sound-controlling devices, responds to subtle hand movements to produce electronic music in conjunction with a computer. When using the glove, according to Sonami's website, "the performance aspect of computer music becomes alive, sounds are 'embodied,' creating a new, seductive approach" (Sonami, "Lady's Glove"). A similar blurring of distinction between instrument and performer is achieved by the Talk Box, a device made famous by rock singer and guitarist Peter Frampton. This electronic-effects unit feeds an electronic signal (in Frampton's case, from his guitar) through a plastic tube into the mouth. The oral cavity becomes a resonator, its internal shape modifying the sound of the initial signal so it takes on characteristics of human speech. A conventional microphone then picks up the new hybrid electronic vocal emanating from the performer's mouth. As Frampton says, "The Talk Box's got . . . soul. Flesh in the wires" (quoted in Tomkins 2010, 132).[12] With both the Lady's Glove and the Talk Box, not only is the performer's instrument electronic, but that very instrument literally becomes an extension of (rather than something external to) the performer's body.

Notwithstanding Derrida's generally important observations about the usual construction of binary pairings, the state of affairs in modern mediatized music calls for further theorizing of such pairings found therein. Given, first, the varied attitudes toward value within a human/machine binary in mediatized music (i.e., is human better, or is machine better?), and given, second, the examples above (and many others like them) in which the inherent oppositional nature of such binaries is severely challenged, an understanding of the dialectical nature of liveness, as proposed in Chapter 1, seems necessary. The conceptual categories of human and machine (and all their respective cognates) in the perception of liveness in mediatized music do not merely oppose one another. Rather, they inform one another—often through conflict and tension, to be sure, but not through categorical negation. In many cases, as I have already argued, processes of mediatization even act to *enhance* and *augment* the perception of human musical performance.

DEFINING *PERFORMANCE*

But what *is* human musical performance? Because liveness is so closely tied to performance, our understanding of just how we filter musical meaning through liveness depends greatly on what is communicated by the concept of performance itself. I offer here, then, not a single definition of or approach to performance but a consideration of several such definitions and approaches found throughout various streams of cultural discourse. From this discussion emerges an explanation of how performance might best be understood in the context of modern musical liveness.

Arguments about a traditional focus within art-music discourse on musical works and their composers, at the expense of substantial discussion about music's performance, its performers, and their social contexts, are well rehearsed and have already been referenced. I have also made clear that my work here proceeds mindful of recent exhortations to begin correcting this imbalance in our academic focus between musical text and act. In particular, a body of scholarship often referred to as *performance analysis* (as described in Bowen 1996) provides an important model for much of the analysis undertaken in this book, in that it takes performance itself (usually in the form of recordings) as the primary object of study. Very recent contributions to this literature have also begun to recognize that in analyzing a recorded performance, one must also be cognizant of the extent to which the recording process itself has helped shape that performance—in other words, the extent to which recorded performance is mediatized.[13] I extend this approach even beyond the specific field of recordings to all the mediatized performances with which I engage here, recognizing that the use of electronic technologies throughout musical practice is crucially significant to the resulting sonic *and* social implications of that practice and must therefore be a central consideration in the formulation of my own theory of liveness.

Other fields of scholarship, notably theater-based performance studies (usually referred to simply as *performance studies*), philosophy, and popular-music studies, also have much to offer in theorizing the social relationships that are newly configured inside mediatized musical practice, which very often revolve around the same technologies that play such important roles in contemporary social communications.[14] This literature also presents us with useful ideas about the social agency of performance itself—its power to convey something beyond the limits of its purely aesthetic content.

As Marvin Carlson argues in his definitive critical survey of the performance-studies discipline, the terms *performing* and *performance* are used in so many different contexts that "little if any common semantic ground" exists among many of these different uses (2004, 2). He identifies three different basic concepts of performance, each of which resonates in its own way with liveness in mediatized music. First, an understanding of performance involves the appreciation of a performer's employment of skill (2004, 3). This concept is compatible with a traditional understanding of art-music performance, as presented by philosopher Stan Godlovitch. He argues not only that to perform music is (at least in part) to demonstrate a particular set of physical skills but also that an appreciation and understanding of performances depends upon our evaluation of those skills. As Godlovitch points out, this is a performer-centered perspective of performance. The opposite, a listener-centered or phenomenal perspective, disregards the evaluation of a performer's skill and agency and focuses instead on the sights and sounds of a performance and how an audience interprets them (1998, 18–28).

Many mediatized performances of music challenge a traditional skill-based understanding of performance, in that the sounds of these performances can no longer be completely attributed to a performer's physical command of his or her instrument: In many cases, the use of electronics provides alterations to the performer's sound, and these new sounds, which can be seen to exceed the performer's skill, are often treated as dishonest or inauthentic. Godlovitch (1998, 27) similarly argues that an evaluation of a recording relies on phenomenal criteria, because we can no longer be certain that what we are hearing is entirely due to a performer's skill. Indeed, much of the criticism directed at Glenn Gould's well-known editing practices—not to mention the scandal caused by Elisabeth Schwarzkopf's "lending" her high Cs to Kirsten Flagstad's recorded performance of Isolde in Wilhelm Furtwängler's 1953 release of Wagner's *Tristan und Isolde* (Furtwängler 1986)—derives from a belief in the recorded medium's ability to misrepresent a performer's actual skills. The perception of liveness, then, often involves a negotiation between the recognizable demonstration of a performer's skill and the potential of mediatizing technologies to subvert performance as a skill-based art.

Carlson's second concept of performance involves engaging with (and subverting) "repeated and socially sanctioned modes of behaviour" (2004, 4)—a concept referred to by Judith Butler (1990a, 1990b, 1993) and others as *performativity*. The performativity of a particular social code—gender, for instance—is to be found in the ability of acting subjects to define this social concept, and hence themselves, through their actions. By this argument, socially sanctioned concepts of gender are understood because of the repeated performative gender-associated actions of individuals; thus gender is performed. As these performative actions change over time, so too does our understanding of gender. In other words, concepts of a gendered body, along with other commonly held social understandings, ought to be understood "as the legacy of sedimented acts rather than a predetermined or foreclosed structure, essence or fact, whether natural, cultural, or linguistic" (Butler 1990b, 274).[15]

Changes in social understandings of these concepts, then, do not occur easily, as any new performative actions are considered in comparison to the previously established (and oft-repeated) common modes of behavior. Butler characterizes these actions as "ritualized production, a ritual reiterated under and through constraint, under and through the force of prohibition and taboo, with the threat of ostracism and even death controlling and compelling the shape of production" (1993, 95). As Butler points out, the productive power of performativity lies in this challenge to constraint, in the ability of performed acts to openly question the established norm: "'Agency' . . . is to be located within the possibility of a variation on that repetition" (1990a, 145). In mediatized musical performance, the relationships enacted between people and technology can be viewed as performative. As has already been mentioned, technology's common position within Western musical practices is often described as antagonistic to effective communication and the transmission of musical meaning. Many mediatized performances, however, propose "a variation on that repetition." They thereby present performance contexts in which the relationships between technologies and people—or, perhaps more properly, the relationships between people as they are mediated through and shaped by various technologies—are productive, meaningful, and communicative.

Carlson's third concept of performance points to a constant awareness of a "standard of achievement" against which each performance is *evaluated* (2004, 4). This particular understanding of performance has two main implications. First, performance is always done *for* someone: the person or people who are evaluating. In some cases, this may be the performer him- or herself, but even so, there is a "consciousness of doubleness" (2004, 5)—the actual performance on the one hand and the ideal performance (the standard of achievement) on the other. Particularly in my discussions of liveness of fidelity, we will see that this conceptualized ideal performance often plays a large part in determining liveness, usually as a point of reference against which mediatized performance is measured.

Second, performance becomes an appropriate concept with which to approach nontheatrical and nonmusical processes as well. We therefore quantify the performance of an automobile or computer or discuss the performance levels of a company's employees. Jon McKenzie (2001) discusses this particular use of the word *performance* in great detail, emphasizing the extent to which such discourse increasingly invokes relationships of power and efficiency and the imperative to "perform," as witnessed by the proliferation of performance-based rhetoric in the technological and managerial realms. Central to McKenzie's arguments is his assertion that digital technology is an increasingly visible component of otherwise distinct types of performances, from the managerial to the artistic. He suggests that

> future researchers will take as given something that we can only dimly perceive today—and then may be too horrified to admit: namely, that all performance is electronic, that the global explosion of performance coincides precisely with the digitalization of discourses and practices, and that this coincidence is anything but coincidental. . . . Performance for them will name the embodiment of digital virtualities (that is, spheres of incorporeal values and references . . .), just as theatre once actualized the virtual spheres of literary societies (scriptures of God and histories of Man), and ritual actualized those of oral societies (myths of tribes and cults of gods). (2001, 267)

The most significant implication of this state of affairs is that the type of performance associated with digital technology (reading, quantifying, rationalizing—those things McKenzie tellingly calls "spheres of incorporeal values and references") is now becoming increasingly implicated in the type of performance associated with musicians, actors, dancers, and the like (expressing, interpreting, emoting, and other activities of the body). The increasing digitization of performance observed by McKenzie calls to mind Auslander's observations of the wholesale mediatization of performance.

We can take from McKenzie and Auslander that the challenge of performance in the face of mediatization is to maintain meaningful and productive communication even as we use the tools of quantification, rationalization, and control (i.e., computer technologies, as characterized by McKenzie) to mediate this communication. Indeed, one of the ongoing challenges of mediatized music has been to create sounds and musical gestures that seem "musical" rather than "cold and machinelike." Concerns about machine elements overwhelming recognizably human elements in music performance, along with McKenzie's admittedly well-placed concerns about technology in performance more generally, resonate with a general wariness of technology inside performance studies. This wariness can and often does turn explicitly technophobic, as is evidenced by Peggy Phelan's oft-cited work, "The Ontology of Performance: Representation without Reproduction" (1993). But where McKenzie argues that soon *all* performance will be electronic (and that the job of performers is to work against the rationalizing tendencies of a common technological culture), Phelan tells us that *no* performance is electronic. According to Phelan, true performance is so dependent on its existence in the present that any use of technologies of reproduction—any participation "in the circulation of representations *of* representations"—turns a performance into "something other than performance" (Phelan 1993, 146; original emphasis).

It is important to note that, despite Phelan's failure to define explicitly what kinds of performance she is addressing, her remarks seem aimed at a very limited field of avant-garde performance art. Perhaps due in part to this ambiguity, however, Phelan's assertions have been taken up by many other scholars in an attempt to apply her definitions to a broader field of performance types. I do not mean to argue that a general technophobia does not appear in critical discourse before Phelan, but rather that its place inside performance studies was cemented by Phelan's arguments. I have already identified a broadly present technophobia in early-twentieth-century Western culture. Moreover, warnings against the rationalizing tendencies of ubiquitous technological use were especially prominent at the height of late Modernism in the 1950s and 1960s and, as before, were intended as a countermeasure to the widespread Modernist rhetoric of progress through technological advancements (which, in the musical realm, was ultimately embodied in the establishment of Pierre Boulez's Institut de Recherche et Coordination Acoustique/Musique [IRCAM] in 1977).[16]

It is also important to address precisely what Phelan believes the goal of performance ought to be, as her perspective resonates throughout a great majority of performance studies. To Phelan, performance's very purpose is to act against the same tendencies of rationalization and quantification identified by McKenzie in many modern uses of technology. Whereas McKenzie advocates *different* uses of technology to achieve this task, Phelan proposes that electronic reproduction technologies must be avoided altogether. For "without a copy" (the ultimate product of such technologies) "live performance plunges into visibility—in a maniacally charged present—and disappears into memory, into the realm of invisibility and the unconscious where it eludes regulation and control" (1993, 148). The greatest strength of performance, according to Phelan, is its "independence from mass reproduction, technologically, economically, and linguistically" (1993, 149). Only in this independent state can performance embody the kind of social and cultural critique—the *performativity*, to use Butler's term in one of its meanings—that is the ultimate purpose of so much performance art.

To adopt Phelan's perspective in the present study of liveness, however, would be counterproductive (if not impossible), because by this logic all mediatized performance is "something other than performance" (1993, 146). In his own response to Phelan, Auslander insists that performance cannot exist completely "outside the ideologies of capital and reproduction that define a mediatized culture" (2008, 45). This assertion that performance *in general* has entered the realm of electronic mediation is well advised; indeed, this notion has already been acknowledged in the previous chapter. Any current account of performance that aims to do justice to the widespread use of that word *must* allow for the use of electronic mediation and, moreover, must address the extent to which this mediation plays a part in the communicative meaning of performances. Furthermore, and to reiterate my argument from above, the mediatized performances I discuss may be seen as performative in the sense that they challenge conventional understandings of the relationship between technology and artistic expression that underlie music studies and performance studies.[17] These technophobic biases are much the same as those rehearsed throughout Phelan's argument. Ironically, the subversive challenge of the performativity enacted in many of the mediatized performances I address is the very quality that Phelan argues must be exercised only through the *avoidance* of technological mediation.

Popular-music scholar Jason Toynbee (2000) presents a useful perspective on technology's ubiquity in popular-music performance, which can be applied to mediatized performance more generally as a productive alternative to Phelan's performance/technology binary. Toynbee takes up the issue of the binary commonly formulated between live and recorded music, which he argues is "related to contested notions of authenticity and artifice" (2000, 69): authenticity, because what is live is associated with "true" human production, and artifice, because what is recorded is thought to betray the machine's interference in that process. A live/recorded binary, as with the related binaries identified earlier, ultimately holds implications similar to those of Phelan's binary between performance and electronic reproduction. Toynbee argues that to distinguish completely between these different poles is to misrepresent the reality of the changing face of popular-music performance. He writes that

> what is missing in . . . approaches [informed by these binaries] is a sense of how popular musicians have responded to the progressive mediation of music-making over the course of the twentieth century by carrying on performing—in whatever milieu is available. At stake here is not so much an opposition as a continuum between musician-audience co-presence on the one hand and various kinds of distantiation and manipulation of sound on the other.

This continuum represents a technosphere, that is a domain of imaginary possibilities and constraints which lies between performance on one side and the more or less remote reception of sound on the other. The technosphere is thus premised on the idea of a performative gap or dislocation, but also a belief on the part of musicians that this might be bridged (2000, 69).

Toynbee's technosphere, then, is a changing technological field, a network of mediatization through which performers communicate with their audiences at varying degrees of distance. Such distance can be understood not only in familiar terms of physical proximity but also in conceptual terms, such as the degree of difference between an unmediated authenticity and a completely mediatized artificiality. While still recognizing that the use of technology can indeed cause a gap between performers' utterances and their audiences' reception, Toynbee also proposes that performers can and do find ways to communicate meaningfully not just in spite of the technosphere but in ways that *embrace* the technosphere. Toynbee's concept also implies a move beyond the limits of recording and reproduction, so often present in discussions of liveness, to a technological realm involving all manner of musical mediatization (whether on a stage, in a studio, or anywhere else). Finally, Toynbee's description of the technosphere as a realm of mediatized musical activity allows for consideration of the types of dialectical relationships that I argue characterize many modern instances of musical liveness, in that it embraces the value of performance and mediatization *and* recognizes the fluid nature of both these elements. With this fluidity in mind, we arrive finally at a discussion of my proposed categories of liveness.

SHADINGS OF LIVENESS

It is worth restating that liveness is a concept based in the perception of performance, and the exact articulation of this concept in any given situation and for any given musicker depends on the specific ways in which he or she perceives performance within that experience. I proposed in the previous chapter seven different categories of liveness, each based on a different conceptual filter through which performance might be invoked: temporality, spatial proximity, fidelity, spontaneity, corporeality, interactivity, and virtuality. My belief in the need to recognize such categories is grounded in a simple idea: Liveness is *lived*. Of course, to recognize this is to beg the question: lived by whom? Although I do not take up the issue of identifying and querying specific audiences,[18] I do proceed mindful of the general idea that different audiences may have different understandings of what makes a particular musical experience live. Certainly, Auslander's suggestion that the "exact meaning and cultural importance [of liveness] are subject to change, especially in relation to technological development" (2005, 8) is informed by the idea that liveness exists as a dynamic concept among different people and at different times rather than as a concrete ontological category with well-defined essential characteristics.

The very fluidity of the concept of liveness is, in part, what makes it so complex and worthy of further scrutiny, and several recent scholars have already begun this task. Even within his narrow focus on the temporal liveness (something happening "now") of broadcast and transmission technologies, Nick Couldry (2004) recognizes changes in the formation of liveness from one based in the experience of television broadcasts to one encountered in the use of the Internet and mobile phones. Remarking on the complexity of liveness for audiences of live theater (a much less mediatized context than those concerning Couldry), Martin Barker states that

> "liveness" emerges as a particular *kind* of discursive concept. It appears to its users to be simple, singular, transparent and descriptive; in reality it is a complex means whereby people are able to position themselves among available forms of culture and to arrive at social, cultural and moral judgements. (2003, 33; original emphasis)

If liveness, then, is a discursive concept, marked not only by its fluidity and complexity but also by its emergence from particular social environments and historical moments for particular ideological purposes, it must be examined with these factors in mind. In the rest of this chapter, I discuss several different shadings of the concept of liveness within various branches of cultural study, particularly its intersection with the idea—and ideologies—of music performance. I divide this discussion into seven different categories, as already outlined, each of which identifies a different way that liveness is understood generally within cultural use and particularly within musical use. In this multivalent approach to liveness, I engage in a similar (if more extensive) exercise to that of Barker (2003), who teases out some various meanings of liveness related to the experience of live theater, some of which correspond to the categories I explore here. Simon Emmerson (2007) similarly addresses several different ways in which we perceive "live presence" in electronic (especially acousmatic) music (many of which I address below) but confines his inquiry to a rather narrow spectrum of musical practice—one that I expand further in this project.[19]

My first six categories of liveness—temporal liveness, spatial liveness, liveness of fidelity, liveness of spontaneity, corporeal liveness, and interactive liveness—are firmly embedded inside extant discussions of music and performance, even if they are not always explicitly identified as such. Each of them, as a result, reflects the valuation of a different quality or combination of qualities thought to reflect a traditional (live) performance paradigm and thought to be lacking or threatened in particular mediated forms of music. The final category, virtual liveness, also has its roots in cultural study, but these roots do not run nearly as deeply within musical discourse as do those of the other categories. I establish with this category an understanding of liveness that is central to my overriding argument that liveness is ultimately perceptual and therefore dependent on imagination; thus, it veers furthest away from generally accepted concepts of the live in music. Virtual liveness is largely constructed by technological means and conveys a sense of performance that, although meaningful, is not grounded in actuality: For instance, it may present performing bodies that are not really there (as discussed in Chapter 6) or interactions between musicians that take place on a virtual level rather than on a material one (as discussed in Chapter 7).

I propose all these categories not as fundamental concepts essential to a precise definition of liveness but rather as useful layers of a multivalent theory with which to consider the variety within discourses on liveness and, more importantly, the types of liveness evident in individual mediatized performance contexts. The valuation of liveness in any given musical experience may involve a complex mixture of several of these categories of liveness, or it may emphasize only one category. Furthermore, perception of liveness is by no means limited to these different categories, which I propose merely as a first step in developing a more complete understanding of mediatized performance.

Temporal Liveness and Spatial Liveness

The most common perceptions of liveness, particularly as invoked by the phrase *live performance*, are what I term *temporal liveness* and *spatial liveness*. Generally, when we speak of witnessing a live performance, we mean that we have witnessed a performance at the time of its occurrence (temporal liveness) and in the physical presence of the performer(s) (spatial liveness). In his oft-cited essay "The Work of Art in the Age of Mechanical Reproduction" (1968), Walter Benjamin's concept of the "aura" of a work of art revolves around the unique existence, and thus the authenticity, of that work in one time and in one place. But an audience of a reproduced work of art, such as a film or a phonograph record, struggles to detect any aura, this authenticity of the original, because the film or record exists in many times and in many places—copies without an original.[20] Although Benjamin does not address questions of musical aura at any length, others have invoked this essay to consider how an aura of a musical performance might comprise the authenticity that attends its spatial and temporal liveness.

Auslander, for instance, argues that due to performance's mediatization:

> its traditional status as auratic and unique has been wrested from it by an ever-accelerating incursion of reproduction into the live event. . . . [A]ll performance modes, live or mediatized, are now equal: none is perceived as auratic or authentic; the live performance is just one more reproduction of a given text or one more reproducible text. (2008, 55)[21]

By Auslander's argument, ours is a society in which reproductions are so ubiquitous that original versions of cultural events and artefacts are no longer perceived as such. The value of such events and artefacts is measured by their potential for mass reproduction. Such an argument, however, is more appropriate for some types of performance than others; thus, Auslander's claim that "all performance modes . . . are now equal" might benefit from further qualification. For instance, Auslander's own account of rock ideology presents not an eradication of aura but rather a reconstitution of it, even though some of the other performances he discusses may fit the description he offers in the passage quoted above.[22] He argues that through live performance, the rock record is authenticated and thus inscribed with the aura of the original (although once removed): The typical rock performance copies the record, which brings the record into the realm of auratic performance. In other words, when we hear a live (and thus auratic) performance of previously recorded rock, we *also* hear the record. The record is perceived as auratic only in the particular time and place of the performance, because in that instance, according to the ideology of rock, it is invoked as a live event.[23]

Auslander's reconfiguration of Benjamin's concept crucially revolves around attributing to a reproduction the very qualities—temporal liveness and spatial liveness—that Benjamin considers to be mutually exclusive with mechanically reproduced cultural artefacts. Yet despite the increasing complexity of the relationship between liveness and mediatization, we still find ourselves understanding liveness (and aura) in reference to its recorded or otherwise mediatized other. Jonathan Sterne reminds us of this important residualism when he writes, "Aura is the object of a nostalgia that accompanies reproduction. . . . [A]uthenticity and presence become issues only when there is something to which we can compare them" (2003, 220–221). Liveness, as I have already suggested, always implies mediatization, because without electronic media, the concept of liveness is meaningless. The various changing tensions between liveness and mediatization are what give rise to the many different manifestations of liveness beyond the temporal and the spatial.

Before discussing these other types of liveness, however, it may be observed that spatial liveness and temporal liveness are not always considered mutually dependent, as they appear to be in Benjamin's concept of aura. Emmerson (2007, esp. Ch. 4), for instance, discusses at length the sense of live presence often perceived in acousmatic music, which stems from the sense of space created in the music through the use of artificial reverberation and stereo-field manipulation.[24] Alternatively, media theory based in television makes frequent reference to a temporal liveness common to live television and radio broadcasts. According to Jane Feuer (1983, 14–16), television's temporal liveness stems from the broadcasting of events at the time of their occurrence and from the framing of programs (live and prerecorded) at regular times and on regular channels, which creates a continuous programming flow. Viewers then feel as though they are tuning in at specific points to a stream of programming that is temporally live, because it is always running.[25] Emmerson's and Feuer's observations are good reminders that liveness can be experienced in many ways; in fact, rigorous analysis requires stepping outside the rather specific framework so commonly invoked by reference to Benjamin's theory of aura.

When we do so, we also must consider the difference that is often evident between temporal and spatial liveness, and other categories, such as corporeality, interactivity, and fidelity. Here I speak of the ontological grounding that usually accompanies instances of temporal and spatial liveness, which is less often a determining factor in other experiences of liveness. Like Benjamin's aura, temporal and spatial liveness, especially as conventionally understood elements of live performance, are grounded in the ontological fact of that performance's existence: Temporal and spatial liveness are experienced *because* a spectator is, in fact, present at a performance. As we see in the discussions to follow, perceptions of other categories of liveness may result more easily than those of temporal and spatial liveness from *simulated* qualities of performance rather than from actual performance itself. This is not to say that temporal and spatial liveness *cannot* be simulated, each in its own way. Temporal liveness, in particular, may be perceived by someone who is watching or listening to a prerecorded broadcast, so long as this person has the mistaken impression that he or she is witnessing something as it is happening. Nevertheless, it is wise to remember that these categories together represent the most common understanding of liveness in reference to a traditional, live musical performance.

Liveness of Fidelity

As I have argued, many positive valuations of liveness stem from ideologies embedded in a binary that pits human production against mechanical or electronic reproduction. These ideologies often lead to implications that what is produced by people is "real" or "authentic," whereas the products (or reproductions) of machines are somehow corrupted by their mechanical or electronic source. A certain appreciation of musical liveness, then, stems from the perception that a musical performance is *unaltered* by electronic mediation. In the case of a typical live acoustic performance, this authenticity is unquestioned: The live performance is superior to the recording, because it is the "real thing" (or so goes the traditional ideology of liveness). Yet a similar notion of authenticity can also emerge from mediated performances or even recordings. In these cases, recordings and performances that display the least amount of technological "interference" are valued over—that is, considered more live than—those in which mediatization is audible or at least acknowledged (in the form of editing, artificial reverberation, or Auto-Tuning, for example). In other words, this type of liveness is one of *fidelity*: The further a recording or performance deviates from "true" (acoustic) performed sounds, the less live it is, at least in this sense.

We can interpret the term *fidelity* in a couple of different but nonconflicting ways. In some cases, a preference for the fidelity of live performances (or live recordings) over studio recordings stems from a mistrust of "studio trickery." The same listening ideology may also hold true for audiences of live popular-music performances, wherein the use of Auto-Tune technology, for instance, is seen as a type of "cheating" on the part of the singer(s), even though other forms of mediatization, such as the use of prerecorded samples or any number of electronic instruments, may be welcomed. Here, a certain ethics of performance, derived from the concept of skill in performance, informs many people's listening aesthetics. Regardless of musical genre, many listeners expect that what they hear through their home speakers, or those on stage, will faithfully represent the abilities of the musician(s) within the accepted conventions of that particular musical tradition. In his seminal essay on music and recording technology, "The Prospects of Recording," Gould quotes Richard Mohr, who was then the musical director of Red Seal Recordings: "Tape splicing borders on immorality because there are many artists today on the concert stage or in the opera house who cannot give you the performance in life that they can give you on records" (1966, 52).[26] Mohr, then, prefers performances and recordings wherein he can be assured of faithful representations of the performers' abilities.[27]

One of the appeals of live recordings is that the "live" label in these cases would seem to indicate this type of fidelity to a conventional performance, particularly in comparison with studio recordings that openly embrace such recording techniques as retakes, editing, and artificial reverberation. Yet Robert Philip argues that even these so-called live recordings (particularly modern ones) may not be completely faithful, because they often feature unacknowledged bits of editing. As he puts it, "The label 'live' on a recording cannot be taken at face value" (2004, 49). The recording process in both of these examples is construed as a threat to a liveness of fidelity.

I also conform here to the more conventional use of the word *fidelity*, at least as it is usually invoked in discussions of recording technology (particularly in popular-music studies). Most often in these discussions, the term applies to the quality of sound captured and reproduced by that technology. As Keir Keightley states, the term *high fidelity* usually refers to "the degree of truth to reality produced by the [audio] system" (1996, 152). Significantly, the concept of high fidelity (hi-fi) began to emerge in earnest around the same time as a discourse of liveness, as both were ushered in (at least partly, in the case of liveness) by the widespread dissemination of long-playing records in the late 1940s and 1950s. Mirroring Thornton's assertions about the ideology of liveness, much of the discourse surrounding hi-fi in the 1950s embraced an oppositional binary between reality and the perceived artifice of machines. Keightley quotes a letter to the editor in a 1957 issue of *Newsweek*: "Do you want your radio or phonograph to sound like a radio or phonograph or do you want to be transported to the concert hall without leaving your living room? I'll take hi-fi" (1996, 153). The binary, along with its inherent valuations, is explicit: Hi-fi records sound like the "real thing," whereas lo-fi records sound like something produced (or badly reproduced) by a machine. A perceived liveness of fidelity in this sense, then, derives from the high degree of perceived technological transparency in the sound of the hi-fi record. Hi-fi technologies, in the words of Sterne (2003, esp. Ch. 5), are seen as "vanishing mediators." That is, they are not considered to influence the performer's communication or its reception in any way but rather to reveal this musical communication in its truest state.[28]

Liveness of Spontaneity

Another quality often thought to contribute significantly to the appeal of live performance is the degree of spontaneity involved. Each performance is unique; moreover, neither performer nor audience knows exactly what to expect. Appreciation of spontaneity seems to derive at least partly from a common skill-based understanding of performance (as discussed above). The realization that a performer's skill level does indeed measure up to the challenge posed by a particular composition, or to a level of improvisation expected by a demanding fan base, is what elicits excitement from the audience. Conversely, the realization that a performer is not equal to the task is often a source of disappointment and points to one of the potentially unpleasant aspects of live performance. In addition, the performer may solve the challenges of a musical work differently each time, satisfying the audience's desire for something new and different. Although this particular quality of liveness remains relatively unthreatened in live performances of mediatized music (so long as performers do not rely too heavily on long sequences of fully prerecorded and/or preprogrammed material), it is virtually eradicated in repeated encounters with individual recordings. Once we have become familiar with a particular recording, it becomes very difficult for us to be surprised (pleasantly or otherwise) when we listen to it.[29]

Aaron Copland, another of Gould's interviewees for his "Prospects of Recording" essay, addresses the distinctions he perceives between live and recorded music, focusing on a liveness of spontaneity:

> For me, the most important thing is the element of chance that is built into a live performance. The very great drawback of recorded sound is the fact that it is always the same. No matter how wonderful a recording is, I know that I couldn't live with it—even of my own music—with the same nuances forever. (Gould 1966, 47)

Schuyler Chapin, then an administrator at the Lincoln Center for the Performing Arts, echoes Copland's sentiments: "I . . . think that many more [listeners] will feel that the adventure, the accidental excitement of a live performance is much more stimulating and satisfying than just listening constantly to a record" (Gould 1966, 47). For his part, Gould cites the spontaneous nature of performance as one of his primary reasons for leaving the concert stage in favor of the recording studio, referring to "those awful and degrading and humanly damaging uncertainties which the concert brings with it" (Gould and Page 1990, 452).[30] The lack of spontaneity, the "take-twoness" of recording (Gould and McClure 1968), is precisely what he likes most about it.

Of course, as I have repeatedly emphasized, many recent concepts of liveness have evolved beyond simple binaries between live and recorded forms of musical encounter to become imbued with a certain ambiguity regarding these ontological distinctions. Paul Théberge (1997) demonstrates that a sense of spontaneity has led to a rhetoric of liveness surrounding the use of digital sequencers in recording studios. On the one hand, these sequencers are used to perform completely prerecorded (or synthesized) material, with the performances taking place inside a studio. On the other hand, this prerecorded material remains malleable (rather than fixed on a recorded track), to be manipulated in real time, which leads many users to consider the sequencer to be a live technology.

Théberge relates an incident during a studio session wherein a recording engineer repeatedly referred to the material played by the sequencer as "the live tracks," even in comparison to the tracks recorded during that same session by a vocalist and a guitarist. He writes, "For the engineer, the sequenced tracks were 'live,' first because the computer was, in effect, 'playing' the MIDI instruments in 'real time' while the other tracks were simply being 'reproduced' on the tape recorder. Second, the sequenced tracks, stored in RAM, were still in a relatively volatile state and could be manipulated at will." The malleability of such tracks as these "lends a spontaneous character to the sequenced material that has, in part, led to blurring the distinction between what is 'live' and 'recorded' in studio production" (1997, 229–230). A liveness of spontaneity, then, like other types of liveness, can be experienced in many different ways, leading to various tensions between fluid categories of live and mediated.

Corporeal Liveness

Perhaps more than any of the categories of liveness discussed thus far, recent scholarship on music and technology has been particularly attuned to perceptions of corporeality in performance, or what I call *corporeal liveness*. This book adopts a similar focus, as most of my analyses have at least *something* to do with issues of corporeality. I have suggested, furthermore, that these analyses address liveness as a quality of perception, which, along with the body, is a concern of phenomenologists within music studies and in cultural and philosophical studies more broadly. Many recent phenomenologists have upheld Maurice Merleau-Ponty's famous argument that all perception is *embodied* rather than just a product of the mind. One's understanding of one's environment depends not just on *thoughts* about that environment but also on *physical interactions* with that environment and on the basis of those thoughts within that corporeal experience. Merleau-Ponty states:

> the body is [not] . . . merely *an object in the world*, under the purview of a separated spirit [read, "mind"]. It is on the side of the subject; it is our *point of view on the world*, the place where the spirit takes on a certain physical and historical situation. . . . [Moreover,] the body is much more than an instrument or a means; it is our expression in the world, the visible form of our intentions. (1964, 5; original emphasis)

In other words, not only perception but also expression is rooted in this corporeality.

Applying these ideas to music performance, we can argue that the communication of music is not merely the communication of thoughts and intentions (i.e., the product of a composer's or an interpreter's mind) but rather of the embodiment of those thoughts and intentions within the physical expressions (the singing or playing of instruments) of a particular performer or group of performers, combined with the embodied perception of an audience (with all the swaying, humming along, air-guitar playing, and other physical responses therein entailed).[31] I must develop this last statement further, however, particularly in light of mediatized music's potential for eliminating all traces of bodies, at least from the process of musical *expression*.[32]

One of the earliest arguments for recognizing the corporeality of music comes not from a musicologist but from literary theorist Roland Barthes, in his seminal essay, "The Grain of the Voice" (1989). Barthes advocates a change in perspective from considerations of music as a collection of works to music as utterance. In so doing, he proposes the concept of the "grain of the voice," of "the materiality of the body" in the singing voice (1989, 182). In the sound of a typical Russian church bass, Barthes identifies (and highly values) traces of the "cantor's body, brought to your ears in one and the same movement from deep down in the cavities, the muscles, the membranes, the cartilages" (1989, 181). To Barthes, the power of music performance to truly move us comes not from the beauty of the musical work being performed but from the corporeal nature of performed musical sound.

Similarly, and following the type of phenomenological argumentation rehearsed above, George Fisher and Judy Lochhead maintain that "the most fruitful access to comprehending music as meaningful behavior is through the active and creative body." Emphasizing the social nature of this musical communication, they appropriate Merleau-Ponty's concept of *intercorporeity* to focus not "simply [on] the constituting agency of the composer but in the shared and bodily-based activities of the creator, performer and listener" (2002, 38–39).[33] In other words, they propose an embodied understanding of music that takes account of relationships between everyone involved in the musical event, a perspective that lends itself well to the concept of liveness as I have outlined it thus far.[34]

The embodied meaning of music at all levels has also been identified in music-performance psychology studies. From the performer's perspective, for instance, Patrick Shove and Bruno Repp (1995), among others, have established that performers often form their interpretations based on concepts of musical movement (acceleration, descending lines, etc.) that relate metaphorically to different body movements.[35] In this way, performers understand music in relation to their own embodied experience of the world. For their part, listeners/observers not only understand musical movement in a similar fashion but also glean further musical meaning (relating to mood, for instance) from the physical gestures of the performer(s) (Davidson 1993; Davidson and Correia 2002).

In addition to strictly *sonic* meanings, several scholars have also argued that we perceive various *social* meanings in relation to the corporeality of performance. Important groundwork has been laid in this respect by Richard Leppert (1993), who points out several important connections between the depictions of musical bodies in art from the seventeenth to the nineteenth centuries and various normative behaviors, particularly relating to gender, common in the bourgeois societies from which that art emerged. More recently, Tracy McMullen (2006) has presented an account of trombonist Abbie Conant's difficulties being accepted by the administration and members of the Munich Philharmonic, which rested not on her abilities as a trombonist but rather on her gender. Indeed, she was awarded the solo chair in the blind audition process; her troubles began only after her gender was revealed. At one point in her ensuing legal struggles with the orchestra, it was argued that Conant's physical strength was not equal to the demands of a trombone section leader (McMullen 2006, 69). McMullen demonstrates how Conant's musical performances subverted common social understandings of gendered bodies—namely, that female bodies lack the necessary strength to perform satisfactorily on large phallic instruments.[36]

Many of the accounts of musical corporeality discussed thus far, however, rely strongly on the situation of listeners within sight of the musical performance in question. In other words, at least according to many of these arguments, embodied perceptions of music (or perceptions of embodied music) occur as much through our sense of sight as through our senses of hearing and touch (many sonic vibrations being felt as much as they are heard, if not more so). Indeed, throughout her account, McMullen (2006) implicitly equates "embodied performance" with "seen performance." This equation of the perception of corporeality with visual perception drastically oversimplifies the ways in which corporeal presence is detected in music. In response to the shortcomings of this simplistic concept, I devote much of Chapters 3 and 6 to exploring how corporeal liveness may still be an important tool for interpreting some recordings when visual cues of performing bodies are absent.

Interactive Liveness

Many perceptions of liveness are linked to the concept of interaction. Interactions between performers and audiences loom particularly large within accounts of the value of live performance. For instance, the idea that recordings rob audiences and performers of this opportunity to interact during the process of making music recurs throughout John and Susan Harvith's (1987) collection of interviews with many of the most prominent classical musicians to record in the twentieth century. Similarly, Merleau-Ponty's aforementioned concept of intercorporeity, as adopted by Fisher and Lochhead—indeed even the word *intercorporeity*—is based on the notion of corporeal interaction among *all* musickers.

Even beyond this idea that music technologies threaten performer/audience interactions, however, many writers have remarked on ways that these technologies may also be used to threaten conventional interactions among the various performers involved in a given performance. Philip, for example, argues that live recordings are often preferable to studio recordings, because they offer an opportunity to hear an ensemble (an orchestra, in Philip's examples) working together in "a continuous process of negotiation" (2004, 47). Most studio recordings (at least of traditional orchestral repertoires), by contrast, have been constructed so as to demonstrate complete unanimity and cohesion throughout, so the "working-out" process that ensembles usually go through in an attempt to reach cohesion during the process of performance is inaudible in the final recording. As Philip argues, "The more thoroughly the moments of imperfection are removed, the less the listener is aware of this human process" (2004, 48). According to Philip, studio recordings misrepresent conventional interactive realities of performance; moreover, this particular lack of liveness is dehumanizing.

Théberge (1989) presents a similar and even harsher argument regarding multi-track recording practices in popular music. In Théberge's description of the typical recording session, members of a rock band are placed in separate rooms so they can no longer see each other and can only hear each other through headphones: "Thus, in order to play at all under the conditions of separation recording, the musical ensemble must become fully integrated into the technological apparatus—the apparatus is a mediating factor between all musical interactions in the studio" (1989, 102). According to Théberge, interactive musical behavior is only *simulated* in multi-track recording, while true interaction is eliminated by the producer's practice of technologically separating and controlling each individual musical element in an effort to achieve the right sound.

Yet, as I argue in Chapters 5 and 7, electronic technologies need not be used to disrupt interactions among performers. Such arguments as Philip's and Théberge's tell us only about specific recording practices; they say nothing of the many attempts in electronic art music, for instance, to incorporate electronic sound technologies as productive parts of interactive performance networks.[37] In addition, the term *interactive* has been adopted by many recent performers and composers of electronic art music to describe various performer/technology interfaces where the very relationship between a performer and his or her electronic instrument is considered interactive.

Virtual Liveness

The roots of virtual liveness as a discursive category are more difficult to identify, particularly within music, but various writers have offered strategies for understanding music that are all directed at what can usefully be described as virtual perceptions of music. William Echard identifies an interpretive tradition, including the work of Naomi Cumming (2000) and David Lidov (2005), in which concern with "narratives, personas and spatial/energetic interpretations in general" (Echard 2006, 7), among other things, amounts to concern with virtual forms of music. The virtual, according to Echard, is that "which is real but not actual" (2006, 8). Echard goes on to identify two important ways that music can be considered virtual.

First, he argues, "*musical texts and objects themselves are virtual in nature*" (2006, 10; original emphasis). Echard points to the common problem of defining the musical work, suggesting that we may usefully describe it "as a virtual object that generates/inhabits multiple lines of actualization, none of which it fully resembles and none of which fully resemble each other" (2006, 10). Second, according to Echard, performers are involved with virtuality in their efforts to fully realize the "wealth of [their bodies'] virtual forms" (2006, 10)—that is, all the potential ways that their bodies might realize the musical performance of a particular work. Echard further explains:

> The musician is involved in giving shape to some indeterminate potential, but can only do so by relaxing their attachment to particular actualizations (including their own selves). . . . Performance, when conceptualized in this manner, is the constant re-pursuit of something that glimmers at the edge of experience, and always retreats after the fact. (2006, 11)

I wish to expand on Echard's arguments for the virtual in music by suggesting that the concept of musical liveness also engages with virtuality. This virtuality resides primarily in what I have described as the perceptual nature of liveness. To return this discussion to mediatized music: As Emmerson (2007) argues, our perceptions of electronic music, particularly of acousmatic music, engage our imaginations. Whatever we perceive is, for all intents and purposes, true, at least with respect to liveness, even if those perceptions are misguided by sonic illusion. For instance, if I believe I hear the sound of a hand hitting a drum, even if what I actually hear is a sound completely synthesized by electronic means, that sound may still convey to me a very real corporeal liveness—just not one based in concrete actuality. Thus, this corporeal liveness is also virtual. For that matter, *all* liveness is potentially virtual, inasmuch as it is based in perceptions that may or may not be "accurate."

How, then, can virtual liveness be used productively as a theoretical category with which to think through mediatized performance, if it is just a shading of some other kind of liveness? I believe the answer lies in the reason for that shading and in the degree to which virtuality—"the opposite of the concrete/actual" (Echard 2006, 8)—makes itself known in a musical mixture of actual and virtual. That is, I present virtual liveness here as a quality of perception brought on by obvious, unmistakable acts of mediatization, even as that mediatization presents itself as somehow live— as somehow conveying musical, human performance. In this way, my use of *virtuality* is also informed by the definition of that term proposed by N. Katherine Hayles, a definition that recognizes the technological context in which virtuality is so often understood. For Hayles, virtuality is *"the cultural perception that material objects are interpenetrated by information patterns"* (1999, 13–14; original emphasis).

This category of liveness, then, is not invoked in discussions of, for example, musical corporeality in which the subtle use of microphones brings out the sounds of a performing body without drawing much attention to that act of mediatization. Rather, I reserve virtual liveness for discussions of performance contexts in which liveness and mediatization are both performed with great emphasis, in which no doubt can remain that electronic technologies are an integral part of fashioning a performance of liveness that otherwise would not be possible. For herein resides, in hyper-relief, the crucial dialectic of mediatized performance: the performance of *live music*, of *mediated music*, and of their powerful merging, all within a single performance context.

***

In the following chapters, I move forward with these categories of liveness, deploying them not as descriptors to indicate the value of performance in *resistance* to mediatization but rather as analytical tools for understanding how the value of human performance has remained central to modern musical practices, even as they have *embraced* mediatization. To be sure, my own accounts of liveness are not free of ideology, even as I attempt to escape the ideologies inherent in such static binaries as authentic/inauthentic, live/recorded, human/machine, and so forth. Rather, by adopting a more flexible approach to liveness—one that does not *degrade* the mediated—I propose ways that we may better understand how and why musickers continue to value qualities of the live in mediatized music.

3 Hearing Glenn Gould's Body
Corporeal Liveness in Recorded Music

Gould is not a pianist who takes time away from the piano to think. He is a musical thinker who makes use of all available means to thought, including the piano.

Geoffrey Payzant, *Glenn Gould: Music and Mind*

Music's path to the mind is inevitably through the body.

Andrew Mead, "Bodily Hearing"

Glenn Gould has long been characterized by himself and by others as a *thinking* musician—a philosopher, a genius, a contemplative eccentric whose limitless musical ability shines through in spite of his notorious physical quirks (his bad posture, his conducting and singing while playing, his obsession with keeping his hands warm, etc.). The recording studio, he felt, offered him the greatest opportunity to construct performances that reflected his best ideas—interpretations formulated in his *mind*—about musical works, particularly because it afforded him the ability to reflect on his different recorded interpretations during the production process. Yet his recordings also present us with very tangible traces of corporeality, so much so that to listen to them is to hear a body performing, as long as we make room in the Gould mythology for a musician whose *playing* is as important as his *thinking*. Moreover, by addressing in this volume the corporeal liveness so evident in Gould's recorded work, I present a reading of recordings—those so-called agents of disembodiment—in which a body still sounds.

I address, in other words, what Suzanne Cusick (1994) and others have identified in musical discourse as the *mind/body problem*. This ideological binary leads to an understanding of music as a collection of works, ideas, and interpretations (isolated products of the mind) but not of actions, tactile sounds, and physical gestures (socially embedded experiences of the body). This chapter, then, engages in what Elisabeth Le Guin (2006) calls a "carnal musicology"—a study of music as a physically enacted phenomenon. In this chapter, I discuss the mind/body problem in music, first broadly and then with respect to Gould. I then address the place of recordings within a mind/body context, arguing that, despite many assertions to the contrary, recording and disembodiment are not necessarily inextricably linked.

Finally, I discuss several of Gould's recordings, with an ear for the audible actions of Gould's own performing body—his corporeal liveness. I then carry this analytical listening exercise into the realm of popular music, with a brief account of corporeal liveness in a recording by singer-songwriter Sondre Lerche.

GLENN GOULD: MIND AND BODY

The centrality of musical thinking (at the expense of musical physicality) is not unique to the case of Gould; rather, it is part of a long tradition. Within the history of Western art music, and particularly within scholarly writing associated with that history, music's most significant properties have long been linked to the realm of mental activity. People who adhere to this concept view music as the communication of ideas, abstract structures, complex patterns, and so forth, all of which are situated in musical *works*. Once composed, these works take on metaphysical properties, existing somehow in and of themselves, awaiting their representation in performance.[1] Yet until recently, these performances were not often considered important on their own—as physical processes of sound creation and communication, carried out by musically laboring bodies. Rather, each performance was (and often still is) judged according to how successfully it communicated the *ideas* that constitute the composer's work.

The primacy of mind in musical discourse has emerged in various guises, as several writers have demonstrated convincingly. In addition to Cusick's condemnation of the mind/body problem and Le Guin's commendable example of carnal musicology, the issue is neatly addressed by Richard Leppert (1993, 96–101), who demonstrates that in many eighteenth-century treatises, the "essential" qualities of music were held to exist in the mathematical relationships between the intervals of the Western tonal scale. This reduction of music to its mathematical properties presents an entirely knowable music, in line with the wider appeals to order and reason so prevalent during the European Enlightenment. The association of music and mind was also prominent within Romantic musical aesthetics, even if the nineteenth-century rhetoric surrounding this concept was more concerned with individual genius than with the rationality of the eighteenth century. Writing in 1813 about Beethoven's instrumental music, for example, E. T. A. Hoffmann repeatedly remarks on Beethoven's unrivaled genius, citing the "inner continuity" and "internal structure" of Beethoven's compositions as the true marks of their worthiness. Hoffmann emphasizes that the structural relationships found in Beethoven's compositions (for example, the unity of motivic materials across different movements of a work) are products of a superior intellect and, furthermore, that "a deeper relationship which does not reveal itself in this way speaks at other times *only from mind to mind*, and it is precisely this relationship that . . . imperiously proclaims the self-possession of the master's genius." Hoffmann also argues that "*only what the mind produces* calls for respect and that all else is out of place" (1998, 1195–1196; my emphasis).[2]

Reference to the nineteenth-century cult of genius, with Beethoven as its central figure, also raises the issue of the contemporaneous cult of the virtuoso, whose central figures were Franz Liszt and Nicolò Paganini. Although virtuosi's physical attributes were highly fetishized in the popular imagination (for instance, Liszt's hands were cast in molds several times during his life), I suggest that bodies remained "weaker" symbols of music's significance than brilliant minds did. This can be explained best, perhaps, in light of Jacques Derrida's concept of *phallogocentrism*: the privileging of reason and mind, and the patriarchal hierarchy of that privileging, in Western epistemology.[3] As Leppert (2007) demonstrates, music became gradually remasculinized in Western Europe throughout the nineteenth century, after centuries of association with feminine qualities. Although Liszt did much in his own right to masculinize the piano, his gender image as a performer remained somewhat ambiguous, as did those of nineteenth-century performers in general. Furthermore, Beethoven, the individual responsible for masculinizing music more than any other at this time, was not a virtuoso figure (or at least not *just* a virtuoso figure) but a brooding and brainy musical genius *par excellence* (Leppert 2007, 151–163).

These arguments depict a tradition in which the most important aspects of canonical Western art music (what is transmitted "from mind to mind") are found in its abstract compositional structure, created by relations between pitches (and, to a lesser extent, rhythms). Within this scenario, anything not associated with these organizational structures—any *noise*, to use Jacques Attali's (1985) term—is an unwanted distraction, at best. For in Attali's usage, *noise* does not refer just to the sonic phenomenon of "unmusical" sound but also to whatever detracts from the organizational principles of music as they have historically been observed in Western musical practices.[4] Gould comes quite honestly, then, to his own firm entrenchment within a mind-centered concept of music, which is clear in his writings and interviews. He adheres to such a paradigm to the extent that he considers the noise of his body (literally and in Attali's sense) to be quite incidental to his mental approach to music.

Before delving too far into Gould's own remarks, it is worth considering the way he has usually been presented in the popular and scholarly media, for our perceptions of Gould the icon (informed largely by these media) most definitely influence how we listen to Gould the musician. Consider the following promotional lines, included by Columbia Masterworks on the back of several of Gould's LPs from the 1960s:

> When Mr. Gould made his recording debut, with the immensely difficult and demanding Goldberg Variations of Bach, his performance was so masterful that it elicited bravos from critics who found it difficult to

believe that a young artist could offer such probing, sensitive interpretations. Mr. Gould has further demonstrated his rare understanding
of Bach's music with recordings of the complete Partitas. . . . An avid
reader, he prefers the works of Mann, Kafka, Tolstoy, Dostoyevsky and
Nietzsche, and is himself a writer of several works on the masters of the
Viennese school. (Columbia Masterworks 1963)

Not only are we told that Gould's greatest musical strengths lie in his
"probing" intellect and in the depths of his "rare understanding," but
we also learn that when he is not playing the piano, he further engages
his mind by reading some of the most intellectually challenging literature
in the Western canon and writing about the most cerebral music of the
twentieth century.[5]

A few years earlier, Ross Parmenter of the *New York Times* had presented a similar portrayal of Gould, following an engagement at the Stratford Summer Music Festival in which Gould spoke to the audience about
the music he was performing. Parmenter attributed the success of the evening to Gould's abilities on the piano *and* to his gifts as a "thinker":

Mr. Gould is as gifted a musical thinker as he is a pianist. . . . Mr. Gould's
comments [about the music of Berg, Schoenberg, and Krenek] gave the
key to his own playing of the works. He understood their motivic coher-
ence so well that each note seemed a vital part of a satisfying and emo-
tionally expressive unit. (*New York Times*, July 10, 1956)

Focus on the significance of Gould's intellectual abilities has reached
beyond popular journalism: It has also become central to many of the
lengthier studies of Gould's work, particularly those that deal more with
his writings than with his playing. For instance, the first book-length
study of Gould, Geoffrey Payzant's *Glenn Gould: Music and Mind* (1978),
announces its bias in its title. John P. L. Roberts's *The Art of Glenn Gould:
Reflections of a Musical Genius* (1999) expresses a similar bias in its title
while also promoting a compatible image—one of Gould in contemplation—through its cover art. Even though Gould sits at the piano in this
picture, he sits sideways, with his left arm resting on the music stand and
his gaze averted from the instrument, giving the impression perhaps that
the instrument itself is merely the necessary tool by which he imparts to
his audience his deep understanding of the music.[6] In other words, Gould
playing is not nearly as important as Gould *thinking*.[7]

For all this focus on Gould's mind, however, it is important to note that
his performing body has seldom been ignored. Rather, Gould's physical
actions have caused much concern and criticism; his body has thus been
portrayed as an obstacle for his mind to overcome.[8] To be sure, Gould's
physical command of the piano was never questioned and regularly received
acclaim from critics and other listeners. I suggest, however, that praise for

his manual dexterity has often been overshadowed by praise for his mental dexterity and certainly by criticism of his other physical mannerisms. In this way Gould's body is depicted not so much as an essential part of his music making but rather as a potential distraction from it.

Gould's unusual stage demeanor during his performing years seems to have drawn the most negative press in this respect. Regardless of whether they enjoyed the program, reviewers typically began by drawing attention to his idiosyncratic performance mannerisms. Only after going through his entire litany of physical quirks would they proceed to evaluate the recital. *New York Times* critic Harold C. Schonberg offers a particularly engaging description:

> At about 8:45 last night Glenn Gould, the cadaverous Canadian, shambled from the wings at Carnegie Hall, managed to get to the piano (which was mounted on small blocks), slumped back on a bench that seemed about three inches off the ground, put his feet on the pedals and also a throw rug underneath them, put a look of ecstatic suffering on his face, and played much of his program very beautifully.
>
> He subsequently went through his familiar eccentricities, which included singing (he was not in especially good voice this time), conducting, and crossing his left leg over his right. (*New York Times*, February 14, 1959)[9]

Perhaps the most effective promotion of this dual image of Gould— one of formidable mind and imperfect body—came from Gould himself.[10] Gould repeatedly states in interviews and in his own writings that for him, the most important aspect of any piece of music is its structure. He asserts, moreover, that his interpretation of such structures is primarily a mental process, quite distinct from the physical act of playing the piano. He often told his friend and colleague, Roberts, that he could "practise in his head" and that he "believed the piano had to be played with the mind" (Roberts 1999, 26). Corporeal activity, then, becomes secondary to cerebral activity. This is not to say that Gould completely ignores the tactile aspects of playing the piano or that he never speaks of them. On the contrary, his own views on the performance of the piano itself are based far more on how the instrument felt under his fingers than on the sounds he could get from it (Bazzana 2003, 197–198). He often states that his own distinctive approach to playing the piano grew out of the tactile way in which he learned to play the organ. He explains that when playing the organ,

> the whole effect of clarity of line, of detached sound, has got to be achieved by a lifting of the finger after the note has been struck and not an attack on the note before it has been struck.
>
> This was the method of playing which of course I learned on the organ and which I simply transferred to the piano, a method which involved minimal movement of the fingers, really, and which—*I'm*

sorry to reduce this to something so physical, but this is really what it was—and a method which began by starting at the key rather than above it, and [in] which no amount of excessive force could be brought to bear on the piano. (Gould and Rich 1999, 139; my emphasis)

Gould reveals two crucial points here. First, even his physical approach to the instrument is only as "physical" as absolutely necessary, in that it involves as little movement as possible. In addition to the "minimal movement of the fingers," he avoids any "excessive force" in his playing.[11] Second, and I think more significantly, Gould feels the need to apologize for speaking about his playing in such blatantly physical terms. He does modify this account somewhat in other interviews, making clear that the physical demands of playing the piano are worked out *in the mind* long before they are ever acted out at the instrument. In one instance, he speaks of "practicing" mentally while away from the piano for long periods of time and states that "one carries the fingerings in one's head at all times" (Gould and Aikin 1999, 269–270).

Gould further reconciles his tactile approach to the instrument with his mind-centered concept of music, because he feels that the real business of music making goes on in the mind, so it is not tied to performance on any particular instrument. Put another way, physicality is important to Gould only insofar as it allows him to realize a piece on the piano, which is secondary to understanding the piece in its own abstract and disembodied state. Gould's praise of pianist Sviatoslav Richter resonates very strongly with the image he projects of himself. As such, it helps further clarify his views on the physical mechanics of making music. He argues that musicians can be divided into two categories: "those who seek to exploit the instruments they use, and those who do not." Richter, he believes, belongs to the second category, which

> includes musicians who try to bypass the whole question of the performing mechanism, to create the illusion, at any rate, of a direct [mental] link between themselves and a particular musical score and who, therefore, help the listener to achieve a sense of involvement, not with the performance per se, but, rather, with the music itself. . . .
>
> [It] is possible . . . to achieve such a perfect liaison with the instrument that the mechanical process involved becomes all but invisible—totally at the service of the musical structure—and that the performer, and consequently the listener, is then able to ignore all superficial questions of virtuosity or instrumental display and concentrate instead on the spiritual qualities inherent in the music itself. (1999b, 52–53)

In a similar vein, Gould's comments about the tactile aspects of any particular piece are often quickly followed by a comment about the more important issue of analysis. Gould's description of Jacques Hétu's *Variations* for piano provides an example: "Hétu's flair for the instrument is unmistakable. Everything works and sounds and lies rewardingly beneath the fingers. Yet, the impressive thing about these *Variations* is that despite their unabashedly theatrical inclination, they are held together by a sure sense of the purely musical values inherent in their material" (1967). Gould then explains that the material in question is a twelve-tone row and goes on to discuss the tonal qualities inherent in this row. To Gould, then, "purely musical values" are to be found in the analysis of a piece, not in the physical act of playing it.

Gould's views on the importance of analytical thought in music must also be understood in relation to his thoughts about the limitations and frailty of his own body. As a particular extension of his admitted hypochondria, Gould lived in constant fear of losing all control of his hands.[12] He made headlines in 1960 when he sued the Steinway and Sons piano company for an incident involving one of their technicians, who purportedly greeted Gould with a "thump" on the back that caused injury to Gould's left shoulder and hand.[13] Columbia Masterworks itself is quite eager to share with Gould's listeners his constant concerns about blood circulation in his forearms and hands, in a press release issued with Gould's first *Goldberg Variations* recording in 1956:

> It was a balmy June day, but Gould arrived in coat, beret, muffler and gloves. "Equipment" consisted of the customary music portfolio, also a batch of towels, . . . five small bottles of pills (all different colors and prescriptions) and his own special piano chair. Towels, it developed, were needed in plenty because Gould soaks his arms and hands up to the elbows in hot water for 20 minutes before sitting down at the keyboard. . . . Pills were for any number of reasons—headaches, relieving tension, maintaining circulation. . . . (Columbia Masterworks 1956)

Regarding his physical eccentricities in performance, Gould also considers them necessary only to the point that they help him achieve his *ideal* performance. He once told an interviewer that when it first came to his attention in 1956 that his singing and conducting were distracting to his audiences, he became very self-conscious, because he had never before given any thought to his physical appearance during performance. "The whole secret of what I had been doing," he explained, "was to concentrate exclusively on realizing a [mental] conception of the music, regardless of how it was physically achieved" (Gould and Asbell 1999, 186).

Gould establishes a clear hierarchy, then, regarding his thoughts about music and his subsequent bodily efforts to represent those thoughts in sound. Clearly, to Gould, a musician's physical actions are only important insofar as they serve his or her mental conception of how a particular work should sound. Gould's views are by no means unique or radical, as they simply reflect the mind-centered concept prevalent for centuries within

Western musical epistemology. Gould is notable, however, for how explicitly he explains this hierarchy. He is also notable, paradoxically, for how much of an inadvertent physical response he clearly has to music despite his own devaluation of music's existence in the physical realm. Gould's willing and almost perverse refusal to acknowledge the significance of his body in his own musical practice, in spite of the overt physicality of his playing, further parallels the immense lack of attention paid to corporeal meaning in so much Western musical thought.

DISEMBODIED MUSIC OR CORPOREAL
LIVENESS? PERFORMANCE ON RECORD

If Gould were uninterested in music's corporeal qualities, audio recording would seem to be the perfect medium through which he could exercise his mind-centered approach to performance. Although Gould never explicitly states as much, many others have argued that recorded sound is essentially *disembodied* sound. John Corbett's description of an "audio-visual disjunction" (1990, 84) in recorded music provides a useful introduction to this discussion. For Corbett, popular-music consumers' various attempts to reconstitute a visual element in their encounters with recordings (through music videos, album-cover art, and audio imaging[14]) are a result of the desire to "negotiate the menacing void" left by the removal of the body from recorded musical experiences (1990, 85). In popular music, according to Corbett, this body is removed not only visually but also aurally by echo, compression, and other recording studio techniques. Ultimately for Corbett, these aural traces also become visual:

> The sound of fingers, lips, legs, and nose are all traces of the performer, the *absent* performer, and they foreground the visual. Echo, by doubling the sound upon itself, and compression, by doing away with unseemly transients, wrench the sound of music from the body of the performer and erase its trace. . . . [Recordings] appeal to a fantasy of absolutely independent music, where concerns of the image never enter the picture. Lullaby, close your eyes, and good night. (1990, 92)

This "fantasy of absolutely independent music" can be linked to the general logocentrism that N. Katherine Hayles argues is indicative of the digital era. Hayles argues that to many modern thinkers, the universe is composed essentially of information, which thus encourages a fantasy comparable to that identified by Corbett:

> Because we are essentially information, we can do away with the body. Central to this argument is a conceptualization that sees information and materiality as distinct entities. This separation allows the

construction of a hierarchy in which information is given the dominant position and materiality runs a distant second. As though we had
learned nothing from Derrida . . . embodiment continues to be discussed as if it were a supplement to be purged from the dominant term
of information, an accident of evolution we are now in a position to
correct. (1999, 12)

The parallels between Hayles's examples and those from within Western art music (Gould, Beethoven, etc.) are evident. Yet for many musicologists concerned with reconstituting the value of corporeality in accounts of
Western music, their arguments about disembodied sound, like Corbett's,
nonetheless revolve around a *lack* of a certain kind of visual information
in a given musical experience. In these cases, as discussed in Chapter 2,
perception of performing bodies is equated with *seeing* those bodies (or at
least with constructing mental images of those bodies). For some writers,
the danger of a mind-centered musical perspective coupled with recording
is that these recordings thus become an easy method by which listeners
"can have the pleasure of the sound without the troubling reminder of the
bodies producing it" (McClary 1991, 136).

Although often productive, such accounts of recordings as agents of disembodiment promote an overriding technophobia that ignores the very real
potential for sound technology to further *increase* a listener's engagement
with corporeality in mediatized music. When we consider the historic development of sound recording and reproduction technologies, we realize that
these technologies were modeled after our own bodies' methods of hearing
sound, the physiology of the human ear (indeed some early sound technologies created by Clarence Blake and Alexander Graham Bell involved the use
of real, dissected, human ears). As Jonathan Sterne argues, "The body is
the first communication technology, and . . . *technologies* of listening . . .
emerge out of *techniques* of listening" (2003, 92; original emphasis). Many
such techniques were developed *inside* the human body (Sterne [2003, 92]
calls them "techniques of the body") long before technologies *outside* the
human body were ever conceived of. To assume that sound technologies
interrupt the corporeal significance of sounds simply because they remove
these sounds from their *visual* sources is thus to ignore corporeally sensitive
techniques of listening that have little if anything to do with sight.

To help rectify this omission, I turn to other writers who have suggested
how we might begin to recognize and appreciate performing bodies, even
when we lack any visual clues about them. Phenomenologists have long argued
that everything we perceive is rooted in a sense of embodiment, because even
our minds are physically situated in the world. This idea has also been taken
up by music-cognition scholars. Marc Leman, for instance, argues that "the
subjective world of mental representations is *not* an autonomous category but
a result of an embodied interaction with the physical environment" (2008,
13; original emphasis).[15] Several writers have followed this line of argument

to suggest that, in perceiving music, listeners relate the sounds they hear to their own embodied understandings of their environment. Variations on this argument bear several different labels, including "kinematic empathy" (Todd 1995), "bodily hearing" (Mead 1999), "the mimetic hypothesis" (A. Cox 2001), and "corporeal signification" (Leman 2008, 17–19).[16] Whatever the label, these concepts all describe a listener making sense of music not abstractly but through corporeal involvement. The body acts as a mediator between physical sound and mental cognition (Leman 2008).

In this way, for instance, a regular rhythmic pulse within a given piece of music may engage a listener's experiences of regular rhythms within his or her own body, such as the listener's heart beating or experiences of walking and running. Moreover, music perception also relies on a listener's embodied understanding of sound production itself. In other words, the recognition that someone has struck a drum to produce a particular sound may engage a listener's own understanding of how it feels to make that physical gesture. Arnie Cox (2001) is particularly helpful in explaining this perceptual phenomenon, because he focuses on the sound-producing body. In his account of a "mimetic hypothesis," Cox presents the dual assertion that "1) we understand sounds in comparison to sounds we have made ourselves, and that 2) this process of comparison involves tacit imitation, or mimetic participation, which in turn draws on the prior embodied experience of sound production" (2001, 195). A listener's responses need not be strictly mimetic, however. Even our descriptions of music as "moving" (ascending passages, accelerating tempi, etc.) illustrate the extent to which we understand musical experiences according to our existing physical knowledge of corresponding motions. Because this connection already exists, musical lines that accelerate, descend, ascend, or follow any other recognizable pattern of motion reengage with listeners' embodied experiences of those particular movements.

Such theories of corporeal listening are based on the sounds of bodies and on physical responses to sounds rather than on the act of viewing bodies. As such, they suggest that corporeal liveness—the perceived trace of bodies performing—may be evident in musical recordings, even if many choose to ignore its importance. Furthermore, corporeal perceptions of liveness carry a significance in recorded music that accounts of recordings as disembodied music deny. As Cox argues, "Music invites us to participate—both in our imagination, which is automatically informed by embodied experience via tacit mimetic participation, and overtly in the form of such things as toe-tapping, swaying, dancing, and singing along. The ways in which we respond to the invitation to participate . . . are part of how we define ourselves and society" (A. Cox 2001, 206–207). An account of corporeal liveness in recordings, in other words, recognizes recorded music as a form of communication in which the *performer* (and not just the composer's work) holds great significance, even if this communication is made indirect by the mediation of technology.

GOULD'S BODY ON RECORD: THE MEDIATIZATION
OF GOULD'S PERFORMANCES

Before discussing Gould's recordings directly, I address here his statements about the recorded medium as they relate to this notion of communication I have just described. For Gould, music was not about communication between performer and audience. After retiring from the concert stage in 1964, he was asked by interviewers whether he missed the direct connection so many performers claim to share with their audiences.[17] Gould responded that he never felt such a connection when he was concertizing, so he certainly did not miss it now that his performances were confined to recording and broadcast studios. Rather, he viewed the microphone as a "friend" and, if anything, felt more communion with it than with any potential audience (Gould and Tovell 1999, 80).

Throughout his writings and correspondences, it emerges that Gould is not entirely antagonistic toward the idea of musical communication, but he views it as a line of communication that ideally does not involve the performer. To Gould, recordings offer a connection with a much broader audience, but one that is, paradoxically, more intimate than that offered in a live performance setting. His perspective relies once again on understanding the musical work as occupying the place of primary importance, for this intimate connection does not take place between performer and listener but rather between listener and work and, through the work, between listener and composer. Gould feels that one of the strengths of electronic sound technology lay in its ability to present to composers a permanent record of their own interpretations (in the form of acousmatic works or their own performances) so they would not have to rely on other performers to get it right. Moreover, Gould argues, listeners will connect more intimately with that work, because they "will be forced to come to decisions about the work of art because of the reaction which they themselves receive from it, and for no other reasons" (1999a, 219). Because they are listening privately, in other words, these listeners generate a response to and an interpretation of the work completely by their own means and are not distracted by the responses of their neighbors in a concert hall or by the presence of the performer on stage. For Gould, music is an "essentially private act" between composer and listener (1992, 180) rather than an opportunity for meaningful communication between *performer* and listener.

Nonetheless, and with all apologies to Gould, I maintain that his recordings do convey performative significance—not just through his brilliant interpretations of musical works but also through the corporeal liveness so readily apparent in these recorded performances. In Gould's recordings, one can constantly hear not just abstract musical structures (disembodied notes) but also many of the incidental sounds—the noise—involved in Gould's act of sounding out those structures on the piano and with his voice. Gould's recordings provide an excellent opportunity to perceive this corporeal liveness in part due to the close microphone pick-up that he and his recording-studio collaborators often employed. Basic microphone technique dictates that the farther a microphone is placed from its intended source of sound, the more the reverberant qualities of the recording space will alter that sound. In Gould's case, a close microphone perspective avoids a great deal of room reverberation, resulting in very clear recordings of the sounds emanating directly from the piano and from its immediate vicinity; hence the clarity of Gould's bodily sounds, discussed below.[18]

Gould's intention was not, however, to provide a "close-up" audio perspective on his body making music. On the contrary, and in line with his mind-centered concept of musical communication, Gould deployed this particular use of recording technology in an effort to make the musical structure more apparent to his listeners. He felt that the more customary recording acoustic usually employed for recordings of classical music (at least in his time), which capture the natural resonances of the performance/recording space, provide an acoustic "halo" around the sound in an effort to make it sound more like a live event.[19] For Gould, the goal was rather to achieve a certain analytical quality in the sound: One that would allow the listener to hear each individual note as clearly as possible. The added effect of this close-microphone set-up, however, is that we can also hear, very clearly, the noise of Gould's body playing his piano. In addition to his singing, we can hear his physical interaction with his instrument; moreover, we hear the tactility of that instrument: the creaking of his chair as he sways, the percussive nature of hammers hitting strings, the redampening of strings as he lifts his foot off the sustain pedal, and the very precise nuances of articulation that are lost in recordings with a more typically reverberant sound. I turn now to specific examples in Gould's recorded output in which these traces of corporeality are most easily perceived. The liveness of Gould's sounding body in these recordings, audible *because of* mediatization, draws attention to the significance of Gould's *performances* and not merely that of his *interpretations*.

GOULD'S VOICE

The most obvious evidence of Gould's own performing body in his recordings is his almost constant singing. Gould once told an interviewer that his singing was a reflection of how he *thought* his phrases should sound, because his fingers never quite got it exactly right (Gould and McClure 1968). At the same time he felt, like many of his critics, that the singing was a dreadful distraction from "the music" and wished he could stop doing it without feeling as though it made his playing worse.[20] Despite attempts to shield this sound from the microphones, his recording engineers were unable to avoid picking it up; it ranges in clarity and loudness from one recording to another. Most of the time, Gould clearly reproduces one of the piano's melodic lines with his singing, often with a character that matches what he is conveying in his playing. The full significance of the liveness inherent in Gould's voice stems largely from the variety in his singing as he demonstrates vocally the nuances of phrasing, dynamics, and articulation to which he aspires in his playing. Through the identification of Gould's various vocal stylings, we can also identify a voice emanating from a particular body rather than just a disembodied voice in the background of a piano recording. I discuss several moments in Gould's two recordings of Bach's *Goldberg Variations* (1956, 1982) when the singing is most pronounced, demonstrating how Gould's performing body is represented in his vocalizations.

I have chosen to focus on Gould's *Goldberg Variations* recordings for several reasons. First, they are certainly the most prominent recordings of Gould's entire discography. As such, they are highly available and potentially well-known to many readers. Second, Gould's singing is more easily heard here, particularly on the remastered version from which I am working (Gould 2002), than on any other Gould album I have been able to consult.[21] Third, the composition itself ranges widely in character from one variation to the next, prompting a variety of vocal responses from Gould in a rather condensed format. Other recordings by Gould, on the other hand, may also offer clear and engaging singing, but often the character of this singing remains unchanged throughout an entire piece (or at least throughout a movement).

Variation 25 from Gould's 1982 recording clearly demonstrates his tendency simply to hum along with individual voices within a piece's overall texture. The variation, marked *Adagio*, is lyrically written. In Gould's rendition, it unfolds slowly and clearly. Although the variation progresses primarily as a solo treble line accompanied by simple pulses in the left-hand voices, Bach does engage in a bit of counterpoint between the treble voice in the right hand and the two voices in the left hand. During the variation, Gould alternates between vocally mimicking the treble voice and one of the accompanying lower voices. Due to the transparent texture of the movement (particularly as realized in Gould's performance), we now hear four clear voices: three from the piano and one from Gould's throat, which variously mimics each of the other three. Most of the time in this variation, Gould projects a basic hum: We hear either a closed "m" sound or a dark long "e" vowel, and very little articulation in the way of hard consonants. This is Gould's singing at its simplest.

Perhaps the most significant indicators of Gould's corporeality in this variation, however, happen in the moments when Gould is not humming—that is, they occur during the brief moments between his voiced hums, when he breathes. The clarity of the recording is such that nearly every time Gould stops for breath, we can hear him inhale.[22] Example 3.1 shows a transcription of Gould's vocalizations (along with Bach's score) for the first four measures of this variation, including the moments where he breathes (indicated with asterisks).

Example 3.1 J. S. Bach, *The Goldberg Variations*, BWV 988, Variation 25, mm. 1–4, with vocal syllables and breaths transcribed from Glenn Gould's 1982 recording[23]

At this moment, a comparison with Gould's first *Goldberg Variations* (1956) is intriguing. At two different instances in Variation 15 of that recording, Gould audibly exhales through pursed lips, rather than singing as he usually does. In addition to the whistling air, beginning at 0:05 (m. 2, beat 2),[24] we quite clearly hear Gould articulate these breaths with a "t" sound to match the articulation of first the middle and then the upper voice in the piano. (This variation, "Canone all Quinta in moto contrario," is written as a canon in three voices.) Gould similarly exhales "musically" at the start of the variation's second half, beginning at 1:04 (m. 17). In both of these instances, we hear Gould expel and shape this air with his lips, teeth, and tongue. Suddenly the voice we hear on these recordings is not just an ethereal humming sound, but it has a source: a living, breathing body.

Breathing aside, the singing we hear in both of these variations, on both recordings, is rather uneventful compared to some of Gould's vocalizations. For instance, on his 1982 recording of Variation 2, Gould offers a rich variety of vocal sounds in a very short time (the variation runs only forty-seven seconds in this recording). Like Variation 25, Bach writes this variation in three distinct voices. Gould begins his rendition by vocally reproducing the most rhythmically active voices (sometimes in harmony), thus alternating between the top two. Gould's performance of this variation on the piano demonstrates a variety of articulations, moving as it does quite freely

Example 3.2   J. S. Bach, *The Goldberg Variations*, BWV 988, Variation 2, mm. 1–8, with vocal syllables transcribed from Glenn Gould's 1982 recording.[25]

between legato and staccato playing and achieving various note lengths in the space between those two extremes. His singing, however, demonstrates even more variety by way of the different syllables Gould employs. Gould can clearly be heard singing the syllables, "da," "dee," "dum," "badum," "ta," "tum," "ti," "tu," and even "diga-diga-dum," among others (see Example 3.2). The syllables themselves are not particularly significant, so much as the extent to which they further engage Gould's vocal apparatus to give us a sense of what Roland Barthes calls the "grain of the voice": the "tongue, the glottis, the teeth, the mucous membranes, the nose" (Barthes 1989, 183)—in other words, the body. At several moments, Gould also clearly increases the intensity of his voice to match his pianistic phrasing. These little vocal swells, brought on by increased airflow and diaphragm support, provide further evidence of Gould's vocal apparatus at work.[26] We hear the tactility of Gould's body in these vocal sounds.

GOULD'S CHAIR

Vocal sounds emanate from inside a performer's body, providing us with evidence of that performer's interior movements. In addition to the sounds of the piano itself (addressed below), some of Gould's recordings offer even further evidence of his *external* movements as he plays the piano. On the sleeve of Gould's *Beethoven Piano Sonatas, Opus 10 Complete* (1965), his producer, Thomas Frost, offers the following explanation and apology:

> For some years now, [Gould] has been merrily fugueing his way through the keyboard works of Bach, Beethoven and Schoenberg to the accompaniment of the strange creakings and groanings of an old, beloved friend—his piano stool. This object of endearment, decrepit and moth-eaten as it is (having reached retirement age long ago), apparently has learned to swing and sway so perfectly with Glenn Gould's body motions that he has stubbornly refused to part with it in spite of all counsel and advice. . . .
>
> [We] hope that you, the consumer, will refuse to be discomforted by some audible creaks that are insignificant in light of the great music-making on this disc. (1965)

Indeed, throughout this recording, Gould's chair creaks audibly in apparent sympathy with his body's movements as he plays; I argue that these creaks are a delightful and essential *part* of the "great music-making on this disc" rather than an "insignificant" distraction from it. As the second movement of Beethoven's Sonata no. 5, opus 10, no. 1 begins, for instance, we hear not only Beethoven's embellished choralelike opening and Gould's usual accompanimental singing but also the gentle creaks of Gould's chair as he moves through this opening passage. Throughout the movement, the chair's sounds seem to indicate relatively little extraneous body movement on Gould's part: just the occasional shift in weight, perhaps as he depresses or releases a pedal or reaches to a different part of the keyboard. At times (for example, 2:18/mm. 22–23) the chair's noises occur during moments of relaxed energy in the piece, seemingly indicating a body moving *not* in sympathy with the movement of the musical line itself or with the movement of Gould's arms as made necessary by that musical line. At this particular moment in the recording (due not only to Beethoven's indications but also to Gould's realization of those indications), the left hand remains silent while the right hand ascends delicately and softly through a slowly moving sixteenth-note line, to arrive, *pianissimo*, at m. 24.

At other moments, however, it seems apparent that Gould's own range of motion increases with an increased intensity and forward motion in the piece. One of these sequences begins at 2:53 (m. 51, beat 2) and continues with increasing chair noise until a moment of peak musical energy is reached (3:18/m. 60), at which point the chair noises subside along with the energy projected in Gould's playing. A similar demonstration of Gould's bodily movement is represented by increased chair noise beginning around 5:22 (m. 98), as Gould moves through a final surge of energy, indicated in the score by a rising contour and a crescendo (both typically interpreted in

Western musical practice as markers of increased energy). His chair remains almost entirely silent after 5:46 (m. 106), as the forward momentum of the piece slows and finally comes to a halt.

GOULD'S PIANO

Finally, the body of the piano itself is also quite audible in many of Gould's recordings to an extent uncommon in piano recordings, particularly those made by Gould's contemporaries. Here I speak of the *noise* of the piano as it is played—not the pitches produced by the depression of keys and the relatively undifferentiated timbre of the piano across its range but rather the sounds of the piano's mechanical parts coming in contact with one another. These sounds seem to me excellent indicators of the kinetic energy involved in playing the piano: A finger depresses a key, for instance, and a pitch only results once that energy has been transferred into the throwing of a hammer against a string. A piano's noises, then, represent actions taken by the pianist, reminding us of the mutual physical relationship between the pianist's body and that of his or her piano. Contrary to Gould's praise of Richter's ability to make the piano's mechanism invisible/inaudible, I find these noises significant and indicative of the vital corporeality of piano performance. Such recognition of the physical relationship established between Gould's body and that of his piano also emphasizes a sort of corporeal codependency between musician and instrument. In other words, without one another, both bodies remain mute. Music sounds only when they come together in performance.

For my final corporeal hearing of Gould, I turn to the fifth movement, "Sarabande," in his recording of Bach's Partita no. 4 in D Major, BWV 828 (Gould 1963). Although we obviously hear the evidence of Gould's fingers in motion, this recording also captures evidence of his feet in motion. The most obvious example of Gould's pedaling is demonstrated by the simple "clunking" noise that occurs when Gould releases his pedal, captured clearly at the end of the first A section and the A' section (1:04/m. 12 and 4:44/m. 38; the movement's form can be described as A-B-A', with Gould observing the repeat of the first A section). A similar (and perhaps more poetically significant) noise is clearly captured at the end of Gould's 1982 *Goldberg Variations*. That recording—Gould's second attempt at his "signature" recorded work (and one of his last commercial releases)—ends not with the natural decay to silence of Gould's final chord, as a more conventional interpretation would observe. Rather, that "musically" significant decay is closely followed by the clunk of the pedal as Gould releases it, reminding listeners that his feet have played an important part in shaping the performance they have just heard.[27]

I also detect in the Sarabande a very beautiful recurring instance of corporeal liveness created by a particular combination of Gould's fingering

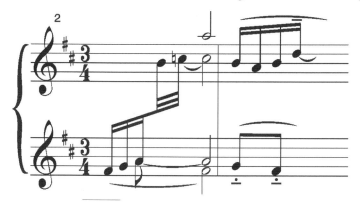

Example 3.3a J. S. Bach, Partita no. 4 in D Major, BWV 828, "Sarabande," mm. 2–3, b. 1

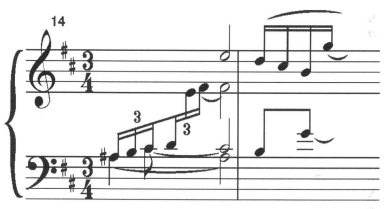

Example 3.3b J. S. Bach, Partita no. 4 in D Major, BWV 828, "Sarabande," mm. 14–15, b. 1[28]

and pedaling. The second measure of each section in the movement ends with a half note in the treble voice, held over a triad that has been built up from the beginning of the measure. In the A and A' sections, this half note, an a″, doubles the third in a diminished iii chord that moves to the subdominant in the next measure (see Example 3.3a). In the B section, the half note, an e‴, functions as the seventh degree in a major-minor seventh chord leading to a G-major chord, which is spelled out in the first beat of the next measure (see Example 3.3b). Each time this moment occurs in his performance (0:08/m. 2, 1:11/m. 2, 2:18/m. 14, 3:48/m. 30), Gould holds the sustain pedal down until he has clearly voiced each note in the measure. At some point before he releases the sustain pedal, he also releases both the keys he has been depressing with his left hand. He then releases the sustain pedal so that we only hear the top two notes, emphasizing the inverted minor third between c" and a" in the A and A' sections, and the minor seventh between f#' and e" in the B section. Finally, he releases the lower note in his right hand so that we hear the top note ringing on its own before he moves on to the next measure.

The first three times Gould performs this little act of manual and pedal precision in the "Sarabande" (that is, in both iterations of the A section and the B section), we hear it exactly as I imagine he intends, and the harmonic importance of those particular notes is emphasized according to Gould's interpretation. When this moment occurs in the A' section, however, another acoustic reminder of the physical contact between performer and instrument sounds. In this instance (3:51/m. 30), Gould releases the pedal and the c" key in such a way that the felt intended to dampen the strings corresponding to that key actually causes a momentary "shimmer" on that note. Such an effect is created when felts are held, by way of a partially depressed sustain pedal, just slightly off the strings—far enough away that the strings are afforded more room to vibrate, but still close enough to the strings to somewhat restrict that vibration. Thus, before our attention is drawn to the sustained a" at the end of this measure, it is first drawn to the c" beneath it, which Gould inadvertently emphasizes when he releases the sustain pedal. Such an audible effect, inadvertent or not, is a clear reminder of the physical process of playing the piano and thus another strong indicator of the significance of corporeality on this particular recording.

A BRIEF DIVERSION: SONDRE LERCHE'S "TWO-WAY MONOLOGUE"

Although my primary subject in this chapter is Gould, and my primary context for discussion is the Western art-music tradition, a brief discussion of a very different recording demonstrates the applicability of the concept of corporeal liveness to a broad range of recorded music. I turn here to Norwegian singer-songwriter Sondre Lerche's "Two-Way Monologue" (2004), in which varying production values and instrumentation create a simple contrast between moments of very evident corporeal liveness and moments in which that liveness gets "buried in the mix." The liveness I perceive in this track emanates from two primary sources: Lerche's voice and guitar. As in Gould's recordings, the "noise" of both these instruments tells us of a body in motion.

The track begins very simply with Lerche's voice and acoustic guitar, both performed softly and obviously captured with close-range microphones. The subtleties of Lerche's gentle voice are demonstrated here in great detail—even to the point that one can hear the final "s" of the word "this" taper away gradually to nothing at 0:31, and a slight rasp in his throat at 0:28–0:30 and at 0:42–0:49—details that would be lost with a less proximate microphone setup. Even more obviously, the acoustic guitar track also reveals clearly audible traces of Lerche's performing body in motion. The guitar part itself is rather simple: On each beat, a single string is plucked, to be answered on each offbeat by a strummed chord. Particularly on these offbeats, the noise of the pick scraping the strings is audible, so each chord features a subtly percussive onset just prior to the pitches sounding. There is also a rhythmic unevenness to this strumming at first, bringing to mind, perhaps, a reluctance to enter into this communication that manifests itself in a slightly faltering (physical) guitar technique. An even more noticeable guitar noise is captured each time Lerche moves his left hand along the strings of the guitar's neck to change chords (particularly audible examples occur at 0:15, 0:21, and 0:34): a high-pitched, metallic scrape, which seems to have been made more apparent by the application of extra reverberation, or by an added distance-microphone capturing extra room ambience. In any event, the emphasis on this noise seems to be a result of deliberate recording and production practices, and it adds to the overall effect of physical closeness and intimacy that pervades the track through the song's opening verse.

This illusion of intimacy is shattered as the track progresses from the first verse to the second. The final words of the verse's refrain, "my name," become an obvious series of deteriorating echoes that quickly pulls us away from Lerche's singing body (0:48–0:55), leading into a louder and more thickly textured second verse in which bass and drums are added, Lerche's guitar strumming becomes more aggressive, his left hand becomes seemingly more deliberate in its movements, and his vocal track seems to have been boosted very slightly in the mix. Although the vocal track is still rather dry (i.e., lacking in much reverberation or other acoustic ambience) and close-miked, and the percussive noise of Lerche's strumming is still audible, a denser overall texture prevents the listener from focusing on these elements of corporeal liveness to the extent possible at the beginning of the track. As the second verse nears its end, these traces of corporeality are pushed aside even more forcefully with the entrance of an electric guitar and the introduction of a ride cymbal by the drummer (1:28), creating an overall texture very much in contrast with the intimacy of the track's opening minute. The remainder of the song repeatedly alternates between this thick, rocklike texture and a thinner, more corporeally infused texture, but we never again return to the pronounced intimacy with which the song begins (the sliding guitar-string noises, for instance, are not heard again).

Consideration of the song's lyrical content provides a useful perspective from which to interpret corporeal liveness as an element of the track's overall aesthetic impact, as it makes evident important connections between lyrical intent and Lerche's performance as conveyed through the track's production. Although the exact significance of each lyrical phrase is often difficult to decipher, the song's overall theme is one of broken communication, apparently between the narrator and his parents. References to this communication breakdown are frequent, as the narrator asks his "Pa" to listen; mentions his "Ma" changing her mind, again; and speaks of a note on a machine-washed, disintegrated piece of paper. These lyrics, then, tell us of messages being confused, lost, or never received in the first place.[29] The song's chorus is even more explicit in its reference to empty communication and a lack of dialogue, with its extensive repetition of the words *two-way monologue*. Notably, the chorus—especially in its final instance—features the thickest textures and therefore the least amount of the corporeal liveness I have been discussing in the entire track.

In summary, then, the song begins with a sparse texture, strongly imbued with elements of a corporeal liveness (the augmented subtleties of Lerche's singing and the noises of his guitar playing). The listener is invited into an intimate communication and brought close to the nuances of Lerche's performing body. As the song's narrative unfolds, and its theme of broken communication—of isolated participants in a two-way monologue— becomes clearer, audible traces of Lerche's body increasingly fade from the track's texture. Between 4:10 and 5:12, a dense and polyphonically busy instrumental interlude of guitars, drums, bass, piano, and various electronically synthesized sounds carries the listener to the final chorus, where the noisiness of the thick instrumentation drowns out any possibility of hearing the types of intimate noises we hear in the opening verse. I do not suggest that this final texture is alienating or uncommunicative, but its deliberately pronounced difference from the physical intimacy communicated in the opening verse makes the attentive listener feel its corporeal lack all the more strongly—an element of human communication whose lack corresponds to the broken communications referenced in the song's title and lyrics.

Crucially, and reflecting my accounts of Gould's recordings, all the nontextual elements of this track that I have discussed are deeply reliant on the performance, recording, *and* production processes (i.e., performance and its mediatization) for their significance. My discussions of Gould's and Lerche's recordings have led me to confront accounts of recordings that characterize them as representations of disembodied music. Although many concerns about the alienating potential of technology in music are well placed, such accounts often ignore the very real potential in mediatized music for *increased* communication of corporeal—and thus human— significance. By hearing performers' bodies in their recordings, we hear their liveness. Not only can we then rethink our common conceptions of, in this case, Gould's musicianship but also our common conceptions of recorded music, recognizing the potential of mediatization to project new and necessary understandings of musical meaning. To listen to music *without* attending to performers' and instruments' corporeality is to hear only compositions and not the material practices and processes of making music. To listen to such practices and processes in recorded music without attending to the significance of mediatization is to similarly neglect important aspects of the existing musical artifact itself.

4   Reconsidering Fidelity

Authenticity, Historicism, and Liveness in the Music of The White Stripes

> As a teen, . . . he learned to value hard work and honesty, hungering
> for authenticity with a passion lacking in his irony-soaked generation.
> When it came time to offer up his artistic vision, Jack chose an ancient
> instrument, the guitar, to perform a sacred music, the blues. While
> his contemporaries gravitated to computer beats and, as he puts it,
> "video games and marijuana bongs," he denied himself such slothful
> indulgences. He denied himself all kinds of things, in fact: the ease of
> mixing an album on an iMac, the convenience of a cell phone, or a
> bass player. . . . "I get punished for my honesty," Jack White says.
>
> Jon Dolan, "New Jack City"

In a discussion of audio technologies, the word *fidelity* usually carries with
it a specific meaning: the degree to which those technologies are perceived
to faithfully convey the sounds they record (their full dynamic and frequency ranges, for instance) without introducing "noises" of their own (the
pop and crackle of phonograph systems, the hiss of magnetic tape). This
might be thought of as the "degree of truth-to-reality" (Keightley 1996,
152) achieved by a recording medium or a recording, and it can be effected
(i.e., noise can be introduced) at the recording and playback stages. Analog
technologies, such as vinyl records and magnetic tapes, also incur increased
noise over time, as the repeated friction of their playback media physically alters the surfaces upon which their sounds are encoded. Thus, the
perpetual search for increased fidelity has been a major concern within the
music-recording industry since its inception, as manufacturers and recordists alike have often striven after recordings that convey for the listener as
faithfully as possible the sounds of live music making, thus shortening the
distance across the technosphere between recorded sound and its reception.
As will be discussed below, the perception of audio fidelity is achieved as
much through illusion as through strictly recorded "accuracy."

I wish to remind the reader of the broader meanings of the word *fidelity*, however, for within this chapter I propose that a more general concept
of fidelity is often also at work within the discourse of liveness, particularly as it relates to the concept of rock authenticity. *The Shorter Oxford
English Dictionary* lists "faithfulness," "veracity," and "accuracy" as
definitions of fidelity, as well as "loyalty," "unswerving allegiance," and

"trustworthiness."[1] *Honesty* is also a closely related term. I offer this elaboration on the word *fidelity* not to propose an *alternative* understanding of its meaning than that implied in an audio-technical context; rather, I wish to frame the discussions of fidelity in this chapter within a broader and more diverse context—one in which the word's various meanings and implications may all come to bear on an understanding of liveness and its relation to, in this case, ideologies of authenticity in rock.

I present in this chapter a discussion of fidelity in the musicking of The White Stripes, as it relates to the technical fidelity of audio-recording technologies and to a discourse of rock authenticity dependent on faithfulness—fidelity—to an ideal of liveness. A certain paradox with respect to fidelity is strongly emphasized when considering the White Stripes, however, in that their authenticity—so heavily reliant on a fidelity to liveness[2]—is framed in part (by them, by the popular media, by their fans) in reference to their eschewal of high-fidelity technologies. In this approach, The White Stripes are certainly not alone. In fact, many other acts (some of whom are discussed below) have recorded music with a much more distinctly pronounced lo-fi aesthetic. However, the immense success and exposure of The White Stripes, coupled with the extent to which they (especially front man Jack White) have shared elements of their musical ideologies in a variety of public forums, have created a scenario in which such ideologies clearly reflect, and are reflected in, those of a very large portion of a broad rock fan base, all of which helps reveal the vital and complex role played by notions of fidelity in understandings of modern rock's authenticity.[3]

The White Stripes are a two-piece band originally from Detroit, Michigan, that helped redefine the sound of mainstream rock in the early twenty-first century—one grounded in a back-to-basics, punklike aesthetic that was demonstrated not only in the music of The White Stripes but also that of The Hives (2000), The Strokes (2001), Yeah Yeah Yeahs (2003), and others.[4] Drawing on an eclectic range of musical influences, the strongest being blues, punk, and country, the duo released their first studio album, *The White Stripes*, in 1999. Their third album, 2001's *White Blood Cells*,[5] brought them widespread popular and critical acclaim, and their mainstream success and popularity were cemented in 2003 with their fourth album, *Elephant*, which won (among a number of other distinctions) the Grammy for Best Alternative Music Album of the year. Their remaining two studio albums, *Get Behind Me Satan* (2005) and *Icky Thump* (2007), each received the same honor and, coupled with the band's reputation as one of the best live rock acts in existence, kept the White Stripes at the center of the mainstream rock universe for most of a decade. The group consists of Meg White on drums and occasional vocals and Jack White on lead vocals and guitar (sometimes to be substituted for one of a number of keyboard instruments). Jack also acts as the primary songwriter for the group, its producer, and its overall artistic visionary/stylist. All of these facts have been widely publicized, but I emphasize them here to frame my discussions of the group in this chapter, particularly with respect to their musical style, their relationship to the fame they achieved, and their place within broader developments in rock music in the first decade of the twenty-first century.

AN HONEST ART: AUTHENTICITY IN ROCK

The arguments I wish to make about liveness of fidelity in this chapter depend on understanding the roles played by interrelated ideological concepts of fidelity, liveness, and historicism in the construction of a rock authenticity that has been increasingly expressed over the past two decades and has found its most widely celebrated example in the discourses surrounding The White Stripes. Many have written convincingly on the ideologies of rock, particularly on the role that the concept of authenticity has played in forming those ideologies.[6] Each of these accounts differs, and several remind us that the nuances of rock authenticity have changed over time with the developments of new musical styles and new social contexts for rock's creation and consumption. Nevertheless, certain key elements seem either to have remained consistently important in the identification and definition of rock authenticity or to have recurred regularly within the ebb and flow of this concept's development. Many of these characteristics are emphasized within discourses surrounding The White Stripes, in the process making clear the extent to which this band's wide popularity depends on their acceptance as authentic bearers of the rock mantle—and even, for some enthusiasts, as saviors of the authenticity of rock itself.[7]

Keir Keightley's essay "Reconsidering Rock" (2001) provides a good entry into this discussion; in it, he proposes that rock authenticity has, like rock music itself, developed along various paths throughout its history. He identifies two "broad families of rock authenticity" (2001, 136): one corresponding to characteristics of Romanticism and the other to characteristics of Modernism. Keightley's list of key tendencies of a Romantic authenticity includes several of the central tropes factoring in the case of The White Stripes: reference to tradition and historical continuity; musical styles built on the foundations of folk, blues, country, and rock-and-roll; a concern with sincerity and directness; a focus on liveness; and a concern with "hiding musical technology" (2001, 137). In Keightley's account, these elements of a Romantic authenticity are contrasted in a Modernist authenticity by their binary opposites (experimentation and progress rather than tradition and historical continuity; a celebration of technology rather than a tendency to hide it; etc.). Keightley also emphasizes that regardless of the exact makeup of an act's (or a fan's, or a genre's) individual rock authenticity, be it Romantic, Modern, or reflective of some other combination of elements, the concept of seriousness—especially as it is understood in opposition to the perceived frivolity of pop music—is key to understanding how this sense of authenticity creates meaning.

This opposition between serious rock and shallow or vacuous pop is expressed in a variety of ways. According to typical characterizations, rock is individualistic, whereas pop panders to the conventions of mass appeal; rock is sincere in its expression, whereas pop's message is superficial, even empty; rock is resistant to commercialization and industry, whereas pop is born of such qualities; rock requires musical skill and talent, whereas pop only requires a good producer and Auto-Tune; rock is good *music*, whereas pop is mere entertainment; and so forth. Of course, many of these distinctions are based much more on myth and mistaken perception than on reality, but, as I have been arguing throughout this book, such is often the way of ideological concepts. Perhaps the most glaring fallacy in rock's typical characterization is the idea that it somehow exists outside the commercial mainstream. To assert that the "authentic" heroes of rock—such as The Beatles, The Rolling Stones, Led Zeppelin, Bruce Springsteen, Nirvana, and most recently The White Stripes—were not or are not dependent upon the trappings of mainstream popular culture in the pursuit of their art is to overlook a vast array of factors, including their immense fan bases, their dependence on technologies of mass mediation, and their incorporation of earlier styles of widely popular music, just to name a few.[8]

Yet such myths remain central to discourses of rock, and their significance within what Lawrence Grossberg calls the "rock formation" is reflected in the extent to which they inform the perceived authenticity of The White Stripes.[9] The characteristics of a rock ideology that I highlight in the previous paragraph, which all aid in identifying rock as distinct from pop, can be seen to inform two related concepts, both of which are relevant to my discussion here. First, the celebration in rock discourse of individualism, resistance, rebellion, and similar themes points to a certain type of alienation with which musicians and fans alike often identify. Second, the individual in rock, the authentic loner, often derives much of this authenticity from a sense of *auteurism*—from the cultural cachet of crafting his or her own musical expressions in every way possible, without sacrificing the honesty and purity of those expressions to outside influences.

A paradox exists in rock's supposed alienation from the mainstream in that a certain myth of community forms around this alienation—around the idea of keeping others (the so-called mainstream masses) outside an exclusive minority of individuals who together celebrate their own outsiderness, their collective belonging within society's margins (Frith 2007, 36).[10] This sense of not belonging and a tendency to celebrate that isolation, argues Grossberg (1992, 202), are clear products of the immediate post-WWII years, when a North American culture in a state of massive transition gave rise to the intrinsically linked twin phenomena of rock-and-roll music and an affluent youth market where neither had previously existed. Many from the baby-boom generation, distinctly aware (with a bit of help from leisure-industry advertisers) of their differences from their parents yet unsure of what to make of them found their "identity in the lack of identity—a sense of perpetual transition" (Grossberg 1992, 202).

The White Stripes, like many rock acts before them, are often seen to have emerged from such a community at the fringes, and the image they actively project of themselves strongly reinforces this impression. On numerous occasions, Jack White—a young white male from the American Midwest—has made reference to his minority status, in racial and musical terms, during his teenage years (when he was defining his own musical tastes):

> I lived in an all-Mexican neighborhood. Mexican Town, it was called. It was un-cool to play guitar. To play an instrument was the most embarrassing thing you could probably make up. Hip-hop and house music—that's what everyone wanted to hear. DJs and rappers. It was very un-cool to actually play an instrument. There was no record store. No guitar shop. Nobody liked rock 'n' roll or blues music. (Guggenheim 2009)[11]

Just as their musical identity is seen to have emerged from the fringes, the White Stripes have also drawn attention to their geographic isolation from more active hubs of the popular music industry, such as New York and Los Angeles. In 2001, Jack produced an album of local Detroit acts, *Sympathetic Sounds of Detroit*, in which he wrote that "Detroit musicians [are free from] the anxiety of not getting signed. We know that it's never going to happen. No suit from LA [*sic*] or New York is going to fly to Detroit to check out a band and hand out business cards" (quoted in Male 2002). A few years later, after finding the success that he had been sure would never come, he nevertheless still offered a similar appraisal of his Detroit roots:

> As someone who grew up [in Detroit], I know that there's something that I got from knowing I wasn't part of a pack. . . . Iggy [Pop] once said that you can be a king in Detroit, but if you went to New York or L.A. you'd just be one of the rabble. It's 'cause the people here don't know what's happening in L.A. or New York. (Scapelliti 2004, 151)

Significantly, this isolation is clearly linked here to the authenticity of the band's efforts and intentions: The inference seems to be that because they never expected to be successful, and moreover because they were so far removed from what constituted "the mainstream" (i.e., the music industry in L.A. and New York), it would be false to assume that any of their music was made in an effort to pander to popular taste.

A perceived resistance to outside influences is central to the construction of a musician's image as an auteur—the sole creator of a work of art, alongside whom everyone else involved in that work's production "is simply part of the means of communication" (Frith 1981, 53) of the auteur's vision. In the history of popular music, auteurism has been associated with studio production and with songwriting. The Beatles, for instance, as writers of their own songs, raised the expectations of fans who thereafter began to demand that authentic rock musicians also be songwriters. Popular music's most famous auteurs—iconic figures, such as Phil Spector and Brian Wilson—were seen in this light (and saw themselves in this light), primarily because they took control of the production process of their recordings. In this respect their recordings bear, at least as importantly as the work of any songwriters or performers, the aural signatures of their producers (Phil Spector's so-called wall of sound; Brian Wilson's intricate multi-tracking and otherwise dense textures).[12]

Jack White—as lead singer, guitarist, producer, *and* primary songwriter of The White Stripes—openly acknowledges his aspirations to auteurism, citing as his principal influence in this regard not any musical figure but film director Orson Welles.[13] Consider the following exchange with film-maker Jim Jarmusch in *Interview* magazine:

JARMUSCH: I wanted to ask you about this unusual situation where you have very strong control over your work. You have control over the music and the production and the videos and, to some degree, the marketing strategy—like giving vinyl to critics. I think that's so admirable, but it's pretty rare, isn't it?

J. WHITE: Yeah.

JARMUSCH: Did you fight for control from the start?

J. WHITE: Yes. It's hard for me, because I'm constantly battling what's good and bad about ego. But because Orson Welles is such a big idol of mine, I love that whole auteur aspect. He was given complete control to do *Citizen Kane* [1941]. With us, being a two-piece band and because the songs are generated from me, it seems wrong to get a producer involved. Some bands can write amazing songs but they don't know how to record them, so they have to have a producer. But I was always hacking away at recording other bands' 45s in my attic. I'm not very good at recording: I don't know where to put mikes; I don't know what the right frequencies are for things. I just try to do what sounds right. But if we can keep everything in this big box and keep people away from us, at least we can be proud of it. (2003, 91)

These ideas seem not to be wholly fixed on Jack's individual control of the band's activities, however; the White Stripes seem also to seek a certain authenticity of creative isolation *as a group*. Although he tends to act very often as the band's spokesperson while Meg remains mostly silent in group interviews, Jack freely offers credit to Meg for providing artistic direction on several occasions—whether it be for bringing his attention to an important artist or recording, or, most frequently, for the way in which her drumming style is the most important element of the band's distinctive sound (which is addressed below). Meg's own words reflect this ideology as well. In an interview conducted during the recording of *Elephant*, Meg talks about the increased attention the band had been getting of late: "It's not changed the way we write the songs. . . . We've created our own little world. When you do that, nothing can get you" (Male 2002). In another interview, she echoes this sentiment from a more personal perspective:

> I've always kind of lived in my own world. Everything else outside me seems far, far away. . . . We never really cared about all the things that other people cared about, you know? Like, people recognizing me on the street never interested me. I've always been kind of suspicious of the world, anyway, so it's pretty easy for me to live in my own little world. (Jarmusch 2003, 90)

In all the interviews from which I have extracted these quotations, and throughout much of rock's discourses in general, an emphasis on isolation and the creative integrity of the auteur are inseparable from the idea of the rock musician's honesty of expression. For instance, Jack's desire to "be proud" of the group's work is further explained as a desire to be able to defend it as *their own* rather than as resulting from the input of external producers, marketers, or anyone else representing the commercial interests of the popular-music industry (Jarmusch 2003, 91). As Simon Frith argues, "Rock, in contrast to pop, carries intimations of sincerity, authenticity, art—noncommercial concerns" (1981, 11).

LIVENESS, FIDELITY, AND ROCK HISTORY

I return later to the concept of honesty, particularly as it contributes to a discussion of liveness and the use of electronic technologies in rock music. First, however, we must understand what role the concept of liveness itself plays within the construction of rock authenticity. As already mentioned, a positive emphasis within the rock formation on isolation exists somewhat paradoxically alongside a theme of community, which is very often identified in rock's live performance. In *Sound Effects*, for instance, Frith provides a lengthy quotation by the Who's guitarist Pete Townshend, who singles out the feeling of community experienced in a rock concert as something to cherish. He presents himself not as an elite rock star but as "one of a crowd of people" (quoted in Frith 1981, 80). A sense of community, however, is not the only important element of rock authenticity offered within a live performance. Performance also offers a rock audience the opportunity to verify the credibility of a rock act's recordings and to determine whether the musicians on stage truly possess the skill and talent seemingly promised by their studio creations. Herein lies another of the commonly held distinctions between rock and pop: Pop music is accepted as music created in the studio, whereas rock's authenticity derives from its performance *in relation to* the studio product (Auslander 2008, Ch. 3; Frith 1981, 80–81).[14]

The White Stripes derive a great deal of their authenticity from their reputation as an excellent live act; as their popularity was beginning to spread widely after the release of *White Blood Cells*, the British rock magazine *MOJO* even declared them "the best live band on the planet" (Male 2002). Much has been made of their practice of performing without a predetermined set list in an effort to maintain what I would call a *liveness of spontaneity*. This liveness of spontaneity is explicitly linked (by Jack at least) to an authenticity of expression:

GUITAR WORLD: You and Meg don't perform with a set list. . . . What's the appeal of it?

J. WHITE: We just try to play things different every time. I want it to be a "moment" every night. . . . I don't want people coming to a show and saying, 'Oh, that's the same show I could've seen if I went and saw them in Cleveland or Florida or something.' I mean, what's the point? You might as well be like the bands that just go up there every time and play their songs the same way as they do on the album, and have the same set every night. I would be so bored with that. . . .

GUITAR WORLD: . . . With The White Stripes, the threat of the show being destroyed by improvisation is the performance.

J. WHITE: . . . I just wanna be in that moment as much as I can, so that it's not fake and there's something real coming out of me, some kind of expression. (Scapelliti 2004, 75–76)

In addition to deriving authenticity from the honesty and spontaneity of their live performances, The White Stripes also carry an ideology of liveness—a liveness of fidelity—into their recording aesthetics, and it is here that concepts of historicism, liveness, and fidelity all contribute to the construction of a rather complex sense of rock authenticity. One quite straightforward link between performance and recording practices is established in the way that Jack describes their songwriting process in the studio, appealing to a liveness of spontaneity in much the same way as in the *Guitar World* interview quoted above. For instance, in response to an interviewer's observation that *Icky Thump* seems "loose . . . not like you've worked the songs over and over," White explains, "Like most of our records, it was half-written in the studio right before we pressed 'record.' That always lends a sense of urgency and immediacy to the songs, to do it in that fashion. I like to work under those conditions" (Murray 2007).

Further insights into the construction of The White Stripes' authenticity can be gained from a discussion about the concept of fidelity itself and its relationship to liveness; an important element of this discussion is the large extent to which electronic technologies factor in realizing such ideological concepts in practice. As mentioned at the beginning of this chapter, the recording industry has long been concerned with increasing the fidelity of recording technologies. In fact, this primary concern has led to most of the major developments in recording technologies over the past century. According to Colin Symes (2004, 68–69), three technological developments of the 1940s in particular were essential to the spread of hi-fi enthusiasm after WWII. First, as discussed in Chapter 2, the introduction of the magnetic tape recorder in North America after the war made capturing excellent performances much easier, due to its ability to assist in the *manufacturing* of such performances (with multiple takes, edits, overdubs, and other techniques) in the event that they did not actually take place in the recording studio to the desired degree of perfection. Second, Decca's "full frequency range recordings," which captured a wider frequency range than any previous recording technology, made possible more accurate representations of the actual sounds of a musical performance. Finally, the 33⅓ rpm long-playing record created by U.S. Columbia—the first long-playing format to gain widespread acceptance—presented two distinct advantages over the 78 rpm disc, which was the previously dominant format. First, by holding more than twenty minutes of music per side (78s held no more than five minutes), it allowed listeners to hear complete performances of major works (such as symphonies) with fewer interruptions to flip and change discs, thus presenting a more "realistic" simulation of a concert experience. Second, the PVC-derived material from which the LP was made created much less noise during playback than did the shellac that was standard for 78s; thus, the performance could be heard more clearly.

All these factors demonstrate new recording technologies being developed and valued for their ability to more accurately bring "living music into the home," as Decca claimed about its full frequency range recordings in a 1947 advertisement (quoted in Symes 2004, 68). The hi-fi discourses of the 1940s and 1950s were concerned about more than just technical considerations (i.e., frequency range, signal-to-noise ratio, etc.), although these were crucial factors—they were concerned also with the very concept of liveness, of putting the hi-fi listener in the "best seat in the house" (Symes 2004, Ch. 3) so that he could experience recorded music *exactly* as if it were performed for him in person.[15] According to the logic of hi-fi, the recordist's primary goal was to replicate as closely as possible the aural experience of live performance. The possibility of finally achieving this goal has been celebrated with the arrival of each new recording technology since the early twentieth century[16]—a progression of continued improvements to fidelity suggesting that perhaps what we are dealing with is not *replication* but the (repeatedly) imperfect *illusion* of replication, or there would be no need for such improvements.

As Symes argues, a history of "realist" recordings is a history of creating the *illusion* of realism through various technological means: "In short, deception and falsification play a significant role in the processes of achieving musical fidelity on record; simulation on record is achieved in no small measure through acts of dissimulation" (2004, 83). The following account of mid-twentieth-century recording techniques used to *create* the effect of liveness during the recording process demonstrates the extent to which a liveness of fidelity has long been a mediatized phenomenon rather than a product of transparent mediating technologies:

> "Liveness," the compound effect of multiple room reflections upon played music, is—if you wish—a distortion of "pure" music; but it happens to be a distortion essential to naturalness of sound. Without it music is most graphically described as "dead." Liveness fertilizes musical performance, seasons and blends and rounds out the sound, assembles the raw materials of overtone and fundamental into that somewhat blurred and softened actuality that is normal, in its varying degrees, for all music. Disastrous experiments in "cleaning up" music by removing the all-essential blur long since proved to most recording engineers that musicians do like their music muddied up with itself, reflected. Today recording companies go to extraordinary lengths to acquire studios, churches, and auditoriums (not to mention an assortment of artificial, after-the-recording liveness makers), in order to package that illusively perfect liveness. (Tatnall 1951)

Historically, newer technologies have simply offered further means for creating "that illusively perfect liveness" more perfectly than their predecessors. Moreover, with each new development, the "old" technology is held up as imperfect, as drastically inferior in its ability to convey the realities of performed sound, as *mechanical* rather than *natural*. Recall the argument of a typical hi-fi enthusiast quoted in Chapter 2, in which the writer contrasted the hi-fi experience of "being transported to the concert hall" with equipment that "sound[s] like a radio or phonograph" (Keightley 1996, 153). Of great significance here is the way in which the newer, better technology (hi-fi) is portrayed as completely transparent—not even there—whereas the radio and non-hi-fi phonograph are clearly meant to be understood as machines standing between the "music" and the listener.

Herein lies the central tension of what Garreth Broesche calls the *dialectic of mediation* in discourses on recording technologies: a continuing attempt to reclaim the naturalness, the realism, the liveness, that has been wrested from the recorded musical experience in the very process of recording it by introducing *yet more mediating technologies*, all the while selling the illusion that the new illusion will bring us closer to reality.[17] The case for high fidelity, for realism in recordings, has long been advanced in these terms. It should be noted, however, that the concern for such realism has been found primarily among recordists and consumers of art-music recordings. The post-WWII hi-fi craze mostly focused on canonic art-music repertoire, while Les Paul's contemporaneous explorations of the creative possibilities of the recording studio soon led to a trend in popular music recordings for the creation of unperformable acoustic phenomena.

This is not to say that popular music recordists have been hesitant to adopt new technologies. Although many of the major advancements in recording technology have been initiated by the classical divisions of record labels, often for the purpose of increasing recorded fidelity, popular-music recordists have historically put these new technologies to uses unforeseen by their developers, in many cases further widening the gap between the sounds heard on their recordings and the realism for which those technologies were designed (Frith 2007, 99). Indeed, many would argue that a general rock aesthetic was born in the late 1960s, when many acts made the recording studio their primary arena of expression, in some cases abandoning the realm of live performance altogether (The Beatles serve here as the most extreme example, beginning with *Sgt. Pepper's Lonely Hearts Club Band* in 1967).

The progressive-rock subgenre (alternatively called art rock or album-oriented rock) that developed in the early 1970s in the wake of such trends began to champion not only leading-edge recording technologies but also new developments in sound-synthesis technologies. For instance, the Minimoog, a portable analog synthesizer developed in 1970 by Robert Moog, helped define the sounds of leading progressive-rock groups, such as Yes and Emerson, Lake & Palmer. At this historical moment, rock was reaching new and unprecedented levels of complexity, drawing on both technological sophistication (synthesizers and complex studio procedures) and musical sophistication (complex song forms and other art-music influences) to bolster its aspirations to the status of Art. In other words, the Modernist rock authenticity I discuss earlier in this chapter, with its emphasis on experimentation, sophistication, technology, and other markers of a progressive and sophisticated art form, was emerging in strength for the first time.

This Modernist ideology, however, was met immediately with resistance by those who favored elements of an already existing Romantic ideology. One of the most outspoken (and widely read) opponents of progressive rock was Lester Bangs, a writer for rock magazines *Rolling Stone* and *Creem*, among others. In a 1970 article written for *Creem* in response to the increasingly complex virtuosic music of such bands as The Who and Led Zeppelin in the late 1960s (music that can be seen in many ways as a type of proto-progressive rock), Bangs advocates for the simplicity and technical naïveté of garage-rock groups, such as Iggy and the Stooges. Consider the following passages, in which he makes the distinctions between the two camps abundantly clear:

> The first thing to remember about Stooge music is that it is monotonous and simplistic on purpose, and that within the seemingly circumscribed confines of this fuzz-feedback territory the Stooges work deftly

with musical ideas that may not be highly sophisticated (God forbid) but are certainly advanced. . . .

. . . A trained monkey could probably learn to play that two-chord line [in the song "1969"], but no monkeys and very few indeed of their cousins half a dozen rungs up on the evolutionary ladder, the "heavy" white rock bands, could think of utilizing it in the vivid way it is here, with a simplicity so basic it's almost pristine. Seemingly the most obvious thing in the world, I would call it a stroke of genius at least equal to Question Mark and the Mysterians' endless one-finger one-key organ drone behind the choruses of "96 Tears." (2003, 39–40)[18]

Eventually . . . I wised up to the fact that the Yardbirds [the band from which Led Zeppelin developed] for all their greatness would finally fizzle out in an electric morass of confused experiments and bad judgments, and hardest of all to learn was that the only spawn possible to them were lumbering sloths like Led Zeppelin, because the musicians in the Yardbirds were just too *good*, too accomplished and cocky to do anything but fuck up in the aftermath of an experiment that none of them seemed to understand anyway. And similarly, the Who, erupting with some of the most trail-blazing music ever waxed, got "good" and arty with subtle eccentric songs and fine philosophy, a steadily dilating rep, and all this accomplishment sailing them steadily further from the great experiment they'd begun. (2003, 40; original emphasis)[19]

Bangs goes on to argue that the true value of rock is to be found in its accessibility (in contrast to the elitism of virtuosic showmanship) and in the sincerity of untrained kids simply picking up guitars and making noise with them. The artiness, complexity, and "accomplishment" of music by Led Zeppelin and The Who are depicted as traits of inauthenticity, as superficial gloss that take rock increasingly farther from its essence of honest expression. The "answer" to progressive rock turned out to be punk, which grew out of the very aesthetic tendencies—even the very music (i.e., that of The Stooges)—that Bangs celebrates here.[20]

The emergence of punk in the mid-1970s, with The Sex Pistols as figurative standard-bearers, stands as one of the key moments in rock history where a new trend is seen by many to have arrived just in time to save popular music from the brink of wholesale inauthenticity. The Rolling Stones and The Beatles had accomplished a similar feat about ten years earlier with their injection of rhythm and blues into an otherwise "slick" and commercialized popular-music soundscape, populated by such acts as Paul Anka, Frankie Avalon, and Fabian (so the mythology goes). In the early 1990s, Kurt Cobain and his band, Nirvana, would reassert rock's dominance by drowning out overly produced pop acts, such as New Kids on the Block and Paula Abdul, as well as the ubiquitous sounds of studio-based dance-music acts, such as Technotronic and C + C Music Factory—and by drawing, through its musical influence, on the subcultural capital of hard-core punk to do so. Beginning in 2001, amid the popularity of The White Stripes' *White Blood Cells*, The Strokes' *Is This It*, and releases by other acts bearing similar markings of a Stooges-like garage-rock aesthetic, The White Stripes (also drawing heavily on the blues as a marker of musical authenticity) found themselves at the center of the most recent moment of rock's salvation—this time providing a more authentic alternative to the increasingly slick production values of hip-hop and the continued success of boy bands, such as *NSYNC.[21] In each of these instances, the "new thing" in rock has emerged at a time when the increasing inauthenticity of popular music's dominant sounds is seen by many fans and critics to be threatening the complete eradication of authentic expression. Crucially, this inauthenticity is very often seen to be represented in an increased reliance on studio technologies.

Grossberg identifies this repeating cycle of crisis and salvation—of fans and critics predicting "the imminent 'death' of rock" only to be saved by a renewed wave of authenticity—as a "constitutive part" of rock ideology as it has developed over time (1992, 207). In other words, the discourse of authenticity so central to rock ideology depends on the constant threat of the inauthentic (just as the discourse of liveness depends on the constant threat of overwhelming mediatization). What also remains constant is the appeal to history and simplicity at each of these moments of renewal, as authenticity is seen to be linked to rock's roots in the face of recent threats. British Beat music of the mid- to late 1960s drew from American rhythm and blues; punk (reflecting the values put forth by Bangs) turned back the clock on the high levels of complexity and skill demonstrated in then-recent developments in rock; Nirvana and other grunge acts invoked the sounds of 1980s hard-core punk; The White Stripes and similar bands at the beginning of the twenty-first century revitalized the sounds of late-1960s garage rock and 1970s punk, with The White Stripes placing extra emphasis on the debt they also owed to that most ancient of popular music styles, the Delta blues.

Much of The White Stripes' recorded output invokes, directly or indirectly, blues forms and lyrics. They have recorded Robert Johnson's "Stop Breaking Down" (on the White Stripes 2002c), Son House's "Death Letter," and Blind Willie McTell's "Your Southern Can Is Mine" (both on The White Stripes 2002a), all from the Delta blues canon, and written several of their own songs that conform to or invoke familiar blues structures. Moreover, Jack very often makes use of the bottle-neck or slide-guitar technique that characterizes so much of the playing of Delta blues artists (this can be heard to great effect, for instance, on "Catch Hell Blues" [on the White Stripes 2007]). By way of further tribute, *The White Stripes* and *De Stijl* were dedicated to Son House and Blind Willie McTell, respectively, and a picture of Charlie Patton—according to most, the proverbial root of the Delta blues tree—hung in the studio during the recording of *Icky Thump* (Di Perna 2007).

The strong presence of the blues in The White Stripes' music, then, is undeniable; what is most significant for the purposes of the present discussion, however, is Jack's rationale for focusing on this type of music. First, he argues, the blues tradition he connects with broke music "down to its very core . . . down to its fundamentals" (*Guitar World* 2006). This minimalist perspective on the blues coincides with the overall aesthetic of the band, which similarly involves an exercise in restraint and limited means: a focus only on drums, guitar, and vocals, which equates to "rhythm, melody and storytelling" (Scapelliti 2004). All this restraint serves a greater purpose, of course—namely, to combat what Jack perceives to be the excesses of modern American culture, be they in music or some other cultural realm. As he puts it, "America has traded culture for entertainment and technology. How can you ever come back from that?" (Dolan 2007). Despite the defeatism seemingly evident in this question, however, the White Stripes' wholesale commitment to the musical simplicity of the blues (and of punk, for that matter) is a clear attempt at an answer.

The White Stripes' appeal to historical simplicity is matched by an appeal to historical authenticity—and in this case, I am referring to an authenticity based in rock music's origins. Even more than that, Jack often presents his interest in the blues as an interest in America's folk music. By casting his own music as a type of folk music, Jack is invoking all the sincerity, honesty, and authentic expression of a music perceived to be wholly outside the commercial—and mediatized—realm. The following passage illustrates this point well:

GUITAR WORLD: By playing the blues, do you feel that you're providing some continuity to the music of the past?

J. WHITE: Yeah. I think everybody should do that. . . . I want to join that family of songwriters and storytellers, just as Robert Johnson did: all of Robert Johnson's songs were coming from Son House and Charlie Patton and Willie Brown. It's the same thing with us. I just didn't want to reference the bands that came out two years ago before we started, you know, because you're referencing a reference of a reference of a reference. When you're interested in folk music in America—the reality of it—you're forced to go back, way back, in the past to get down to the nitty-gritty of what it's all about and what expression through song is about. (Scapelliti 2004)

As modern American culture is besieged by the inauthenticity of technological excess and shallow entertainment (at least according to Jack's descriptions), then The White Stripes, like only a handful of rock saviors before them, have set about reinstating authentic expression by resurrecting a supposedly pure music—one untainted by modern values and commercial interests.[22]

The concept of fidelity also plays an important part in such revitalizations of authenticity. In all these historical moments of crisis and salvation that I have mentioned, the older style of music being invoked as an antidote for music's modern ills is perceived as more invested in honest, *live* performance than in the commercial and technological trappings of the recording studio. In other words, their fidelity to a live aesthetic is seen to be stronger than that of the threatening inauthentic pop-music subgenres. In many cases, however, this fidelity to liveness seems to favor de-emphasizing, rather than celebrating, the technical fidelity of recording and performing technologies. That is, whereas the discourse of hi-fi, particularly with respect to art-music recordings, links newer, more advanced technologies of increased fidelity to the pursuit of liveness, the discourse of authenticity in rock, at least in these cases, links an increased fidelity to liveness with a rejection of hi-fi (and other technologically advanced) equipment.

This connection is especially apparent in the case of the White Stripes, whose avoidance of digital (and other modern) technologies has become a central element of their entire mythology and celebrated ideologies. In line with his comment about modern technologies in America, quoted above, Jack publicly eschews digital recording and effects, heavy overdubbing, and many of the other technological developments that have become standard elements of the modern recording industry.[23] The liner notes for *Elephant* (2003), for instance, proudly proclaim that "no computers were used during the writing, recording, mixing or mastering of this record." All the recording, in fact, was done on four-track and eight-track reel-to-reel tape machines. The recording of *Icky Thump* in 2007 was considered a significant departure for the band, because for the first time they worked in a fully equipped, "modern" studio—although Jack still reminds his fans in a *Guitar World* interview that they did, in fact, still record to analog tape rather than to digital code. Elsewhere in the same interview, he says of their previous avoidance of such studios, "We were always scared of big studios, because we were scared of sounding too polished or having to fight through modernity to sound real" (Di Perna 2007). It would seem that for the White Stripes, modern technologies pose not just an aural threat to rock authenticity ("sounding too polished") but an ideological one as well, as suggested in Jack's description of fighting "through modernity."[24]

The significance of this preference for analog over digital technologies is foregrounded if we once again place our discussion in a historical context—this time, in the context of The White Stripes' own historical moment. The decade immediately prior to the emergence of the White Stripes (i.e., the late 1980s and 1990s) saw an underground trend for vintage, nondigital technologies and a certain fetishization of low-fidelity sound—concerns that found their most ardent expressions in so-called lo-fi rock acts, such as Pavement, Guided by Voices, and, more famously (if less overtly), Beck. At the same time that digital technologies (widely introduced to the market in the early 1980s) were being linked by many to the concept of musical "purity" (Frith 1996, 235), some musicians were reluctant to adopt the new high-fidelity soundscape of popular music, because the pure sounds that were revealed once the noises of analog media were removed seemed to them too "cold" or "machinelike." Analog, lo-fi technologies, by contrast (be they synthesizers, inexpensive tape recorders, or some other technological representative of the predigital era), would allow musicians to "sound authentic, rather than over-produced."[25] Writing in 1988, Andrew Goodwin had already identified this emerging trend, wherein musicians who had grown up listening to the supposedly "cold" (by 1970s standards) sounds of synthesizers in progressive rock were now turning to them as a mark of "'authentic' musical roots" (1990, 265). "In pop's digital age," he writes, "analogue sounds are the real thing, however automated or synthetic" (1990, 266).[26]

The White Stripes and many of their peers inherited this logic, and within the context of the so-called garage rock revival of the 2000s, we hear a pronounced emphasis on predigital sounds entering the mainstream of popular music. One of the most telling comparisons between lo-fi and hi-fi aesthetics in popular music of recent years can be found in the vocal timbres representative of various genres. The vocals of The Strokes' lead singer Julian Casablancas, for instance (and less extensively those of Jack White—however, consider "Astro" and "Stop Breaking Down" [both on The White Stripes 2002c] for comparable vocals) are regularly heavily distorted in a manner resembling the overdriven vocal and guitar tracks that permeated the garage rock and punk of the late 1960s and 1970s, respectively. These lo-fi vocals have become common once again just in time to provide an audible contrast to the obviously digitized vocal timbres of much pop, hip-hop, and R & B of the new millennium, such as the drastically Auto-Tuned vocals heard in Cher's "Believe" (on Cher 1998), Kanye West's *808s & Heartbreak* (2008), and virtually all of T-Pain's recorded work.

This inherited lo-fi musical aesthetic has also been brought to the fore at the same time as another considerable shift in many consumers' experiences of fidelity: the emergence of MP3, a digital audio format with distinctly lower fidelity than the CD it has replaced as the dominant format for consumers of popular music. As Daniel Guberman argues, with the increasing dominance of MP3 audio (a shift begun in the late 1990s), for many listeners, "post-fidelity values," such as the quantity of music at their disposal, the ease of accessing and controlling this music (by way of playlists, shuffle features, etc.), and the visual style and aesthetics of listening devices, have become elements of their listening experiences more important than the fidelity of the recorded material itself (2011, 434). If a lower-fidelity (although still digital) listening experience has become "natural" for the most recent generation of rock fans, it is not surprising that many of these fans are sympathetic to a general lo-fi music aesthetic such as that informing the work of The White Stripes, The Strokes, and others.

In addition to the historical perspective just offered, we can also make sense of The White Stripes' preference for analog technologies by considering once again the strong link between their studio practice and their identity as a "live" band. Specifically, Jack very often describes their use of studio technologies in similar terms to those in which he frames his use of technologies in performance: He portrays the creative act in both settings as a struggle—drawing on the time-honored romantic image of the suffering artist—and digital technologies as crutches that would allow the artist to bypass this struggle altogether. Jack frequently describes his guitars themselves as something to do battle with, something to master, and these accounts are consistent with his characterizations of technology in general. Consider, for instance, the following passages:

> It's work to play it [his plastic Airline guitar], but I like that. I had a Silvertone guitar that never stayed in tune, but when it went out of tune I would just work with it. If I wanted to play it safe I'd go out and get a brand-new Stratocaster or something like that. But I don't like to play it safe; I like it when things are getting messed up. . . . With a guitar like the Airline, my mind is always working. I'm not just "phoning it in." (Scapelliti 2004)

> I keep . . . guitars that are you know—the neck's a little bit bent and it's a little bit out of tune and I wanna work and battle it and conquer it and make it express whatever attitude I have at that moment. I want it to be a struggle. (Guggenheim 2009)

When asked about his own use of a digital effects pedal (the DigiTech Whammy Pedal) in conjunction with his guitars, he downplays its role by explaining that he only uses it to generate extra octaves rather than for all the effects it offers and that he wishes someone could make him one that *only* generates octaves (Di Perna 2007; Scapelliti 2004). In other words, the digital technology is being put into service in a very limited role, and he is careful not to succumb to the temptation of letting it do too much of his work for him.

These accounts of technology in performance resonate with concepts of liveness deeply embedded inside common formulations of rock authenticity. As Frith argues in terms that very closely mirror JackWhite:

> [O]ne of the recurring pleasures of popular culture is the difficult or spectacular act, the drama of which lies precisely in its liveness, in the resulting sense of risk, danger, triumph, virtuosity: we need to see things which we know must be live. . . . What's valued here is not . . . seeing something unique, but seeing something difficult, something that *takes work*. Far from wanting the means of production to be concealed, the

popular audience wants to see how much has gone into its entertainment. (1996, 207; original emphasis)

White also carries such a characterization of authentic music *as work*, which I have highlighted thus far as an appeal to authenticity in performance, into his discussions of The White Stripes' recording process—describing digital recording technologies as "evil" (Male 2002) and as facilitating the creative process to the point where it is no longer truly creative, thus sacrificing the honesty of expression so central to his band's authenticity. For instance, he argues:

Technology is a big destroyer of emotion and truth. Auto-tuning doesn't do anything for creativity. Yeah it makes it easier. . . . But it doesn't make you a more creative person. That's the disease we have to fight in any creative field: ease of use. (Guggenheim 2009)

And elsewhere:

I think people go in to make a record these days and they overthink it and overproduce it, because Pro Tools and all that digital technology affords people so much opportunity to do that. People need to put limits on themselves. If you're a drummer who's just starting out, it's not gonna make you a better drummer to go out and buy a gigantic double-bass drum with 40 drums and 40 cymbals. Sit down in your room with a snare drum and some brushes and learn rhythms. (Scapelliti 2004)

Particularly in this last quoted passage, but also in the rhetoric he uses rather consistently throughout the other examples I have presented here, Jack White clearly establishes an ideological and aesthetic link between performance and recording. He further confirms this link in explanations of the band's attempts to create recordings that will maintain their identity in live performance, especially considering their performances are limited to what the two musicians can realistically accomplish. White also argues that this connection between recordings and live performances has become an essential part of the band's identity among fans and critics, to the extent that any recordings that could not be performed by two musicians on stage are seen by many as suspect (Murray 2007).

Clearly a liveness of fidelity is at work here, although not one in which recorded music is thought to faithfully represent performance that has occurred in the past, as would be the case with a typical "live recording." Rather, in these *studio* recordings, The White Stripes strive for, and their fans appreciate, a certain fidelity to *future* performances. Even though, as discussed above, their goal in each live performance is to present something completely unique, their recordings, to a large degree, must allow for those performances to unfold without drastically distorting the *recorded* identity of the songs.[27] Here we are reminded once again of Philip Auslander's assertion (2008, Ch. 3) that rock authenticity derives not solely from recordings, nor solely from live performance, but from a dialogical relationship between the two. In this case, recordings are governed in part by the restrictions and conventions of live performance, which is measured against its fidelity to those recordings.

In discussing what I am describing here as a fidelity to liveness in The White Stripes' recordings, Jack White focuses on limiting the *number* of musical elements on record to what can be replicated in performance (for example, the number of vocal tracks present, or the overall instrumentation of a recorded song). Also evident in many of The White Stripes' recordings, however, is an approach to rhythm that promotes a further interpretation of a liveness of fidelity, even as other elements of the recording, such as stereo panning and double tracking, clearly represent the logic and conventions of popular-music recordings far more than those of live performance. The rhythmic characteristic in question here is, quite simply, a rhythmic looseness—a lack of precision that is especially noticeable in Meg's drumming but often extends to guitar and vocal tracks as well, or at other times is even more noticeable when heard against guitar and vocals whose rhythms do not coincide precisely with those of the drum track.

Before discussing the rhythmic characteristics of any recordings in particular, it is worth noting the extent to which Meg's drumming is often singled out as a distinctive part—even the most important part—of The White Stripes' sound. Jack's own explanations of this characteristic tend to focus on what he describes as the primitiveness, childishness, and naïveté of her playing;[28] fans and rock journalists are quick to echo Jack's language. This simplicity and unlearnedness is certainly noticeable throughout The White Stripes' recordings (live and studio), not only in the rhythmic imprecision of Meg's drumming but also in her favoring of straightforward patterns with few fills or embellishments. Even though the rhythmic imprecision, at the very least, could easily be corrected by way of digital adjustments to the recorded track, no such attempt seems to have been made, presumably because to do so would detract from the effect of simplicity for which The White Stripes claim to strive.

In a line of reasoning very reminiscent of Lester Bangs (and thus of the punk aesthetics that followed in the wake of Bangs's early-1970s writing), Meg's drumming is *valued* for its simplicity, its unlearnedness, its lack of complexity. I would argue that its lack of rhythmic precision also lends a strong element of liveness to The White Stripes' recordings—a liveness of fidelity in line with the broader live aesthetic governing most of these recordings—because of the extent to which it begs to be heard as the unaltered (at least with respect to its rhythmic values) performance of a real drummer. Particularly in a time when the norm in popular music is (and has for some time been) to achieve rhythmic exactness with the aid of digital technologies, Meg's recorded performances stand out for their lack of digital polish.[29]

* The fourth beat of the first bar in the pattern is only played by drums

Example 4.1 The White Stripes, "There's No Home for You Here," first basic drum pattern.

Consider, for instance, the two basic rhythmic patterns heard throughout most of "There's No Home for You Here" (on The White Stripes 2003). After a two-measure introduction, the song's chorus presents a repeating two-measure rhythmic ostinato shared by multiple guitar tracks and Meg's drums (see Example 4.1). The density of the overall texture, combined with the slight rhythmic variations between all the different voices in that texture and with the rather sustained sounds of Jack's guitars and Meg's cymbals, make a precise beat very difficult to locate. What does come through the texture, rather than rhythmic precision, is the occasional voice anticipating or delaying the beat in comparison to all the others. In addition, the sixteenth-note pairs in the pattern are very often rushed by one or more voices. This pattern, played always with the rhythmic looseness I have described, occurs at 0:06–0:25, 1:02–1:15, and 3:22–3:39 (end) in accompaniment to the chorus, and at 2:12–2:30 and 2:42–2:55, on either side of the bridge.

Even more rhythmically imprecise, however, is the simple pattern Meg plays leading from choruses to verses (0:25–0:37, 1:15–1:28; see Example 4.2), which is then slightly altered during the song's two verses (0:37–1:02, 1:28–1:53; the eighth-note pair moves from the third to the fourth beat of the second measure). This pattern begins as a simple hi-hat solo (held slightly open for a little bit of "sizzle") beneath a quiet guitar line; in the second half of each verse (0:50–1:02, 1:41–1:53), the hi-hat is joined by snare and bass drums, but the pattern remains consistent with that of the first half. This slightly thickened texture signals a gradual build in volume through the remainder of the verses, and the track explodes once again in density and volume at the chorus (thus exercising the typical loud-soft-loud pattern that Nirvana brought to the mainstream in the early 1990s). During the song's outro, which simply consists of four repetitions of the chorus (the fourth one fading to silence), the first two of these repetitions are also arranged with the overall soft texture of the verses, including the drum pattern of Example 4.2. All the passages described here (especially at 0:25–0:50 and 1:15–1:40) bear a sparseness within which anything but complete rhythmic precision will stand out—there is nothing behind which to hide, so to speak. The rhythmic simplicity of the pattern—a pulsing beat with one slight variation at the end of the second measure—also seems to ask for strict time to be kept.

However, Meg's lack of precision on this simple hi-hat pattern catches the ear immediately. The quarter-note pulses are generally not metronomic,

Example 4.2 The White Stripes, "There's No Home for You Here," second basic drum pattern.

and the eighth-note embellishments are even less precise (they are usually rushed). This particular drum passage presents an approach to rhythm so unpredictable, so *human* in its lack of quantifiable perfection, that it stands in stark contrast to the majority of popular music—particularly pop and hip-hop—in which rhythmic exactness is an essential part of typical production values. Comparison between Meg's drumming in "There's No Home for You Here" and the electronically produced rhythm tracks of OutKast's pop/hip-hop hit "Hey Ya!" from the same year, for instance (on Outkast 2003, CD 2), makes these distinctions obvious.

And this, it would seem, is precisely the intention. Jack's ideological pronouncements about the plight of modern America's technologized culture, combined with the band's various appeals to familiar constructions of rock authenticity, place the music of the White Stripes—in typical rock fashion—in opposition to pop, hip-hop, and other of rock's "Others." This rock conveys liveness in part because its rhythms seem so human in comparison to the rhythms prevalent in pop and hip-hop. As I argue throughout this chapter, various threads of rhetoric linked to common notions of rock authenticity also lend to the celebration of the White Stripes as a band whose music communicates a great deal of liveness. Not just in this individual track but also in a large proportion of The White Stripes' recorded output, liveness of fidelity, as a general *fidelity to liveness*, is inextricably linked to notions of naturalness, history, and performance, all as they inform a rock authenticity that is familiar within rock's overall historical trajectory and particular to the so-called garage-rock revival of the early twenty-first century.

Paradoxically, at least as far as discourses of fidelity in recorded music go, liveness of fidelity here is constructed in part thanks to a lo-fi aesthetic. Within a traditional context of high-fidelity recording—a context featuring primarily the values consistent with producers and consumers of art-music recordings—advanced (now digital) technologies are seen to bring listeners as close as possible to a natural, live musical experience. Within the rock formation, however, and especially within constructions of authenticity as it relates to The White Stripes—as primary representatives of rock's latest "salvation moment"—the authentic, natural, live experience is seen to be found in the avoidance of digital technologies and the standard practices of the digital recording studio.

This entire account of a modern rock authenticity has further served, I hope, to demonstrate the complex relationships that often exist between acts of mediatization and perceptions of liveness. For all that it operates under the pretense of liveness, rock authenticity clearly also makes room for what many would consider to be nonlive elements of recording *and* performance. Even the White Stripes, who are regaled by fans and critics alike for their liveness and old-fashioned authenticity, regularly employ "unperformable" studio techniques—such as the dense layers of vocals and guitars on "There's No Home for You Here," the double-tracked vocal and guitar tracks on "Blue Orchid" (2005), the double-tracking and stereo-field manipulation of the vocals on "Take, Take, Take" (2005), and many others—that, more than forty years ago, made The Beatles seem positively avant-garde on *Sgt. Pepper's Lonely Hearts Club Band* (The Beatles 2009), although they now rightly seem old-fashioned. In other words, the extent to which mediatization is permitted within the perception of liveness is ever changing, over time[30] and across musical genres. The White Stripes play within this dynamic terrain of liveness, deliberately—but selectively— invoking liveness to augment the authenticity of their efforts. The extent to which they are celebrated as live and authentic, despite the seemingly "nonlive" elements in much of their music, demonstrates just how dynamic that terrain really is.

5 Interactive Liveness in Live Electronic Music

> I dream of instruments obedient to my thought and which with their contribution of a whole new world of unexpected sounds, will lend themselves to the exigencies of my inner rhythm.
>
> Edgard Varèse, "The Liberation of Sound"

> Some people have a fear of technology, they look at this thing with all the knobs and holes and dials and things and go . . . "Oh, my God," you know. Whereas for me, it was like, "Okay, I'm going to get to know this. This is a living, breathing entity. It has desires and abilities, limitations and possibilities." And the process was getting to know the instrument. It was always in intimate and friendly rapport. . . . And it was alive, you know, and you just have it on and you go and you interact and get to know it. You build up a relationship.
>
> Suzanne Ciani, speaking about her Buchla 200 synthesizer

WHAT IS LIVE ABOUT LIVE ELECTRONIC MUSIC?

I have, to this point, posited liveness as a concept whose various articulations very much rely on real or implied relationships not only between performance and recording, human and machine, authentic and artificial, but also between performer and audience, one musician and another, a work and its performance. In this chapter, I address some of the variously implicated relationships of liveness more directly, querying those implied by the use of the word *live* in the genre label live electronic music. Live electronic music is widely considered to be a diversified musical genre, one rather resistant to definitive characterizations. Nonetheless, I demonstrate that as musicians began performing electronic art music in concert settings, particularly in the late 1950s and 1960s, a new paradigm of musician/machine relationships began to emerge that differed greatly from Modernist understandings of electronic technologies typified in much electronic art music for fixed media. Such Modernist understandings posit electronic technologies as instruments of rational and systematic control, whereas many composers and performers of live electronic music, by contrast, began using these technologies as tools to facilitate more reflexive and interactive relationships between themselves and other musicians. Some even explored similarly interactive musician/machine relationships. These relationships, I argue, provide a context in which an *interactive liveness* began to emerge in conjunction with the developing practice of live electronic music. This particular notion of interactivity in performance is born from a dialectical tension between instances of musician interaction and technological mediation.

According to several accounts, live electronic music is understood as any concert music, composed or performed[1] primarily since the late 1950s, presented in real time and involving some type of electronic sound.[2] By this definition, each of the following would be considered live electronic music: a performance involving flute with fixed media (such as prerecorded tape); a performance involving a keyboard-based synthesizer; and a performance involving an amplified vocalist whose sound is fed through various electronic filters and manipulated in real time. In such cases, the word *live* seems, at least for the purpose of categorization, to mean "real-time and on-stage." Put another way, it indicates a traditional temporal and spatial liveness. More recent scholars, however, understand the genre as performed music involving the electronic manipulation of acoustic sound and/or the electronic real-time production of sound.[3] According to these accounts, electronic sound must be *actively* generated for it to be live. Under this definition, the second and third examples I give above still qualify as live electronic music, but the first (a performance for acoustic flute with fixed media) does not, because the only electronic element in this performance is completely predetermined.[4]

This very distinction prompts the question: Why is prerecorded tape not live, even when presented alongside a performer who is live in every conventionally understood meaning of the term? One could argue that the temporal liveness and spatial liveness invoked by the flutist's performance (so long as an audience is present) are also attributable to the prerecorded sounds emanating from the loudspeakers on either side of him or her. Yet one could also point to other qualities of liveness that are lacking in this performance. For one, because most of the audience likely understands that the taped part will remain unchanged from one performance to another, they may not experience the liveness of spontaneity so often attributed to performance. Still another sense of liveness, this one based in interaction, is also common to many live performances but largely lacking in this hypothetical scenario for flute and tape.

I refer here to the interactions between musicians that characterize the performance of so many musical ensembles.[5] A performance involving flute and prerecorded tape seems to straddle ontological categories: On the one hand, the presence of a flutist with another "performing entity" (the tape) suggests that this is a piece for a flute-and-tape duo. On the other hand, the lack of interaction between flute and tape suggests that this is really a piece for a solo performer with predetermined accompaniment, or at best a piece for two solo performers. Two-way interaction seems to be promised, but the piece never delivers on that promise; the desire for interactive liveness is made even more palpable in its absence. Identifying interaction, then, seems to be central to understanding liveness in live electronic music, at least according to the second of the definitions outlined above.

In most accounts of live electronic music and its more modern extension, often called *interactive computer music*,[6] interaction is usually identified in the musician/machine interface exercised in performance. I argue here that this sense of technologically oriented interaction finds its early counterpart in a conventional sense of inter-musician interaction. Early examples of live electronic music began expanding this paradigm of performance interaction with various levels of technological mediation so performers still interacted with one another, but in ways that relied on the use of electronic sound technologies. Eventually, some musicians extended this concept of a mediatized interactive performing ensemble to one in which various technologies could be viewed as performance partners rather than simply as tools or instruments to facilitate this interaction. In other words, the distinction between musician and machine in these performances is challenged by such a concept of interaction. In recounting this development here, I focus on the interactivity inherent in various configurations of musicians and technologies in live electronic music, contrasting this interactivity with the Modernist penchant for technological mastery described above.

By exploring this particular emergence of interactive liveness, I offer an answer to some of the more salient criticisms of electronic art music, which focus on the Modernist approach to technology I have described. For instance, linking modern uses of technology in music to the statistical and rationalized nature of Western technocratic society, Jacques Attali writes, "The theoretical musician" (by which he means the composer of Modernist serial and postserial electronic music[7]) remains a musician of power, paid to perfect the sound form of today's technical knowledge. . . . The musician . . . tries to understand and master the laws of acoustics in order to make them the mode of production. Liberated from the constraints of the old codes, his discourse becomes nonlocalizable. Pulverizer of the past, he displays all of the characteristics of the technocracy managing the great machines of the repetitive economy. (1985, 12–13)[8]

According to Attali, this music eschews meaning, because it eliminates actual performers (in the case of much electronic music) and because it lacks an understandable musical language. Alienated audiences associate such music with a musical intelligentsia, which, particularly in the time and place in which Attali is writing (Paris in the 1970s), had strong ties to forces of technocratic societal control (as argued in Born 1995).[9]

Yet Attali's views are limited by his narrow scope of musical examples (despite his tendency to make all-encompassing, categorical statements). Indeed, he fails to address the great variety of electronic music being made in the second half of the twentieth century. Georgina Born (1995, 58–65), on the other hand, reminds us that throughout this time, two different strains of the musical avant-garde, which she identifies as *musical Modernism* and *musical Postmodernism*, emerged from competing ideologies. In Born's assessment, Modernist music is characterized by determinism, rationalism, scientism, and several other traits identified by Attali as characteristics of the "music of repetition"; moreover, she argues, it often serves the interests of technocratic power far more than it serves any particular artistic endeavor. Born characterizes Postmodern music, on the other hand, by its irrationalism, its use of commercial or "low" technology, its existence outside universities and other large institutions, its focus on music as a physical and performative art form, and its emergence on the American West Coast. These forms of music, by whatever label they are known (experimental, Postmodern, etc.), fall outside Attali's purview.

Born's own assessment of this second, Postmodern type of music (a categorization that quite comfortably includes much live electronic music) lacks somewhat in its depth. Apart from the few descriptors just listed, she provides little information regarding how this music was or is made, or, more importantly, what a performance of this music might actually convey to an audience. Furthermore, her oversimplified categorizations, relying as they do on factors of geography and institutional affiliation (and not on music), betray limitations much like Attali's: They characterize music according to where and by whom it is made, with little concern for what this music may communicate (sonically, metaphorically, etc.) in its presentation. They also leave little room for identifying any music made within one of those geographic/institutional "camps" that demonstrates tendencies seemingly more at home in the other (at least, according to Born's criteria). I do not set out here to answer all of Attali's and Born's concerns about the technocratic nature of Modernist music. Rather, I intend to describe how some live electronic music, through its performance, offers a more productive model of human/machine relationships than does the music they criticize, thus adding, I hope, another dimension to the discussion of electronic art music from the 1950s and 1960s. Through various modes of mediatization, the interactivity I wish to emphasize communicates a distinctly dialogical liveness largely ignored in music founded on the hegemonic mastery of technology so predominant in Modernist thought and practice.

Although I identify the flowering of this interactive liveness in the 1960s, I also demonstrate that it had its roots in earlier, more isolated, electronic art-music practices. Early efforts by John Cage and Pierre Schaeffer explored strategies for maintaining liveness in musical performances that otherwise broke sharply from traditional paradigms of live music. We must understand these few early forays into liveness in electronic music in light of the prevailing approach to technology typified in Western Modernist thought, which, rather than being supplanted by the paradigm of interactive liveness that emerged in the 1960s, has continued to develop and inform many electronic musical practices to this day. The discussions I embark on here expand on Born's and Attali's focus on the potentially limiting deployments of electronic technologies in music by drawing attention instead to instantiations of liveness, which are detected in more socially oriented musician/machine relationships.

BIRTH OF AN ELECTRONIC AESTHETIC

Accounts of the genesis of electronic music often begin with a brief discussion of Italian Futurist music.[10] The Futurists, particularly Luigi Russolo, were among the earliest musicians to call for the use of *noise* in music. In his 1913 manifesto, "The Art of Noises," Russolo describes the music he intends to make by mechanically imitating the noises of the modern Italian environment (1986). He systematically classifies all these noises and divides them into six groups (see Figure 5.1). A few weeks after writing his manifesto, Russolo demonstrated the first of his *Intonarumori* (noise instruments), a *scoppiatore* (burster), which was designed to imitate the sound of an early automobile engine (Brown 1982, 34).[11] Over the next several years, Russolo created twelve different types of *Intonarumori* and traveled around Europe, performing music composed by him and others specifically for these instruments. By 1927, he was able to combine all twelve instruments into one large "noise harmonium" (Brown 1982, 47).

Russolo's accomplishments are pertinent to a discussion of electronic music for several reasons. First, the inclusion of environmental noises (industrial and natural) would become a key element in many later pieces of electronic music. Barclay Brown further points out that Russolo's attempts to imitate these sounds by way of mechanical devices (calling his noise harmonium the "first mechanical synthesizer") situate Russolo among "the first major exponent[s] of musical synthesis itself" (1982, 48). Russolo's inclusion of electric motors in some of his *Intonarumori* also places him among the early inventors of electro-mechanical musical instruments. Moreover, when one considers the broader Futurist and Modernist contexts within which Russolo and his "art of noises" are situated, further seeds from which electronic music would grow become apparent.

1	Roars, Thunderings, Explosions, Hissing roars, Bangs, Booms
2	Whistling, Hissing, Puffing
3	Whispers, Murmurs, Mumbling, Muttering, Gurgling
4	Screeching, Creaking, Rustling, Humming, Crackling, Rubbing
5	Noises obtained by beating on: Metals, Woods, Skins, Stones, Pottery, etc.
6	Voices of animals and people: Shouts, Screams, Shrieks, Wails, Hoots, Howls, Death rattles, Sobs

Figure 5.1   Luigi Russolo's six categories of noises[12]

Modernist artistic practices and aesthetics throughout Europe and North America in the early twentieth century involved "a fascination with technique, with speed and motion, with the machine and the factory system" (Harvey 1990, 23). Nowhere was this fascination more apparent than in the art and manifestos of the Italian Futurists. In addition to their enthusiasm for Russolo's mechanical *Intonarumori*, the Futurists glorified machines and electricity in their poetry, sculpture, theater, painting, and even clothing.[13] While celebrating new technologies, they violently opposed anything that might be associated with a nineteenth-century Romantic aesthetic, which included celebrations of nature. Filippo Tommaso Marinetti's 1909 prose poem, "Let's Kill Off the Moonlight," and Giacomo Balla's 1909 painting, *Lampada ad arco* (*Arc Lamp*), both feature scenes in which the light of electric lamps confronts and overwhelms the light of the moon (a common Romantic trope). Marinetti writes, "And so it was that three hundred electric moons, with their rays like dazzling white chalk, snuffed out the green, antique queen of all loves [the actual moon]" (2006c, 28).[14] Paul Théberge argues that this aspect of Futurist aesthetics was "an almost literal expression of the scientific philosophy of 'domination of nature' and of the subjection of the entire natural world to the order of production which is characteristic of modern instrumental reason" (1993, 163). This theme of domination and control extended, for some Futurists at least, to the domination of other people by means of mechanized violence. For example, Marinetti glorifies modern warfare technologies in his "Electric War: A Futurist Visionary Hypothesis" (2006a) and in "The Foundation and Manifesto of Futurism" (2006b).[15]

It is important to identify the prominence of this polarity between machine and nature within the Modernist context, because it has become central to the aesthetics of countless pieces of electronic art music. It is also important to identify the logics of technological control and organization so apparent in Russolo's classification of all natural sounds and in broader Modernist contexts. The first epigraph to this chapter, by Edgard Varèse, illustrates not only the extent to which this notion spread to other musicians in the early twentieth century but also the particular manner in which technology was seen to be "obedient" to its human designers.[16] As discussed above, this very notion of systematic control via new technologies informs much of the criticism of later electronic art music found in Attali (1985) and Born (1995).

The interest that Russolo demonstrated in the codification and technological control of sound, coupled with modern industrial logics of mass dissemination and commerce, informed another early-twentieth-century musical experiment: Thaddeus Cahill's telharmonium.[17] The telharmonium, first installed in 1906 at Telharmonic Hall in New York City, was the first music synthesizer and the first electronic instrument designed for the mass distribution of musical performances. The large dual-manual keyboard sat in a performance salon, while the remaining bulk of the instrument—nearly two hundred tons of oscillators, switchboards, transformers, and other electromagnetic parts—lay concealed in the basement. Cahill soon established a schedule of daily recitals that not only drew crowds into the hall (where concealed telephonic receivers disseminated the instrument's sound throughout the room) but also were broadcast via telephone lines to subscribers (Weidenaar 1995).

As Gordon Mumma (1975, 288–289) argues, the financial model around which this instrument was developed and performed (that of broadcasting to a large number of paying subscribers, both commercial and private), in addition to the large scale of financial investment needed to construct the instrument in the first place, were products of America's own capital expansion at the beginning of the twentieth century. The telharmonium was also a cultural product of its time in another sense: The method of synthesis that Cahill developed for this instrument was based entirely on the objective and systematic measurement of sound and would theoretically enable Cahill to reproduce any timbre and achieve any number of intonation systems.[18] In other words, it offered the promise of *complete control* over any sound.

Ferrucio Busoni, having just learned about the development of the telharmonium, writes about its promise of unlimited tunings in his 1906 essay, "Sketch of a New Aesthetic of Music" (1999). In this document, Busoni taps into the imperative of technological progress so prevalent in Modernist rhetoric, arguing that new systems of intonation would aid in music's own progress and that Cahill's telharmonium would make these systems possible. Busoni's language demonstrates the extent to which this "progress" was thought to depend on rigorous and rationalized scientific methods:

> [Cahill] has constructed a comprehensive apparatus which makes it possible to transform an electric current into a fixed and mathematically exact number of vibrations. As pitch depends on the number of vibrations, and the apparatus may be "set" on any number desired, the infinite gradation of the octave may be accomplished by merely moving a lever corresponding to the pointer of a quadrant.
>
> Only a long and careful series of experiments, and a continued training of the ear, can render this unfamiliar material approachable and plastic for the coming generation, and for art. (1999, 23)

Despite Busoni's hopes for the instrument, however, Cahill did not use the telharmonium for the exploration of new musical sounds. Concerts consisted of traditional musical fare from the Western canon: transcriptions for the telharmonium of Brahms's *Hungarian Dance No. 7*, Mendelssohn's *Song of Spring*, the overture to Rossini's *William Tell*, nocturnes by Chopin and Field, and so forth (Weidenaar 1995, 168). In 1914, Cahill's company declared bankruptcy, and the telharmonium was dismantled before any further experimentation with the instrument's synthesizing capabilities could take place.

Early- and mid-twentieth-century composers also treated other early electronic instruments rather conservatively. The theremin, ondes martenot, and trautonium inspired some new compositions but seemed to most composers to be suitable only for traditional melodic roles.[19] Seen from a different perspective, however, these four instruments resonate with the Futurist project to aestheticize electricity, as exemplified by Balla's painting and Marinetti's poem. These instruments brought electronic technologies into the realm of music and, more specifically, into the realm of music performance. Electronic music technologies would soon find another home as essential creative instruments in studios, and the Modernist musical impetus toward the control of sound through new technologies would be taken to new lengths.

EARLY PHONOGRAPHY

The introduction of the gramophone to the Western marketplace in 1896 made possible the widespread dissemination of recorded performances.[20] Music could now transcend time and place through a process of recording, distribution, and subsequent playback. Yet nearly thirty years later, as Darius Milhaud (1924) remarks, the disc recorder had not yet escaped from its archival role.[21] At that time, Milhaud was experimenting with the effects of altering the speed of a recording, observing the resulting changes to the intrinsic characteristics of the recorded sound. By 1930, Percy Grainger, Ernst Toch, and Paul Hindemith had all conducted similar experiments (Katz 2004, Ch. 5; Manning 2004, 11). In the 1930s, a handful of commercial recordings exploited the possibility of rerecording a previously recorded performance while generating a new, accompanying performance by the same musician, thus resulting in apparent one-person duets (Cunningham 1998; Day 2000; Lacasse 2000). By the late 1940s, as mentioned in Chapter 2, in addition to these techniques, Les Paul had developed methods of reversing the temporal direction of recorded sounds (so they were heard from "back-to-front" upon playback) and primitive forms of artificial reverberation, echo, and phasing. He had also begun experimenting with the effects of different microphone placements.

These musicians and the technicians who worked with them began to realize the potential of the gramophone beyond its intended use as an archival tool. They found ways to use it as a creative tool and as such gave genesis to *phonography* (Eisenberg 1987): the use of recording technologies to create in recordings elements that do not, and perhaps even cannot, exist in the initial performances they apparently record. As discussed earlier, this potential for studio "fakery" was largely responsible for an emerging rift between recorded and live music in the popular imagination. Some early endeavors to bring recording technology into the realm of performance, however, indicated a potential for liveness in the recorded medium.

For instance, Cage's first experiments with recording technology soon followed those of Milhaud, Hindemith, Toch, and Grainger. In 1939, Cage was working as an accompanist to Bonnie Bird's dance classes at the Cornish School in Seattle, which had recently acquired a fully equipped radio studio. Cage began to experiment with these facilities, and in March of that year, using the equipment in the studio, he composed *Imaginary Landscape No. 1* (see Cage 1960) as the musical accompaniment to a number that Bird had choreographed. This piece allows me to address many of the broader implications brought about by the introduction of recording technologies into a performance context.

Imaginary Landscape No. 1 is scored for piano, Chinese cymbal, and two phonographs. Cage instructs in his score:

> This composition is written to be performed in a radio studio. 2 microphones are required. One microphone picks up the performance of players 1 and 2. The other, that of players 3 and 4. The relative dynamics are controlled by an assistant in the control room. The performance may then be broadcasted and/or recorded. (1960, 2)

Like Milhaud, Hindemith, and Toch before him, Cage utilizes the variable speed function of the turntables to alter the pitch of the recorded materials, which in this case are recordings of test-tone frequencies. Performers are instructed in the score when to switch speeds on the turntables and when to raise or lower the tone arms. The phonographs are treated as much like conventional musical instruments as possible in that Cage specifies durations (turning the sound on and off by lowering and raising the tone arm) and changes of pitch (resulting from the change in the turntable's speed) by whatever means the phonographs allow. Rather than through the production of original sound, however, these musical elements are realized through the manipulation of reproduced sound.

The assistant in the control room has a function similar to that of the phonograph operators, controlling the dynamic levels of each pair of performers, thus treating the mixer in the control room as yet another musical instrument (albeit one limited only to volume control) in addition to the phonographs. Even though the other four instrumentalists perform at the same time as the control-room assistant, their performances become *reproductions* as soon as they are converted to an electric signal by the microphones and then back to acoustic vibrations by the loudspeakers in the control room. When the control-room operator responds to these reproductions, he or she manipulates prerecorded sound in the same sense as do the phonograph operators. The performance that takes place in the radio studio thus involves various levels of production and reproduction: The pianist and cymbal player produce original, acoustic sound, while the phonograph operators manipulate reproduced sound, thus actually producing something new. In a similar manner, the assistant in the control room manipulates a further reproduction of these sound productions and reproductions to shape the configuration of sounds that an audience in an adjoining hall will ultimately hear. What emerges here for perhaps the first time in electronic art music, if only in its infant form, is a concept of performance in which the sounds of one performer are not just guided by another (as a symphony conductor guides the playing of instrumentalists) but actually physically controlled by another.

In this particular configuration of performers and recording technology, the control-room performer, to a certain extent, co-opts the agency of the other four performers. As Simon Emmerson (2000; 2007, 18–22) demonstrates, the concept of liveness is often linked to the identification of performer agency. That is to say, for music to be live, it often relies on the perception that a particular performer holds responsibility for having produced those sounds at that moment as a result of deliberate intention and action. In this way, liveness implies a certain authenticity. Thus, the surrender of control from one performer to another might be seen as a reduction of liveness in this particular performance context. Indeed, several writers have argued as much with respect to various other forms of mediatized music. Much of Théberge's (1989) argument regarding the loss of interactivity in recorded popular music, for example, rests on his assertion that in many multi-track recording studios, performers surrender their agency to sound engineers and producers. Not coincidentally, John Croft (2007) also argues that liveness is threatened in music for live electronics when listeners/viewers struggle against complex layers of electronic mediation to perceive a performer's agency.

Yet Cage presents further challenges to the distinctions between sound production and sound reproduction that may still allow for the persistence of liveness in *Imaginary Landscape No. 1*. The first performance of this piece, along with the instructions for future performances implied in Cage's score, present the performance conditions that lead me to this assertion. While the Cornish School's dancers performed on stage in the presence of an audience, the music was broadcast live into the hall from the radio studio (Key 2002, 106). In this performance of *Imaginary Landscape No. 1*, then, the performance of music occurred in a different location than did the performance of dance, but the aural aspects of that musical performance were heard in real time, via sound-reproduction technology, at the audience's site of audition/viewing while they watched the dance.

Cahill's telharmonium broadcasts (like radio broadcasts) had also separated the site of musical performance from the site of audition, but in so doing, they had eliminated the visual aspect of music performance altogether. Cahill's ultimate intention was for this music to be heard anywhere, at any time. Cage's approach, on the other hand, although separating the sound from its original source, still held to the idea that this sound was to be framed within a particular spatial and temporal setting (in the performance hall for the duration of the dance), while an audience watched performers on a stage. Thus, although relying on musical sound that is technologically reproduced (on many levels), *Imaginary Landscape No. 1* still remained framed within a performance, imbued with the corporeal liveness of the dancers and the temporal liveness of the simultaneous studio performance and broadcast. This performance context brings the dialectical nature of liveness itself to the foreground by emphasizing the various fluctuating tensions between live and mediated performance.

These experiments with electronic sound conducted by Cage and others were rather isolated, however, and sustained exploration of the possibilities of electronic technologies in art music did not emerge until the late 1940s and early 1950s. At this time, composers and technicians in different parts of the world established several studios dedicated to the composition of electronic art music. The most influential of these were Schaeffer's *musique concrète* studio, *Groupe de Recherches Musicales* at *Radiodiffusion Française* (RF) in Paris,[22] and the studio for *elektronische Musik* at *Westdeutscher Rundfunk* (WDR) in Cologne.[23] In Schaeffer's *musique concrète*, real-world sounds were recorded and then treated to various types of electronic modification. Schaeffer and his colleagues would vary the speed, reverse the playback direction, edit, repeat, and remix this material until they arrived at their final composition, which existed only in recorded format and needed to be played over loudspeakers to be heard. Put simply, this was a music that bypassed conventional performance altogether. As it was *initially* conceived by Schaeffer, the sounds used in creating *musique concrète* were to be treated in such a way as to eliminate as much as possible any associations between those sounds and their physical, real-world sources.[24]

Composers of *elektronische Musik* in Cologne established a different method by which to compose music for recordings. Rather than rely on real-world sounds, these composers synthesized all their sounds by means of electronic oscillators. They recorded sine waves and then treated them to the same types of sound-manipulation techniques as had been developed by the composers at RF, in addition to some made possible by electronic filters. Like *musique concrète*, *elektronische Musik* existed only in recorded format. In addition, like more conventionally recorded music (i.e., recordings of acoustic performances) and like the radio and telharmonic broadcasts already discussed, both *musique concrète* and *elektronische Musik* removed sound from the site of their physical production. Furthermore, both styles of music, at least at first, presented entirely new and unfamiliar sound worlds, which had few associations with any traditional performance conventions. In sum, due to their nature as *recorded* music, to their dissociation from any previously *performed* music, and to their unfamiliarity, *musique concrète* and *elektronische Musik* largely eliminated any perceivable qualities of performance from the musical experience. Significantly, they accomplished this very crucial omission by way of a systematic and rationalized control of sound through various electronic technologies.

Sounds were measured, codified, created, and altered, all within a Modernist environment that fetishized progress and treated technology as an objective tool.

This is not to say that these early examples of fixed-media music were never heard in any type of performance setting. The Paris and Cologne studios presented their compositions over loudspeakers to concert-hall audiences. For their part, however, the composers in Cologne were not attempting in these presentations to bring any aura of *live music* to the occasion. In a 1958 article entitled "What Is Electronic Music?" founding Cologne studio composer Herbert Eimert set out to define the studio's goals and aesthetic foundations. He explains that attempts to create a new style of music by electronic means must not proceed as a "mere transference of the traditional into the electroacoustical" and continues:

> Here we touch on a most widespread misconception: namely, the idea that one can make music "traditionally" with electronic means. Of course one "can"; but electronic concert instruments will always remain a synthetic substitute. The fact that practically no music which can be taken seriously, artistically, has been written for electronic concert instruments is due precisely to the fact that its use as either soloist or ensemble instrument does not transcend the old means of performance. (1958, 1–2)

Eimert picks up this idea again later in the article:

> Today the physical magnification of a sound is known, quite apart from any musical, expressionistic psychology, as exact scientific data. It cannot, however, be the function of electronic music to make the sinus tone[25] like the living "parasite," to feign similarity where disparity exists. Talk of "humanised" electronic sound may be left to unimaginative instrument makers. (1958, 9)

Liveness, at least conventionally understood as a "human" practice, was not a priority.

In Paris, Schaeffer likewise recognized a lack of "human" connection between his listeners and the sounds of his recorded compositions and thus made attempts to instill attributes of live performance into their public presentations. In an effort to "perform" the loudspeakers that were used in these presentations, Schaeffer asked the studio's technician, Jacques Poullin, to construct a device that would allow a performer to actively distribute sound throughout the performance space. This would be possible with a few simple potentiometers (otherwise known as pots) on a mixing console. But the gestures required to operate such controls would be rather subtle, as most pots were controlled by simple sliders or knobs.[26] Schaeffer wanted a device that would make the performer's physical gestures visible to the entire audience. He also wanted these gestures to correlate visibly (and logically) with the resultant localization of sound, with the ultimate goal being to overcome the "inhumane" nature of this rather technical process with an increased sense of human production (Poullin 1957, 112). He sought, in other words, to infuse these performances with qualities of corporeal liveness missing from the recorded sounds themselves.

Poullin constructed the *pupitre d'espace*:[27] a system consisting of four loudspeakers, five channels of sound, four wire receiving loops, and a transmitting coil held by the performer. Two speakers were placed on stage

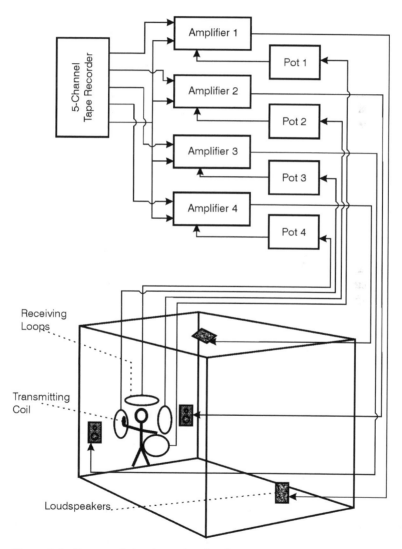

Figure 5.2 Setup and circuit routing for the *pupitre d'espace*[29]

(right and left), one was suspended from the ceiling in the center of the hall, and one was placed at the back of the hall. The performer stood on a platform surrounded by the receiving loops, which were arranged to match the placement of the speakers (one on either side, one above, and one directly in front of the performer). Although four of the five channels of sound were each fed to individual speakers in a predetermined manner, the performer directed the placement of the fifth channel (see Figure 5.2). The manual placement of the transmitting coil within the vicinity of a particular loop directed the fifth channel of sound to that loop's corresponding speaker (Manning 2004, 26). In this way, the performer of the *pupitre d'espace* could act as a sort of conductor, controlling aspects of the sound in performance rather than producing new sounds himself.[28]

This live performance of sound localization therefore brought an aspect of human performance to music that otherwise appeared (at least to the audience experiencing it) to be created by machines.[30] Most significantly, Schaeffer and Poullin had employed *an additional technology* in achieving this air of live performance. In other words, they generated a sense of liveness not by avoiding or negating technology but by configuring a musician/machine relationship that reintroduced performance into the presentation of otherwise nonperformed music. Garreth Broesche's (2012) concept of the dialectic of mediation (as discussed in Chapter 4) can be seen at work here again, as a new technology (the *pupitre d'espace*) is introduced in an effort to negate the perceived dehumanizing effects of previous technologies (sound recording). Once again, the dialogical nature of liveness and of mediatized performance comes to the fore as we identify these negotiations between human and machine. Admittedly, the *pupitre*'s function was still to demonstrate a performer's physical control of sound localization. Thus, the intended liveness in this performance context remained quite typically rooted in traditional concepts of corporeality: A performer's physical gestures determined musical sound.[31] As live electronic music continued to develop over the next few decades, however, musicians would explore different relationships with electronic technologies, leading to new kinds of mediatized performance and new expressions of liveness.

LIVE ELECTRONIC MUSIC AND INTERACTIVE LIVENESS

Despite Schaeffer's attempts to create a more conventional performance context for his compositions, *musique concrète*, like *elektronische Musik*, remained primarily a recorded music. Throughout the 1950s and 1960s, other composers made attempts to integrate fixed-media music more fully into the realm of performance. Most commonly, they achieved this task by combining the presentation of a prerecorded tape (composed according to the *musique concrète* tradition, the *elektronische Musik* tradition, or both) with the performance of a traditional acoustic instrument. This type of music became known as *mixed music*, due to its conscious mixture of both acoustic and recorded elements.

Mixed music was often criticized, however, for the extent to which performers felt constricted by the inflexible tape part. A sense of interactive ensemble—resembling that achieved in the performance of traditional, acoustic, chamber music (or other ensemble-based music), in which each performer may influence and be influenced by other performers—was very difficult to achieve in mixed music. Although an acoustic performer in mixed music may have conveyed many of the traditional attributes of live performance him- or herself, the interactive liveness so important in chamber music was difficult (if not impossible) to appreciate within the mixed music "ensemble."[32]

Although mixed music remained the most prominent type of performed electronic music throughout the 1950s and 1960s, some composers began seeking musician/machine configurations that would allow for a more interactive sense of performance. These endeavors led to the emergence of live electronic music according to the second definition that appears at the beginning of this chapter: performed music that involves the electronic manipulation of acoustic sound or the electronic real-time production of sound. Some early examples of live electronic music included the reappropriation of tape recorders not as passive playback devices but as instruments to be actively manipulated.

Mauricio Kagel's *Transición II* for piano, percussion, and two tapes (1959), for instance, requires the active use of a tape recorder to record, modify, and playback the sounds of the other performers.[33] The recorded sounds used in the types of electronic art music discussed so far in this chapter represent finished products: Even with Schaeffer and Poullin's *pupitre d'espace*, a performer could control which speaker the tape would play from but could not alter the sounds that would actually be emitted. One of the tapes (Tape 1) used in *Transición II* follows this method, as it contains prerecorded sections of the piece played by the pianist and percussionist. For the other tape (Tape 2), however, the recorded sound is captured, manipulated, and then reproduced all during the process of performance. As the pianist and percussionist play, a tape operator records sections of their performances. The tape operator then makes this recorded material into repeating tape loops that he or she plays back during the course of the performance, by which time the acoustic performers have moved on to other material. The recorded material may be modified by means of speed changes, reverberation, filtering, and/or other tape techniques during its playback, or it may not: The decision of whether to modify the material is left to the performers. Kagel describes the entire process: "While the interpreters always play in the present, they simultaneously tape-record fragments for the future; these fragments, in turn, become the past when, later, they are made audible through loud-speakers in the hall" (quoted in Schwartz 1975, 115).

Kagel points here to one of the key capabilities of the recording medium: the ability to manipulate perceptions of time so distinctions between past, present, and future become blurred. The pianist and percussionist interact with past versions of their own performances; the performers and audience alike are confronted with memories of music just played, while simultaneously trying to commit to memory what may be heard again in the future, all within the framework of one performance. Of course, one may argue that listening to a Beethoven piano sonata (or any other piece of music) invites the same kinds of play with memory and expectation. In *Transición II*, however, the recording and reproduction of musical material exactly as it is played (at least, more exactly than would be possible without recording technology) foregrounds this temporal play far more than in nonmediatized music. The audition of Tape 1—the material recorded before the performance—adds another layer of temporal disjunction, providing for the performers a memory of a more distant past (recording the music prior to the performance) and, for the audience, an encounter with an imagined (or at least unwitnessed) past. A performance of *Transición II*, then, establishes a series of interrelations between music as it is produced and that same music as it is subsequently and simultaneously reproduced. It confronts and plays with qualities of temporality that arguably form the foundation of what I have called *temporal liveness*.

Furthermore, as is the case in Cage's *Imaginary Landscapes No. 1*, the reproduction of the sounds on Tape 2 actually involves a creative act of production: The tape operator actively participates in the recording, manipulation, and subsequent audition of sound. Whereas Cage's technicians operate within the studio, however, Kagel's operate onstage, during the performance. A performance of this composition emphasizes the roles of the tape operator and tape recorder in facilitating the entire process described above. By itself, a tape recorder is an inanimate object. Only when taken up by a human and *performed* as an instrument in a musical context can it become an integral part of this composition. Thus the distinction between technician and musical performer or, perhaps more importantly, between electronic machine and musical instrument is also blurred.[34] In its blurring of these distinctions, Kagel's *Transición II* presents performance as a mediatized form of human production on many levels.

Such pieces as Kagel's *Transición II* also demonstrate a crucial development in musician/machine relationships with respect to my focus here on interactive liveness. First, following Cage's earlier example (but to a much greater degree), this piece challenges traditional concepts of musical agency by providing a context in which some performers' sounds are directly manipulated by another. Significantly, Kagel's pianist and percussionist do not renounce all control. They still produce intended sounds; moreover, the audience hears these sounds unaltered and in their entirety alongside the very same sounds as captured and controlled by another performer— the tape operator. Through these negotiations of agency, a new concept of

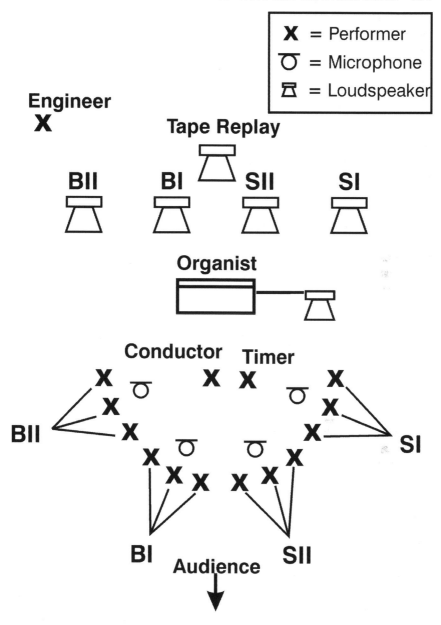

Figure 5.3   Stage setup for Karlheinz Stockhausen's *Mikrophonie II*

performing ensemble is forged: a type of interactive network in which the various performers not only *share* in creating the final product but also must relinquish *their own sounds* to each other for further manipulation. Seen in this way, this new type of *mediatized performance network* hinges not only on the cooperative interactions between performers so essential to traditional chamber music but also, and crucially, on the role of electronic technology in forming the network.

The exploration into technologically facilitated interaction—the establishment of what I call *interactive performance networks*—was taken to even greater lengths as live electronic music continued to mature and develop. In *Mikrophonie II* (1965),[35] for instance, Karlheinz Stockhausen also uses sound technologies to challenge traditional concepts of performer agency, thus presenting another reconfiguration of social interaction in music performance. As in Kagel's piece, both performer/machine relationships and electronically mediated inter-performer relationships play vital roles in facilitating perceptions of interactive liveness, even when other qualities of liveness may seem threatened.

The performing forces for *Mikrophonie II* include a choir of six sopranos and six basses, a conductor, a timekeeper, a Hammond organist, and an audio engineer (see Figure 5.3). Although original music is performed, prerecorded excerpts of Stockhausen's *Gesang der Jünglinge* (1956), *Carré* (1960), and *Momente* (1964) are also added to the mix periodically throughout the performance.[36] Each of the four sections of the choir sings into a microphone, and each of these microphones feeds into a ring modulator (described below). The electrical output of the Hammond organ feeds into all four of the ring modulators and into its own loudspeaker (see Figure 5.4). Each modulator feeds into a potentiometer, and each potentiometer feeds into a loudspeaker. The sound engineer operates the potentiometers, ultimately controlling the mix of all members of the ensemble and the mixture of acoustic sound with amplified and transformed sound. It is important to note that this mixture of acoustic and amplified sound varies considerably throughout the composition, according to Stockhausen's indications in the score. At times the amplification, and thus the ring modulation, is turned off altogether; at other times, it completely overwhelms the acoustic sound. Significant moments also occur in the piece where the mixture between acoustic sound and electronically modified sound is intended to be balanced enough to render both elements clearly audible.[37]

To appreciate fully the various levels of performer control, interactivity, and, ultimately, liveness, evident in a performance of this piece, one must understand the role of the electronic components within this performance network. The ring modulators fulfill the most important function. A ring modulator combines two audio signals in such a way that the two signals modify each other. It attenuates the original sounds and produces the sum and difference frequencies of those two signals. For example, if one signal

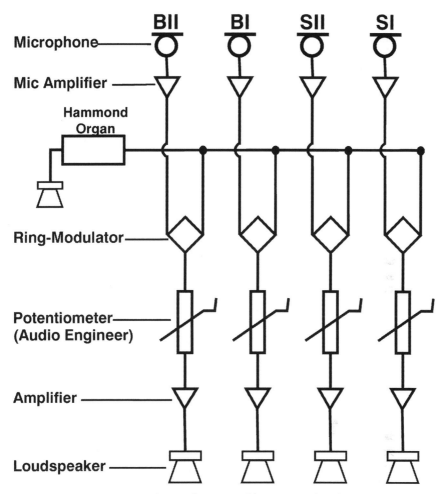

Figure 5.4   Circuit routing for Karlheinz Stockhausen's *Mikrophonie II*
Stockhausen MICROPHONIE II
© 1965 by Universal Edition A.G., Vienna
© Renewed
All Rights Reserved
Used by permission of European American Music Distributors Company, U.S. and
Canadian agent for Universal Edition A.G., Vienna

were carrying a pure frequency of 440 Hz (*a*') and the other signal were
carrying a pure frequency of 110 Hz (*A*), the ring modulator would produce
both the sum of those frequencies, 550 Hz (slightly lower than *c#*'') and the
difference, 330 Hz (*e*') (see Figure 5.5). This easy calculation only works
with pure sine tones, however. If one were to combine more complex frequencies, such as the sound of three human voices with that of a Hammond
organ, the resulting frequencies would become virtually unpredictable.[38]

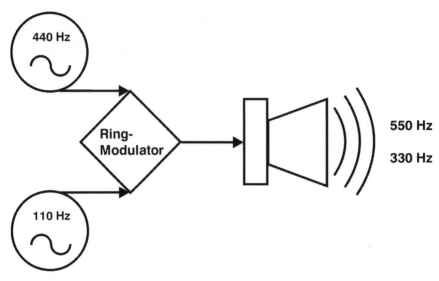

Figure 5.5   Example of simple ring modulation

The ring modulator, however, only operates when two signals are present. Therefore, at moments in *Mikrophonie II* when the choir sings and the organ remains silent, or vice versa, the audience hears only the non-transformed sounds of those particular musicians (although these sounds may be amplified). In Stockhausen's original conception of the piece, each performer's part is quite strictly notated. In this scenario, the musicians would at least be aware of when others were to enter and therefore of when their own sounds would be altered by ring modulation. As the piece was rehearsed, however, Stockhausen found it more desirable to give the performers more freedom in interpreting the score. He states, "Finally a score came into being which made it possible for each individual singer and the organist to react to each other, according to the context" (1995b, 82).

Paradoxically, however, as the performers gain more improvisatory responsibility for their own performances, they ultimately lose more control over the resultant sound of the modulated signals. Stockhausen states, "The organist had to decide from the context when and how much electronic transformation should be produced by changes in dynamic level" (1995b, 82). In many instances, the organist is also responsible for devising his own rhythmic and pitch material, as are the singers. If each performer has little or no knowledge of exactly when the others will sing or play, they have an even smaller chance of predicting what kinds of sounds the ring modulator might produce than they would if the entire score were meticulously notated. Furthermore, no one is ever guaranteed that whatever contributions he or she makes to the ring modulator will actually have an impact on the *amplified* sound that the audience hears, because the sound engineer turns the loudspeakers off at particular moments in the performance, which leaves only the nontransformed sound audible to the audience. Stockhausen makes it even more difficult for listeners to determine who is producing the sounds they hear in all cases by positioning the choir members with their backs to the audience.

The actual sounds of this composition, then, are at times completely disengaged—in more ways than one—from their original sources: the singers and organist. Most significantly, the sounds the audience hears are not always the direct results of individual performance but rather the modified sounds produced by the cooperative process of ring modulation. Although vocal sounds in particular often represent a corporeal presence (as discussed in Chapter 3), large amounts of amplification and ring modulation may at times overwhelm any potential for identifying corporeal liveness; the piece plays "on the hot edge" (Corbett 1990, 92) between corporeal signification and complete disengagement from that corporeality. Thus, within the performance network of *Mikrophonie II*, each performer's individuality, usually so easily linked to his or her recognizable corporeality, is somewhat obscured by the entire process.

At the same time that he presents this treatise on varieties of corporeality, Stockhausen also mixes real-time performance with prerecorded sounds. As mentioned above, Stockhausen dictates that recorded excerpts from three of his other works be played at specified moments in the performance. In addition to challenging conventional notions of temporality in performed music (in a manner akin to that in Kagel's *Transición II*), this mixture of recordings with live performance further contributes to the very loss of performer identity I have already discussed. In *Mikrophonie II*, the prerecorded music is played through its own loudspeaker, which is placed in the center of all the other loudspeakers (see Figure 5.3). This particular localization of the prerecorded music blends it with all the other amplified sounds. Boundaries between acoustic sounds and amplified sounds—which for many amount to boundaries between live sounds and nonlive sounds—thus become blurred.

Numerous tensions are at work in a performance of *Mikrophonie II*. First, the piece highlights a tension between corporeal liveness and the ability to eradicate corporeality through mediatization. It also highlights the tension between the assumed temporal liveness inherent in a live performance and the ability to disturb this conception of temporality with the introduction of prerecorded material. Yet recall Stockhausen's comments about the method of performance he finally settled on for this piece: "Finally a score came into being which made it possible for each individual singer and the organist to react to each other, according to the context." Stockhausen emphasizes interaction between musicians; this interaction depends not only on his score but also on the same musician/machine relationship that challenges corporeality in the first place. The sonic results of this live interaction also emanate from the same row of speakers that emits the prerecorded (i.e., nonlive) music.

Stockhausen sets the stage here for a self-reflexive use of technology in which musicians react to each other and to the unpredictable nature of the electronic ring modulation (further facilitating a liveness of spontaneity, especially for performers). Interactive liveness can then emerge from this dialectical relationship between musicians and electronic technologies, as, once again, thetical moments of human utterance converge with antithetical moments of machine utterance. Moreover, the various interrelations established here between corporeal liveness, temporal liveness, and interactive liveness bring the very issue of liveness in mediatized music to the forefront of this piece's performed meaning. Although the qualities of corporeal liveness and temporal liveness I describe here are not *necessary* components of interactive liveness, the various categories of liveness performed *in this piece* exist nonexclusively and must be understood in relation to one another within this complex mediatized performance network. Stockhausen's *Mikrophonie II* provides a performance context in which one can clearly appreciate the potential complexity and fluidity of the concept of liveness.

I suggest in this chapter that a growing number of musicians in the 1960s embraced electronic sound technologies as tools with which to emphasize the interactive nature of group performance and, moreover, that this practice engendered a kind of mediatized interactive liveness. As discussed in the chapter's introduction, the emergence of this type of liveness in live electronic music stood in stark contrast with the aesthetics promoted and practiced by Eimert, Boulez, and other Modernist musicians (as argued in Attali [1985] and Born [1995]). I wish to illustrate here that the performance of interactive liveness was not restricted to the type of mediatized inter-musician interactivity I have outlined up to this point. Throughout the 1960s, several musicians also began to explore the possibilities of interacting directly *with* their electronic technologies. In other words, they engaged in a set of anthropomorphizing practices, granting a certain amount of performative agency to the technologies with which they performed and thus severely challenging distinctions between musician and machine.

Gordon Mumma was one of the first musicians to explore this type of interaction with a device he calls a *cybersonic console*. His *Hornpipe* (1967)[39] for French horn and cybersonic console establishes a symbolic interaction between musician and machine in which the machine is considered a fully collaborating performance partner—an equal contributor in the interactive performance network. The console contains electronic circuits that respond to the frequencies of the horn and the resonances of the performance space. Mumma explains the concept of the piece:

> The cybersonic console monitors the resonances of the Horn in the performance space and adjusts its electronic circuits to complement these resonances. During this adjustment certain circuits become unbalanced and attempt to rebalance themselves. While rebalancing, various combinations occur which produce electronic sound responses. These

responses, heard from loudspeakers, result in three further sound activities: Horn in ensemble with electronic sounds, solo electronic sequences of long cybersonic responses, and electronic sounds articulated directly by Horn sounds.

In each performance the player learns from his own choices and their corresponding electronic responses which sounds are most likely to unbalance and rebalance the cybersonic console. Beginning as a solo, a performance of Hornpipe becomes a duo of responses between the Horn and the cybersonic console, ending when a sustained Horn sound balances all of the cybersonic circuits and terminates the electronic sounds. (1972)

A performance of *Hornpipe* draws our attention to the process, not only of the performer attempting throughout to achieve a balance with the cybersonic console but also of the performer learning from one performance to the next how best to achieve that balance. The process unfolds by means of a perceived dialogue between the performer and the console.

I use the word *perceived*, because, of course, the console does not exercise the same kinds of human reasoning and decision making as the performer: It responds according to the way Mumma has designed it. In a performance of *Hornpipe*, Mumma (a French horn player himself) is really only in dialogue with the results of his own electronic design. Yet I argue that the perception of an interactive liveness between musician and machine does not depend on the *actual* existence of dialogues between performers and technologies. Rather, it rests on these musicians' exploring the *illusion* of such dialogues; put another way, it rests on the *virtual* existence of such dialogues. Virtuality is the central focus of my next chapter. For now, however, I simply emphasize that many live electronic musicians increasingly entertained the idea that some level of perceived "communication" might take place between musicians and electronic technologies. This type of communication is also invoked in this chapter's second epigraph, in which Suzanne Ciani grants to her synthesizer, even if only metaphorically, a personality and liveness of its own.

For his part, Mumma recognizes the extent to which his cybersonic console merely acts as it has been programmed to act, but his statements nonetheless suggest that we ought to consider levels of interactive liveness that may be explored with this type of human/machine configuration:

I made circuitry which had decision-making possibilities, and I allowed it to make decisions. I knew the kind of decisions it would make, and I made its environment for it. And then I could share decision-making with it. . . . I set up situations so we could interact . . . and we adjust ourselves to each other and to the circumstances through the course of a performance. That's a sort of semi-automatic situation. It's also live performance. It's an ensemble piece. (quoted in Ashley 2000, 99)

I have been concerned in this chapter with outlining a particular histori-cal moment in the development of electronic art music, in which a particu-lar concept of mediatized musical interaction, as an element of liveness, emerges in strength. The emergence of this concept is significant in part due to the similarities it shares with current uses of digital technologies in a variety of performance settings. Although anything more than a cur-sory consideration of such performance contexts is outside the range of my current project (not because it is inappropriate—far from it—but simply because limits have to be set somewhere), I feel it important in this instance to draw attention, at the very least, to some of the strong implications of interactive liveness found therein.[40]

Newly configured networks of mediatized interaction play a vital part, for instance, in networked performances of music (via the Internet or a more localized network) and in what is broadly referred to as *interactive composition*, or interactive computer music. Interactive composition, in fact, dates back to the early 1970s, as new technologies allowed for pre-liminary steps in extending the logics and aesthetic concerns of live elec-tronic music into the digital realm. The pioneering work of Joel Chadabe and Salvatore Martirano, especially, featured the development of interac-tive digital technologies that allowed for a sort of collective improvisa-tion between composer/performer and computer, not entirely unlike the scenario created by Mumma in *Hornpipe* (Chadabe 1997, Ch. 11; Jordà 2007). Pauline Oliveros's *Expanded Instrument System* provides another useful example of mediatized interaction. Begun in 1965 with a system of reel-to-reel tape machines that allowed for an instrumentalist's or vocalist's improvisatory responses to various tape delays, the Expanded Instrument System engaged in a play with temporality similar to Kagel's *Transición II* while also emphasizing a concept of musician/machine interaction similar to that informing Mumma's *Hornpipe* and the other interactive compos-ers just mentioned. Oliveros writes, "Through the years I understood the Expanded Instrument System to mean 'time machine'—what is expanded is temporal—present/past/future is occurring simultaneously with transfor-mations. What I play in the present comes back in the future while I am still playing, is transformed and becomes a part of the past. This situation keeps you busy listening" ("Expanded Instrument System").[41] Oliveros has since continued her work on this interactive performance tool using digital tech-nologies, specifically digital signal processing that provides "several kinds of pitch, time and spatial ambiance transformations and manipulations" ("Expanded Instrument System") in a MAX/MSP environment.[42]

Networked performances of music are another context in which interac-tive liveness is often central to the goals of its practitioners. In recent years, much of this activity has been facilitated by the Internet, but earlier per-formance networks that connected musicians separated in space but not in time by way of modems over telephone lines were explored as early as the 1970s. Since then, important developments in networked performance have been made by such composers as William Duckworth, Tod Machover, and, once again, Oliveros (Mills 2010, 186–187). Oliveros is currently involved with two projects involving Internet-enabled networked performance: the Telematic Circle, an "interest group that uses and develops applications for telepresent music performances" (Oliveros, "Telematic Circle"), and the Avatar Orchestra Metaverse, a global collective of users who perform multimedia works online via the virtual-reality platform Second Life, treating this online environment "as an instrument itself" (Avatar Orchestra Metaverse). Both of these scenarios offer rich opportunities for discussion with respect to interactive liveness and demonstrate the ability of Internet technologies to facilitate entirely new interactive performance networks. The Avatar Orchestra Metaverse, in particular, foregrounds the possibilities for virtual interactivity not only through its online environment but also, and especially, in each participant's use of an animated avatar to represent his or her presence within the virtually created world particular to each performance.[43]

I argue in this chapter that the liveness indicated in the genre label live electronic music emerges not only from its existence as a performed music—that is, not only from its performance before a physically and temporally co-present audience. Liveness may also emerge from productive tensions between traditionally understood elements of live performance—for instance, temporality, corporeality, and, most importantly in this chapter, interactivity—and that sometimes-perceived eradicator of liveness, electronic technology. Technologically enhanced interactive liveness emerged in electronic art-music practice as a strategy for configuring musician/ machine relationships different from those pursued by musical Modernists dating back to Russolo and the other Futurists.

The legacy of these Modernists is important, as much new electronic art music still maintains a clear lineage with their foundational work. Nonetheless, it is also important to recognize, as I do in this chapter, the work of live electronic musicians that cannot fall so easily under the criticisms leveled at electronic art music by Attali (1985), Born (1995), and others. One of the distinguishing features of this live electronic music is an approach to musical interaction that led to the performance of what I have called *interactive liveness*. Rather than approaching sound technologies as implements of rationalized control, many live electronic musicians began to conceive of these technologies as instruments of social interaction. Whereas composers from within the Modernist legacy may have viewed these technologies as "instruments obedient to my thought," some musicians outside that tradition even began to project onto their machines the metaphor that technologies were capable of thinking and of communing with people.

As I discuss in the next chapter, an increasing willingness to interact with technologies in this way lays the foundation for my concept of virtual liveness. To lay the groundwork for that discussion, I demonstrate here that technologies need not be viewed as impediments to liveness. Indeed, as is evident in some of the examples discussed above, the use of electronic technologies may even make some perceived traces of liveness *more* evident, even as it simultaneously *eradicates* certain others. In the case of modern performance networks, such as that established in the Avatar Orchestra Metaverse, interactive liveness is given entirely new configurations thanks to the Internet technologies involved. Electronic technologies, I attempt to demonstrate, may be deployed in music so as to reflect the dialectical nature of liveness in mediatized culture: the constant negotiation between conventional traces of human activity and identifications of newer, electronic mediations. As I explore in the next chapter, this dialectical negotiation may even result in the formation of a new figurative entity—one that simultaneously performs *musician* and *machine* while still remaining *live*.

6 Virtual Liveness and Sounding Cyborgs
John Oswald's "Vane"

Flesh in the wires . . .

Peter Frampton

In the three previous chapters, I have been concerned mostly with perceived traces of liveness that result from slight incursions of mediatization into the human process of performance. The corporeal liveness discussed in Chapter 3, the liveness of fidelity discussed in Chapter 4, and the interactive liveness discussed in Chapter 5 all result from recognizably human acts of musicking in which electronic technologies, each in its own way, are intrinsically involved in creating a specifically mediatized shading of that humanness. Although these performances are mediatized, they remain close enough to the realm of human experience that to still refer to them as *performance* does not require a drastic reconfiguration of that concept. What happens, though, when the limits of human performance are clearly surpassed— when performative qualities, such as corporeality and interactivity, are clearly matched, or even exceeded, by qualities of mediatization? Does this mediatization erase all traces of liveness? I argue in this chapter that liveness may yet persist in these situations, and I propose the concept of *virtual liveness* as a tool for theorizing performative meaning in such contexts. Like all the other categories of liveness I address, virtual liveness involves identifying traces of live performance in mediatized music. Whereas most accounts of liveness focus on the perception of *actual* performers, however, virtual liveness invokes virtual performing personae: performers who exist only in a listener's encounter with highly mediatized music (in this case, a recording involving high levels of electronic sound manipulation).

Virtual personae exist, in other words, in the technosphere, that "domain of imaginary possibilities and constraints" (Toynbee 2000, 69) in mediatized music, which lies on a continuum between live sound at one end and mediatized reception at the other. Liveness persists in the perception of virtual personae, because despite high levels of mediatization, recognizably human performance still maintains a place of central importance. Yet human performance is not the only source of meaning attributable to these performance contexts; rather, it works in productive tension with highly perceptible elements of mediatization, so our virtual performing personae also may be described as *sounding cyborgs*. Various neighborhoods of cultural study, such as electroacoustic music theory, cultural theory, and media theory, among others, offer useful theoretical tools (addressing, for instance, aural source recognition, the subjectivity of performers and listeners, virtuality, and the cyborg figuration[1]) to help explain virtual liveness and sounding cyborgs. Thus, I begin by considering these ideas in the context of my own theories of liveness, laying the foundation for the analysis that follows.

The remainder of the chapter puts these theories to work in a critical analysis of virtual liveness in John Oswald's *plunderphonic* piece, "Vane" (1990).[2] I rely here partly on Oswald's own statements about "Vane," which imply his perception of an imaginary performing persona in a piece that owes much of its identity to electronic studio composition techniques. Oswald's comments prompt me to invoke the sounding cyborg figuration in my own hearing of his work. In my analysis, which focuses especially on Oswald's combination of his source materials, I identify a sounding cyborg imbued with virtual liveness by its evocations of two recognizable performance styles and by the ways these styles combine via technological manipulations. This virtual persona presents new associative meanings of corporeality, genre, gender, and liveness, inviting new stylistic interpretations precisely because of the unique combination of elements enacted by Oswald in his digital realization of "Vane." First, then, I present the theoretical underpinnings of my approach to virtual liveness and sounding cyborgs.

SOURCE RECOGNITION, SUBJECTIVITY, AND PERSONAE

Liveness, as I present it throughout this book, relies on the concept of communication (whether real or imagined) between "performer" and "audience." For an audience to glean any performative meaning from a musical experience, some sort of *source recognition* must take place, an appreciation of musical sound emanating from a particular, identifiable source—in our scenario, some type of performer. Of course, a listener's ability to recognize the specifics of that source depends greatly on his or her own *subject position*: How does this listener's interest/education/experience influence his or her perception of that source? Finally—and here the use of electronic technologies has a very significant impact—in highly mediatized musical contexts, perception of liveness may extend beyond what a "real" performer has presented for the audience, and the performer may find him- or herself sharing the stage with, or even relinquishing it entirely to, an imagined and technologically enhanced *performing persona*. A closer look at these three concepts allows for a clearer explication of how virtual liveness can emerge from even highly mediatized recorded music.

Identifying sound sources in recordings of many types of music is not at all problematic and often lends itself immediately to an understanding that performing musicians are responsible for the sounds heard on that record-ing—an understanding that usually carries with it a great deal of corporeal significance, as I discuss throughout Chapter 3. Highly mediatized music, however, can present a more complex scenario as far as source recognition is concerned. Recognizably human utterances can easily be obscured or overwhelmed by rather unrecognizable machinelike sounds, throwing the issue of liveness severely into question. Nonetheless, where recognizably human sound sources do persist, even when in conversation with highly mediatized sounds, liveness may still be a useful tool with which to ana-lyze the resulting musical experience, so long as a nuanced consideration of source recognition plays a part in the analysis.

A sustained discussion of source recognition must begin with a con-sideration of the earliest large-scale attempt at creating purely acousmatic art music, Pierre Schaeffer's *musique concrète*. Despite Schaeffer's initial insistence that such music could be heard in a way that would eliminate ("bracket out") all associations with the original sources of its sonic mate-rial (be they conventional instruments or trains),[3] however, Simon Emmer-son (2007, 5–6) reminds us that much acousmatic music often causes listeners to pay more attention to perceived sound sources in an attempt to compensate for the missing visual stimulus.

In fact, many composers of electronic music since Schaeffer's initial exper-iments have taken this impetus toward source recognition as a central aes-thetic tool in their work. Such music often *depends* for its effectiveness on listeners making associations between the sounds they hear and their per-ceived sources of these sounds.[4] A basic perception of corporeal liveness is based on the same principle: identifying a perceived source of sound. In much acousmatic music, however, play with source recognition runs much deeper, as it often explores sounds beyond (but not excluding) those associated with the musically performing human body. The interplay between those sounds whose original (physical) sources are easily recognized and those beyond recognizability constitutes the central interest of much of this music.[5] As is evident below, my analysis of "Vane" focuses a great deal on the interplay between sounds easily ascribed to the performers of the original recordings and those that resist such easy source recognition (even though *all* sounds in the tune derive in some way from the original recordings).

Of course, the level of recognizability of each source, despite its level of mediatization, depends a great deal on the individual subject position of each listener/observer. In fact, the fluidity and flexibility of liveness that I emphasize reflects in part the very subjective nature of the entire con-cept. Liveness is intrinsically linked with perception and therefore highly dependent on the one perceiving the musical performance. Each individual listener/observer presents a potentially unique experience of liveness in any given situation, including those outlined in the previous paragraph. Fur-thermore, the whole idea of communication between performer and lis-tener depends on recognition of the subjectivities of both parties.[6]

Therefore, high levels of mediatization may threaten the ability of listeners to identify the sources of the sounds they hear, depending on their own knowledge, experiences, interests, and other realities of their own unique subjectivities. For instance, a listener unfamiliar with the possible ways electronic sound technologies can alter recorded sounds may hear in a highly processed drum track only that "some type of drum was hit." A listener familiar with the aural effects of various electronic signal processing techniques, on the other hand, may correctly identify a tom drum captured with a distance microphone and treated subsequently to heavy artificial reverberation and a quickly rising low-pass filter.[7] Put another way, this listener may be able to determine with great accuracy the extent to which the sound he or she hears derives from the drummer's initial physical gesture. The resulting significance of that perception may generate a very different appreciation of the piece of music from that experienced by the first listener. Each listener's subject position, then, significantly affects his or her encounters with music and, more specifically, with liveness, which relies on the concept of communication between performers and listeners.

Western musical thought has long held that traditional performance situations set up an ideal model of this type of communication. Traditional settings that place performers in a position facing an audience mimic conventional "face-to-face" contexts of communication. This direct relationship between performers and listeners receives extra emphasis in more intimate performance settings, such as pubs. Of course, larger performance spaces (rock arenas, for instance) promote a greater sense of anonymity due to the sheer number of listeners, combined with the physical distance between the performers and most of these listeners. A sense remains, nonetheless, that these performers are present at one time and in one place to perform for their audience and for no one else.

But a sense of direct communication, and thus the subject position of the listener, is potentially more severely threatened when listening to recordings. Listeners no longer hear sounds performed "just for them" in a particular time and place. It would seem more difficult, then, for a listener to experience this music as the "I" of a direct "I-You" communication when he or she is just one of possibly thousands of people who will hear this performance and when the performers are not aware of any specific listener's presence in that potential interaction. Performers here perform for an infinite number of potential anonymous listeners,[8] and those listeners now choose at will from countless performances, all frozen in the form of CDs or as invisible files existing only in cyberspace and awaiting their multiple identical instantiations through multiple sets of speakers.[9] Any potential form of "I-You" communication is further threatened by acousmatic music in which performers are avoided altogether, for then both "I" and "You" may seem to disappear entirely.

The concept of *performing personae* helps explain how subjectivity may be maintained in these types of situations so liveness might then remain an important part of recorded music even when traces of conventional performance are obviously mixed with—and at times obscured by—electronically produced sound. I argue here that listeners, in seeking their own subject positions, may also assign subjectivity to that with which they seek communication (in this case, what they hear on a recording), even when they know that no "real" performing human body is producing those exact sounds—when physical boundaries of human music performers are surpassed by technological means. In other words, they construct a virtual performing "You"—a performing persona—to complete the usual line of communication.

In her engaging study of musical subjectivity, Naomi Cumming (2000) demonstrates the importance of the performing "personality"—a performer's musical identity—and, furthermore, how that performer's perceived subjectivity informs a listener's encounters with performances, whether live or recorded. She presents a review of a performance by the violinist Midori, in which the reviewer is disappointed that the Midori he heard in concert does not sound like the same Midori "who sells all those CDs" (Potter 1996, 734; quoted in Cumming 2000, 21). Cumming argues that the disparity between the two Midoris exists because recordings, through the various recording and processing techniques practiced by studio engineers and producers, are able to present a different sounding "personality" than that which *actually* exists. This personality heard on CD is, however, no less real to listeners:

> By altering the balance, dynamic level, and quality of her sounds, the engineers have effectively created for her a musical "body" and identity, at least in [the reviewer's] experience. They are able to effect this illusion because the characteristics of sounds are the aural "marks" of bodily actions. A violinist's perceived "strength" reflects the tension of her muscles, the weight of the arm as it is allowed to fall in the movement of a bow, the degree of friction in an "attack." Although a listener's attention, when playing a CD, may not be directed to bodily actions . . . the impression of a "personality" can be gained subliminally through the markers in sound of what seem to be the performer's characteristic physical responses. Sonic illusion is not, then, the innocent cleaning up of a musical surface, but the construction of a personality. (2000, 21–22)[10]

Yet potential problems exist in trying to apply Cumming's concept of personalities in traditional violin performance to recordings of imaginary sounding cyborgs, such as the one we encounter in "Vane." Perhaps primary among these is the ease with which the recorded Midori can be mistaken for the real Midori. It is conceivable that the sounds encoded on a Midori CD are faithful to Midori's actual performance capabilities, because her CDs still sound like a "real violinist"—like a fully human, musically laboring body. The reviewer's disappointment at learning that he has been duped is evidence that he had believed in the reality of the recorded Midori personality, which turned out to be partly the real, physical Midori and partly a technological construction. Can listeners still hear personalities, however, even when technological construction *obviously* accounts far more for what they hear than actual performance—that is, when the boundaries of embodied performance have clearly been crossed in favor of expanded electronic possibilities?

My unequivocal answer to these questions is "yes." Before explaining why, however, I must address a point of terminology. As stated, I wish to extend Cumming's concept of a performing personality into the realm of recorded music that is obviously "electronic." Yet I find that because the personalities created in much of this music are just that—creations—as much as (if not more than) they are traces of real people, the word *personality* implies an entity that is too distinct for my purposes. In Cumming's usage, the term seems to imply a definition provided by the *Shorter Oxford English Dictionary* (SOED): "the assemblage of qualities or characteristics which makes a person a distinctive individual; the (esp. notable or appealing) distinctive character of a person."[11] This seems appropriate when addressing the subjectivity of living, breathing individuals (such as Midori).

Persona, on the other hand, implies an entity that is more "put on" or consciously acted—in a sense, created or performed. The SOED provides a useful definition for persona: "A character assumed by an author, performer, etc., in his or her writing, work, etc."[12] Philip Auslander (2004, 2006a) also proposes the persona as a focus for the analysis of musical performance, with one crucial difference from the definition just given: A persona, for Auslander, is an identity that is partly performed by a musician but also depends on an audience, and on the social and musical allowances and constraints of any given performance context, for its exact articulation. For my purposes, likewise, a persona is as much a character identified by any listener as it is one (per)formed by a composer or performer. After all, the subjectivity of individual listeners ensures that they may all create for themselves, in conjunction with the performance they witness, different performing personae. In this sense, listeners exercise as much agency in the creation of performing personae as do those responsible for the sounds on a particular recording (composers, performers, engineers, producers, etc.).[13]

HEARING SOUNDING CYBORGS: VIRTUALITY AND VIRTUAL LIVENESS

The reliance of my theory on (partly) imagined performing personae, created in the minds of listeners encountering high levels of mediatization acting in tandem with traces of (particularly corporeal) liveness, takes us into the realm of the *virtual*. Once an understanding of the virtual is reached, and the significance of virtual relationships in many modern cultures is acknowledged, it becomes clear how virtual relationships between listeners and imagined performing personae can lead to meaningful perceptions of virtual liveness. I also argue here that the theoretical figuration of the sounding cyborg can help us make further sense of the imagined persona's very real performative power within highly mediatized musical experiences.

The word *virtual*, to be sure, carries with it several possible connotations, two of which seem especially useful and appropriate in this context. First, this word has been used increasingly in recent years to indicate some experience that is mediated by digital technology. For instance, *virtual realities*—computer-simulated physical environments—have been part of the popular imagination since the late 1980s. Additionally, as the Internet becomes a more vital part of many modern lifestyles, we refer to more and more of our activities as taking place *virtually*—that is, through the mediation of cyberspace. Second, and not in an entirely unrelated manner, the word *virtual* is also used to describe something that is, to borrow from William Echard (2006, 8), "real but not actual." In other words, the virtual is real in essence but not literally so. It seems to exist but not in any concrete form. Taken in conjunction with the nature of a modern cyberculture, the application of the term *virtual* to activities carried out through electronic networks of communication within that cyberculture begins to make a great deal of sense. For within this cyberculture—and with this term I refer to a modern culture highly reliant on (even obsessed with) the possibilities of computers and other electronic technologies to mediate an increasing number of social interactions—many participants are prepared to imbue the implicated technologies with their own virtual subjectivities.

These subjectivities are virtual in both senses of the word: They are mediatized and lacking in concrete reality. Without question, the imbuing of subjectivities to machines involves a willing suspension of disbelief, for we all *know* that machines are objects that merely act as they are programmed to act.[14] As Margaret Morse argues, however, many are prepared to suspend this disbelief, for virtual interactions with electronic technologies (and with other humans through electronic technologies) play an increasingly important role in how many modern societies function. As the twenty-first century progresses, social activity increasingly moves to digital realms, where communications are reduced to binary data before taking their ultimate forms as images or sounds. Making sense of this reality is an imaginative act:

> Whether business or entertainment, in order to support a culture based on more than just the economic exchange-value of data, information that has been *disengaged* from the context of the subjects, time, and place in which it is enunciated must be *reengaged* with personality and the imagination. That is, an information society inevitably calls forth a *cyberculture* that enjoys far different characteristics—much like

alphabets and phonemes can be articulated at higher levels of language.
(Morse 1998, 5–6; original emphasis)

The defining characteristic of this cyberculture is its virtuality: its existence in a realm that is real despite its lack of concreteness. Thus, within
cyberculture, virtual relationships take on real meaning for participants. In
cyberculture, users extend the idea of "'personhood' to machines." Therefore, "a machine that . . . 'interacts' with the user . . . can produce a feeling of
'liveness' and a sense of the machine's agency and—because it exchanges symbols—even of a subjective encounter with a persona" (Morse 1998, 14–15).
The presence of such virtual relationships, not to mention their importance
within modern cultures, makes possible their extension into mediatized
musical settings, in which they become the basis for the perception of virtual
musical liveness. The belief in a discourse between performer and audience—
even a virtual or imagined discourse—makes this virtual liveness very real
indeed and incredibly resonant with a broader cyberculture.

This approach to virtuality understands the word *virtual* in a slightly
different sense from that which focuses on the specific realm of virtual
reality (e.g., S. Jones 1993), which attempts to simulate with the greatest possible accuracy *actual* and *authentic* physical environments and, furthermore, to enable interactions with those simulated environments. The
virtual environments and relationships explored by Morse, like the virtual
personae described in this chapter, are made possible only *because* of their
involvement with electronic technology; they do not necessarily attempt the
complete simulation of material reality. Although they rely on users' recognizing *traces* or *elements* of actual reality (be they in the form of recognizable human behavior, recognizable acoustic sounds, etc.), the "realities" of
their *technological* ontologies play equally significant roles in communicat-
ing their various meanings.

Virtual liveness is at work, then, when a listener identifies with a performing persona in a piece of highly mediatized recorded music. The
persona necessarily takes on qualities of a human performer but, in its
virtuality, also adopts some electronically based characteristics. Such is
the case, for instance, in Katharine Norman's (2004) analysis of Magali
Babin's fixed media composition *Petit jardin* (on Babin 2002), for which
Babin performed the percussive sounds in an improvisatory fashion and
recorded the results. She then compiled the composition in the studio from
these sounds, treating them in several instances to a great degree of electronic signal processing.

In Norman's analysis of the piece, she describes her own visceral reaction
to the physical gestures she imagines Babin to have made in performing the
source sounds for the recording. Yet she also identifies an electronic "presence" among these sounds and an interaction between the concrete and the
digital. The piece depends, then (both in Norman's account and in my own
hearing), on a close interrelationship between corporeal and technological
presence. The performance that Babin gave in the recording studio has been

altered; the performance audible in this piece has been created anew. The performer we hear, if such a being were to exist, is part Babin and part recording technology. Its "body" is no longer only human but now enjoys the extended performative capabilities afforded it through digital sound technologies. This hybrid persona exists only in a network of mediatized sound, only in the technosphere. It is virtual, and thus so is its liveness.

The virtual persona in *Petit jardin*, like the virtual persona we encounter below in "Vane," suggests one final theoretical concept by way of its human/machine hybridity: the figuration, virtual in itself, of the cyborg. The cyborg's liminal state—existing somewhere in the space between "fully human" and "fully machine"—makes it amenable to readings in which the transgression of boundaries inherent in human/machine relationships is emphasized. The cyborg's hybrid nature defies the commonly understood opposition between human and machine and thus potentially, by extension, between nature and culture, bodies and information, and especially between men and women.[15] Although I am not primarily concerned here with the power politics specifically identified by many cyborg theorists,[16] I believe the cyborg figuration still offers a useful model with which to think about productive relationships between people and machines. It presents an alternative, in other words, to technophobic binary constructions that pit people *against* machines, by embracing the cyborg's ability to subvert these binaries through its liminality. As liminal spaces are virtual spaces—located as they are *between* spaces of concrete reality[17]—the cyborg is a *virtual* figuration, free to challenge the commonly understood boundaries and limitations of its constituent parts by way of its hybridity. A sounding cyborg, by extension, is a particular virtual figuration—a virtual persona—that exists in the sounding realm.

The cyborg persona in *Petit jardin*, for instance, presents a free interplay between recognizably human sounds and recognizably technological sounds. This relationship between body and technology is not antagonistic but open and creative. To properly understand the ubiquity of electronically altered human sounds in many recent musical styles, music scholarship needs theoretical tools with which to address the variously enacted musical relationships between people and machines. The figuration of a sounding cyborg is one such tool. It becomes apparent below that many similarities exist between my own interpretations of gender and genre bending by way of the sounding cyborg in "Vane" and the arguments just outlined about cyborgs' abilities to transgress those kinds of boundary-imposing categorizations.

PLUNDERPHONICS

Before a detailed discussion of "Vane" gets underway, however, a more general introduction to *plunderphonics* is in order. Oswald's plunderphonic compositions exist only as recordings: They are not written down in any conventional form of music notation, nor can they easily be recreated by performers in any conventional sense.[18] Unlike the vast majority of recorded music, Oswald creates his plunderphonic compositions entirely from other, widely available commercial recordings rather than from any newly recorded or realized sounds (hence his use of the word *plunder*). He has used as source material the music of widely divergent composers and performers, including Michael Jackson, Duke Ellington, and Ludwig van Beethoven, among many others. For each piece, he submits one or more source recordings to various electronic sound-manipulation techniques, such as speed alteration, montage, and sound reversal.

Most broadly, plunderphonics fall into a category of popular music described by Chris Cutler as "progressive," which "struggle[s] to liberate the communicative and aesthetic power" of new electronic sound technologies—a music "whose aim is to engage and reveal" rather than to capitalize on the commodity market (1993, 14).[19] But this tells us nothing about how plunderphonics *sound*, or even how they are made—it merely describes one of the levels of discourse on which they operate. On a compositional level, then, as outlined above, Oswald's primary instrument in these endeavors is the recording studio itself. His techniques and, simultaneously, his aesthetic objects include "editing, multitracking, piecemeal fabrication, quotation, reference; in fact . . . the whole ambiguous life of recorded sound *as recorded sound*" (Cutler 1993, 82; original emphasis).

More specifically, however, where should Oswald's plunderphonics be placed as a musical genre? Their overall *musical* style (with regards to tonality, rhythm, timbre, instrumentation, and other results of compositional and performative choice) depends both on Oswald's source material (which can range from pygmy hunting calls, to tango, to Bing Crosby's "White Christmas," all in the same tune[20]), and on how he chooses to manipulate it. Thus, although many of his plunderphonics can be heard as "popular music," trying to define exactly what *type* of popular music (rock, pop, hip-hop, etc.) each one most resembles is often a futile exercise. This is not to say that their references to specific styles of popular music are negligible—indeed, my analysis of "Vane" depends a great deal on the interpretation of the different genre norms represented within the song—but rather that to place any one plunderphonic within a single genre category is often impossible (and, as we see, this is usually Oswald's intent).

At the levels of compositional technique and material makeup, plunderphonics can be related to what Andrew Jones (1995) calls *musique actuelle* on the one hand and to more common sample-based forms of popular music, notably mashups[21] and some hip-hop on the other. Like Cutler's description of progressive popular music mentioned above, Jones focuses in his account of *musique actuelle* on music that works to discover the aesthetic and creative possibilities of electronic sound technologies without confining itself to any one musical style or approach—indeed often by bringing several musical styles together in one place. As Jones argues, "*Musique actuelle* lets the future leak through when musical worlds collide" (A. Jones 1995, 7). In addition to their lack of widespread commercial appeal, the *musique actuelle* artists Jones discusses share an experimental approach to their use of technologies and to the very question of musical genre.[22]

Consideration of mashups and hip-hop, then (and here I focus on turntablism, although other elements of hip-hop's broad musical spectrum would also work), provides perhaps a more recognizable context within which to consider Oswald's plunderphonics, if only through their differences. Of course, the work of various mashup artists and turntablists varies almost as widely as the *musique actuelle* artists discussed above, but, at the very least, these broad genres can provide more concrete examples against which to contrast plunderphonics. Plunderphonics share with turntablism and mashups their complete reliance on prerecorded audio and on the technological manipulations of those plundered recordings to create something new. Among the many differences between plunderphonics and turntablism, however, is turntablism's basis in real-time performance. Oswald's pieces, by contrast, are conceived as fixed-media music and indeed often involve far more complex layers of technological manipulations than would be feasible in a real-time realization.

Perhaps the most obvious distinction between plunderphonics and mashups is the latter style's usual social function as a dance music, which necessitates certain musical characteristics, such as the maintenance of a steady beat (we can also understand much hip-hop in this sense). Mashups also typically maintain a popular song's structure, whereas Oswald's plunderphonics range drastically in form, only occasionally resembling structurally the music from which he borrows his material. Finally, both turntablism and mashup creation exist as vibrant, dynamic cultures enjoyed by extensive worldwide communities, whereas plunderphonics have never managed to attract such a large number of fans or practitioners.[23]

Taken more on its own terms, Oswald's plunderphonic method revolves around the fundamental idea that despite the changes performed upon them, his original sources should be instantly recognizable to listeners—hence his reliance on commercial recordings. Oswald explains his method and terminology further in a 1989 interview with Norman Igma:

OSWALD: A plunderphone is a recognizable audio quote. Recognizable by at least a lot of people. That part is a bit vague. The piece may become less recognizable once we get through with it, but to remain plunderphonic the derivation must maintain a substantial degree of its original character.

IGMA: So you take a song and change it somehow; but someone who is listening to it will still recognize the song. Is that right?

OSWALD: Yes. Although it may not be the melody and lyrics of the song that they are associating with. It might just be the sound. My conviction is that the average person will realize they're hearing a familiar recording long before the melody makes its signature, or the singer gets to the words. The timbre, or the sound, of the recording is the trigger. (2001, 32)

Sometimes, the source material is easily recognizable, and the transformations enacted upon it are easily identifiable.[24] In other plunderphonic pieces, Oswald's manipulations are so extreme as to approach the threshold of recognition for most listeners.[25] To engage with Oswald's plunderphonics is thus to engage with a network of intertextual associations, not unlike the intertextual contexts created by turntablists and mashup artists. Oswald presents his listeners with multiple layers of meaning, which not only are carried by his source material but also are created anew by the ways in which he alters, recontextualizes, and combines this material. Often, these new layers of meaning challenge those commonly associated with the recordings from which plunderphonics originally derive. Oswald's "Angle" (1990), for instance, demonstrates how plunderphonic music can reconfigure a source's genre. In this track, Oswald extracts very short segments of the 1961 Phil Spector–produced doo-wop hit "Pretty Little Angel Eyes" by Curtis Lee and the Halos (on Lee 1996), looping various arrangements of these segments in such a way as to emphasize a newly imposed rhythmic regularity. This rhythmic emphasis greatly overshadows any type of textual narrative or extended melodic repetition (both very important aspects of the doo-wop aesthetic) that exists in the original recording.[26] The resulting piece brings the familiar doo-wop sounds of "Pretty Little Angel Eyes" into a context resembling much electronically produced dance music of the 1990s.

The conventions of musical genres, however, carry far more associative meanings than just those that can be described in musical terms. Indeed, much music scholarship of the past two decades, particularly in the field of popular-music studies, does vital work to emphasize how different musical styles and practices perform meanings pertaining to class, race, gender, and other important realms in which social relationships are enacted. These associations are not lost on Oswald, whose plunderphonic challenges to previously well-defined distinctions among genres also reconfigure the ways in which class, race, and gender are typically performed by these genres. With respect to his plunderphonics box set (2001a), Oswald relates that he was excited by the prospect of having it filed in the most typically diverse section of record stores. He states, "The traditional record sections are, for the most part, either racist (soul and pop), sexist (male and female vocals), or class-based (classical and folk). In the box set department race, gender, and social class get mushed together" (Oswald and Igma 2001, 11).

More than just "mushing together" these styles in the form of a box set, however, Oswald juxtaposes these social categories within individual compositions. His "Power" (1975) sets up a simple dichotomy between instrumental material by Led Zeppelin (whom Oswald calls "those famous satanists") and a recording of an evangelical preacher. Oswald explains, "i think i was trying to create an uncomfortable situation. . . . Rock fans were uncomfortable listening to talk about god and jesus. God and jesus fans were known to be uncomfortable about rock" (Oswald and Igma 2001, 5).[27] Oswald thus presents a piece with which those who would normally listen to either one of his source recordings may now have difficulty relating. Whatever meaning or "message" they may once have derived from this material is now presented along with sounds that represent far different, and potentially conflicting, meanings. This concept of conflicted musical identities brings us, finally, to "Vane," in which interrelated issues of gender and genre confusion play vital roles in creating an important sense of virtual liveness.

THE SOUNDING CYBORG IN "VANE"

Oswald realized "Vane" as part of a commission from the Elektra recording label. On the occasion of its fortieth anniversary, Elektra released a two-CD collection called *Rubaiyat* (1990), which consisted of some of the most successful records from its forty-year back catalogue, all performed anew by artists who were then currently signed to the label. Among many other cover versions, Faster Pussycat recorded a glam-metal version of Carly Simon's 1972 pop hit "You're So Vain" (on Simon 1990). As part of this project, Elektra intended to release an additional EP of Oswald's plunderphonics, all of which drew from Elektra's recording vault. Elektra, however, failed to secure copyright permission for recordings by both Metallica and the Doors that Oswald had used as source material for new compositions.[28] Thus, the plunderphonic EP *Rubaiyat* (which Oswald prefers to call *Elektrax*) was only released to radio stations and never circulated commercially (Holm-Hudson 1996, 25).

"Vane," which combines the two versions of "You're So Vain" mentioned above, is the fourth track on this EP.[29] Simon's original version, especially through its first two verses, demonstrates a style fairly typical of singer-songwriters in the early 1970s, with emphasis on clearly sung vocals and acoustic instruments. The track becomes more cluttered as it progresses with heavier drumming, greater intensity in Simon's vocals and the background vocals (Mick Jagger adds his background vocals on all but the first iteration of the chorus), and the addition of electric guitar and violins. The piano and acoustic guitar also drop out of the mix in the second half of the track. Significantly, as I discuss below, in his piece, Oswald focuses on material from the first half of the track.

Faster Pussycat's version, on the other hand, represents the glam-metal style of the late 1980s and early 1990s quite well.[30] It features a faster tempo (approximately 128 bpm to Simon's approximately 102–108 bpm), heavy drumming, multiple electric guitar tracks, and a clenched, half-sung/

half-screamed male vocal track. "Vane" exploits the differences between these two recordings, repeatedly juxtaposing one against the other. The piece thus features frequent shifts not only from one style of performance to another but also from one tempo to another, creating what Oswald calls a "polyrhythmic limp" (Oswald and Igma 2001, 12). He describes it as "two tempi alternating in loping fashion, which . . . sounds like a strutting rock star with one leg shorter than the other" (2001, 8). In my analysis, this strutting rock star, considered in conjunction with the sounds of the recording that demonstrate Oswald's technological manipulations, becomes the sounding cyborg in "Vane."

Oswald's compelling interpretation implies that the performing persona invoked in this piece stems exclusively not from one of his source recordings but instead from his digital combination of those recordings. Such a persona carries with it further implications. First, this persona represents a particular type of liveness in "Vane," as evidenced in Oswald's description of the bodily performance mannerism (a rock star's lop-sided strut) he imagines represented in this piece. This liveness, however, is not easily traceable to an actual performer (or to a single, conventionally gendered performing body), despite the obvious corporeal basis for Oswald's remarks. Rather, it is indicative of a technologically enabled *virtual* performer who does not exist outside the technosphere particular to "Vane." This imagined persona shares combined qualities of Simon's and Faster Pussycat's performances and representative performance styles,[31] in addition to qualities generated by Oswald's use of digital technologies in altering these performances. Many of these additional qualities are unambiguously "of the machine."

The persona invoked in "Vane" is thus not one of a traditional human musical performer but a hybrid man/woman/machine performer representing contrasting performance styles; a virtual performer imbued with not only performing limbs and (bi-gendered) vocal cords but also, with the assistance of digital sound technologies, the ability to splice, rearrange, and alter minute sections of recorded musical performances. The persona invoked in "Vane," in other words, is a cyborg, and this cyborg is *live* inside the recording. Furthermore, this liveness is distinct from any liveness that we may attribute to a traditionally performing musician: This liveness exists only virtually.

A detailed analysis of the piece demonstrates just how this virtually live-sounding cyborg finds its voice inside "Vane's" technosphere. In constructing "Vane," Oswald extracts segments of varying length from both versions of "You're So Vain" and rearranges them in collage fashion, sometimes altering their speeds slightly or playing them backward and sometimes overlaying them. In some of Oswald's plunderphonics, he distorts his source material to such an extent that the original performances are completely obliterated, but as I explain above, Oswald still intends that the sound or timbre of the recordings should trigger recognition in a listener. With "Vane," however, most of the samples remain long enough and sufficiently intact so that a listener can still grasp a sense of the tempo, rhythm, vocal style, and other characteristics evident in the original recorded performances.

Although these two recordings of "You're So Vain" are obvious products of the recording studio, the idea of performance remains central to my account of how they convey liveness in their original forms and in Oswald's piece. Each recording represents a tradition that is just as invested in performance, or at least in the image of performance, as it is in studio work. The singer-songwriter tradition from which Simon's recording comes conjures images of an earnest songstress sitting at the piano or standing in front of a single microphone with her guitar, sharing her deeply personal songs with an attentive audience. As mentioned earlier, the first two verses of Simon's recording in particular convey this style perfectly. Moreover, the lyrical content of Simon's song and the folksy roots of this singer-songwriter style (with its associations with social and political activism) combine to create an air of empowerment for the female protagonist, who offers a harsh critique of the man who so casually tossed her away.[32]

The glam-metal musical style of the 1980s represented by Faster Pussycat likewise invokes certain general performance conventions: namely, white men with long hair, makeup, and skin-tight (and skin-bearing) costumes strutting around with their guitars. Whereas associations with Simon's performance style convey a sense of feminine empowerment, metal (particularly that performed by Faster Pussycat) often conveys just the opposite: chauvinism, misogyny, and the sexual exploitation of women.[33] Both of these musical genres convey particular performance conventions and gestures and thus well-understood qualities of liveness, however different their social implications may be. In his treatment of this source material, Oswald is careful to maintain enough of what defines these genres that these performance associations are also maintained. Of course, these associations are also combined so that listeners are invited to form new associations, which lead (among other things) to the construction of a new performing persona.

Here, the cyborg as reconfigured rock star looms large. The metaphorical implication of the cyborg, as already discussed, is that it achieves a blend of opposites. In this case, it is both woman and man, feminist and misogynist. Yet it is also more than this, as Oswald adds another layer of metaphorical hybridization: He challenges the distinction between people and machines through evocations of human bodies modulated by technology. In the remarks quoted earlier, Oswald brings to our attention the "polyrhythmic limp" created by his combination of the two source recordings' different tempi. This rhythmic effect, which Oswald associates with his "strutting rock star" persona, constitutes one of the central musical ideas in "Vane"; as such, a close look at how it unfolds throughout the track tells us much about the sounding cyborg in this piece.

Throughout "Vane," Oswald constantly alternates between the two source recordings, either one phrase at a time or several times within the same musical phrase (refer to Table 6.1 for a full breakdown of all aspects of the following analysis). He sets up the rhythmic contrast immediately in his introduction, where he edits the duple-metered introduction to Simon's recording so it achieves a pattern of rapid triplets that, when taken in conjunction with the resulting newly configured piano melody, create an impression of a 9/8 meter. Oswald then switches (0:28) to the steady, back-beat-laden duple meter of Faster Pussycat's introduction, and then back again (0:44) to the newly created triple meter of Simon's intro. Although a relatively steady beat is maintained throughout all this material—the dot-ted-quarter beat of the 9/8 meter, at approximately 67 bpm, flows rather smoothly into the backbeat (second and fourth beats) of Faster Pussycat's duple meter, at approximately 128 bpm—the contrast between triple and duple meter prepares the listener for the conversation that is about to take place between these two seemingly disparate voices. Also evident at this early stage in the piece are the two different performing styles, as the piano, acoustic guitar, and light drumming from Simon's introductory mate-rial stand in stark contrast to the electric guitars, heavy drumming, and screaming (Faster Pussycat's lead singer Taime Downe repeatedly screams, "Yah!") from Faster Pussycat's opening material.

Immediately after Oswald's introduction, he brings the two original parts much closer together (0:57), alternating between both performers repeatedly asking, "Don't you?" in the same stilted polyrhythmic limp employed throughout the piece. This rhythmic stutter is created not only by the alternating tempi but also by an "out-of-tempo" snare-drum hit at the beginning of the section, a repeated interruption of Faster Pussycat's line by Simon's line before the rhythmic impulse of the former has quite come to completion, and a complete breakdown of any underlying pulse at the end of this section of alternating lines (1:05). As the piece progresses, the distinct rhythmic qualities of the original recordings become more difficult to determine as the two original acts alternate with increasing rapidity. What begin as two very distinct performance styles meld toward the end of the piece (and at select points along the way) into a hybrid style distinct to "Vane," and the persona of the strutting rock star with one leg shorter than the other, not to mention of two different genders, becomes clearer.

Oswald explores this merger of genders explicitly in the phrase begin-ning at 1:42. At this point, he focuses on the last two lines of the original song's first verse, drawing from both recordings alternately. In the source recordings, the line sung by Simon is "Then all the *girls* dreamed that they'd be your partner," which is changed to "Then all the *boys* dreamed that they'd be your partner" by Faster Pussycat. In Oswald's version, "boys" and "girls" can be heard simultaneously, before Oswald returns to alter-nating between the original performers. After Oswald's new "Then all the girls/boys dreamed that they'd be your partner" phrase, he repeats "they'd be your partner" four more times, repeating "partner" an extra time in the third iteration. This short phrase is never the same twice, as Oswald pres-ents a new combination of performers with each repetition.

Table 6.1 Lyrics and key sound events in John Oswald's "Vane"[34]

Time	Lyrics	Description
0:00		CS's intro material (piano, bass, drums, acoustic guitar), looped in fast triplets; creates an impression of a 9/8 meter; dotted quarter note = approx. 67 bpm
0:28	YAH! YAH! YAH! YAH! YAAAAAAAAH! YAH! YAH! YAH! YAH! YAAAAAAAAH!	FP's intro material (lead vocal, multiple elec. guitars, drums); duple meter and tempo maintained; quarter note = approx. 128 bpm, so that backbeat continues (approx.) tempo of initial dotted quarter.
0:44		Return to CS intro material in 9/8
0:57	DON'T YOU, don't you . . . . DON'T YOU, don't you . . . . DON'T YOU, don't you . . . . DON'T you . . . DON'T you . . . *Don't* youuuuuuaaah . . . YAH!	Alternate between FP and CS, with original tempi intact for each sample; further rhythmic stutter created by snare-drum hit before first line, "interruption" of FP by CS in first three lines, and by breakdown of any underlying pulse in final line
1:15	You walked into the party like you were walking onto a yacht	CS sings "forwards . . . with a backwards texture," creating the impression of the original song's opening lyrics; loss of attack (due to editing process) creates a sustained instrumental texture.
1:24	YOU TOOK ME HOT TO PERFORM ONE THIGH . . . aauuuuahh . . .	Rhythmic irregularity created by stuttering instrumental (drum & guitar) interruption of lyrics after "hot" and "perform"; these rhythmic stutters continue after second line as snap-scanned CS enters in background at 1:34.
1:42	Then *all the* girls/BOYS dreamed that they'd be your partner . . . THEY'D BE YOUR PARTNER . . . They'd be your partner . . . THEY'D BE YOUR partner, partner . . . THEY'D BE YOUR PARTNER . . . YAH! . . . You! bluuuuuaaah . . .	Rhythmic stutter and CS snap scan from previous section bleed into first word ("Then"); first line switches tempo with sampled source, creating "polyrhythmic limp"; beginning with second line, CS tempo speeds up to match FP tempo, but transitions from one source to the other create irregular pulse.

(continued)

Table 6.1 (continued)

Time	Lyrics	Description
2:14	BUT you GAVE away THE things YOU LOVE, and ONE of *them* was ME . . . YAH!	Despite increased alternation between sampled sources, tempo adjusted for steady pulse through first and second lines.
2:21	*I had some dreams, they were clouds in my coffee. Clouds in my coffee* YAH! YAH! YAH! YAH! YAH!	Both sources combined for first and second lines; tempo altered on CS material to match FP.
2:30	*You're so vain . . . so vain . . . s-s-so vain . . . song is about you . . .* 'bout you . . . *I'll bet you think this song is about you* DON'T YOU, don't you . . . bluuuuuaaah . . .	Chorus/Climax: Highly complex layers of lyrics (*drastically* simplified and condensed here) compete for audibility with dense layers of drum samples. Polyrhythmic limp persists throughout. Third line emerges intact from texture before fourth line returns us to material from "chorus" section from ca. 1:00.
3:00		Return to CS intro material in 9/8; transition from previous snap scan to beginning of this section by way of single snare-drum hit.
3:20	**YAH!**	Final scream is heard, punctuated by loud snare and electric. gGuitar.

Carly Simon (CS) lyrics in plain type
Faster Pussycat (FP) lyrics in **BOLD AND CAPS**
Lyrics sung by both simultaneously in ***bold and italics***
Lyrics that are seemingly "of the machine" underlined

He also further explores in this section the rhythmic irregularity so central to my interpretation of this strutting bi-gendered rock-star persona, presenting two different tempo configurations of his combined materials. First, Oswald maintains the original tempi of his source materials in the first line of this section so the alternating and overlapping samples create a slightly staggered pulse. He then speeds up the Simon material when she sings, "they'd be your partner," so the subsequent trading of lines all matches in tempo. Despite the potential for a steady pulse here (due to the matching tempi), however, Oswald avoids such steadiness in the transition from one source (and one gender) to the other. At these moments, he cuts short or extends the occasional beat—giving the impression, perhaps, that the gender switch still comes a bit awkwardly at this stage—so as to maintain the polyrhythmic limp.

However awkward this "Vane" persona may seem at this point, Oswald's emphasis on the word "partner" in this passage carries much significance, as it points out quite obviously the new partnership forged on this recording between the two original singers. The gender blurring that occurs at the beginning of the phrase with the combination of "girls" and "boys" emphasizes the androgynous nature of our new performing persona. The partnership becomes even further cemented in the next section of lyrics (2:05), as Oswald switches between Simon and Faster Pussycat even more rapidly than in the passage just described. With nearly each word in the first line of text (from 2:05–2:21), Oswald switches performer and tempo. In a couple of instances, he allows both singers to sound simultaneously, which creates overlapping tempi. The rhythmic stuttering is also helped along by a rhythmically complex collage of drum samples immediately preceding these lyrics and by brief hesitations before the words "quite" and "naïve." This rapid alternation between sources is followed finally by the line, "I had some dreams, they were clouds in my coffee" (2:21), sung by all singers (including backup singers) at the same time.[35] This phrase is very reminiscent of the final line of Oswald's "Pretender," in which a sloweddown Dolly Parton sings, "I am the great pretender" at the same time as a normally pitched Parton. Oswald describes this phrase as "Dolly singing a duet with himself" (Oswald and Igma 2001, 16).

The gender switching and eventual gender melding that occur in these pieces also create a sonic parallel with many of Oswald's *plundergraphics*: images combining features from two or more musicians to make them appear as one. Oswald compiles one such image for the cover of the *Rubayiat/Elektrax* EP, featuring half of Simon's face, her neck, and her right breast (excised from the cover art to her 1972 album *No Secrets* [Simon 1990]), matched up with half of Jim Morrison's face, his shoulders, and the left half of his bare chest. Morrison's shaggy hair covers the whole head, and some of Simon's hair falls down over her right shoulder. Simon's full lips, long hair, and breast (conventional bodily signs of femininity) stand in stark contrast with Morrison's wild hair, flat chest, and body hair (conventional bodily markers of masculinity).[36] Oswald says of "Vane" and of this image:

> There's also a very coarse kind of gender switching in the line "You had me several years ago . . . ," which is alternating words sung by Carly and the Faster Pussycat singer, which I tend to think of as approximately an aural representation of the photo collage of Carly and Jim Morrison, which became the frontispiece of the elektrax cd. The components are still individually intact and recognizable, but there's an androgenic affect. (Oswald and Igma 2001, 8–9)

The new persona of "Vane," in other words, is recognizably masculine and feminine.

Yet this bi-gendered partnership is not all we hear in Oswald's "Vane." In addition to its gendered and other physical characteristics, the "Vane" persona owes just as much of its identity to Oswald's technological manipulations as it owes to the original performers of this music. We hear not just a woman/man hybrid but also a musician/machine hybrid; this sounding cyborg, in its challenge to both these boundaries, resonates strongly with the work of the cyborg theorists mentioned earlier. At several moments in "Vane," recognizably human sounds give way to recognizably electronic sounds. To begin with, the phoneme trading that occurs in the passage just discussed is far too complex to resemble simply "man alternating with woman" or "man singing with woman." Something in the stuttering rhythms and combined timbres of Oswald's combination betrays its technological origins.

Technological associations also occur earlier in the piece, as at 1:06, after the final repetition of "Don't you?" The final word of this phrase—"you"—sung by Simon, stretches out for the next ten seconds, as Oswald here treats the original recording to a "snap scan": "an aural analogue of frame-by-frame playing of a film or videotape, drawing out an isolated moment in the original sound source . . . and greatly expanding it in time without lowering its pitch" (Holm-Hudson 1997, 21). Oswald cuts the recorded word into minute sonic "frames," in other words, and inserts equally short spaces of silence between these frames. Toward the end of this treatment, Oswald slowly shifts from the "oo" vowel of "you" to an "ah" vowel (also seemingly sung by Simon), further distorting the word. Oswald repeats the effect at 1:56 and at 2:50 (although in these instances, it sounds more like "blue" than "you"). The end result in each of these cases is a sound resembling nothing more than a compact disc skipping in a dusty player.

Immediately following the first of these snap scans (at 1:15), Oswald explores a different configuration of several minute sonic frames. In this case, with the line, "You walked into the party like you were walking onto a yacht" (the opening line of Simon's original recording), he presents what he refers to as Simon singing "forwards . . . with a backwards texture"

(Oswald and Igma 2001, 8). In creating this effect, Oswald cuts this phrase into several extremely short segments and reverses the sound envelope of each segment while keeping them all in the correct order. In other words, each phoneme is split into further segments, and all these segments are heard in the correct order; however, each individual segment is heard from end-to-beginning instead of from beginning-to-end. Because much of how we understand sounds derives from how each of those sounds begins, a reversal of a sound's overall profile—even that of a very short sound—can drastically affect its impact on a listener. Ultimately, what we hear in this case sounds similar to the opening line of Simon's original recording—it has the proper melody, contour, and basic rhythm, and the lyrics are reasonably intelligible—but her voice seems somehow filtered through some type of electronic sonic blender.

The most obvious moment in which Oswald presents decidedly machine-like sounds creates the climax of the piece. As Simon and Faster Pussycat sing together on "I had some dreams, they were clouds in my coffee," they lead into the first and only iteration of the chorus in "Vane" (2:30). The chorus is anything but the tuneful and catchy chorus of Simon's original, however, as it consists of obviously looped and edited phrases from both recordings ("s-s-so vain" recurs repeatedly throughout, for example), packed so densely that a detailed description of each sample would take far more space than is appropriate here. These layered and looping samples combine recognizable textual phrases and instrumental (particularly percussion) excerpts. The entire texture is extremely noisy, giving the impression that our cyborg may be short-circuiting. The chorus ends with an intelligible iteration of "You're so vain/I'll bet you think this song is about you," which leads to a repeat of the traded lines, "Don't you? Don't you?" (2:43), followed once again by the familiar snap scan of Simon's "oo" vowel.

One might be tempted to abandon the idea of a performing persona during this chorus, due to the obvious polyphony and extreme density of Oswald's mix. To attribute all these sounds to an individual entity, even a sounding cyborg, might seem a stretch. Yet Oswald maintains within the densest moments of this passage a specific characteristic of the persona that pervades the entire piece: the polyrhythmic limp. Due to the rhythmically uneven manner in which he loops some of these samples, the sound of a lopsided cyborg persists and is further enhanced by the obvious sounds of electronic manipulation. Then, following the snap scan (3:00), Oswald returns us once again to the triple-metered Simon material from the opening of "Vane." This guitar-and-drum duo continues for twenty seconds, perhaps lulling its listeners into believing that Simon has shed her glam-rock-star half after the intensity of the chorus. At the very end of this short piece, however (3:20), he returns with one last "Yah!" to remind us that he is indeed very much a part of the song's cyborg persona.

So what of this persona? Apart from its liminal existence as man, woman, and machine, why is it significant? In this case, the contrasting physical performance styles normally associated with each rock subgenre, along with the similarly conflicting social meanings usually conveyed by these styles, also play a large part in my own arguments for the significance of the sounding cyborg. At first glance, Oswald presents two incompatible versions of the same song. Considered on its own, Faster Pussycat's rendition appropriates Simon's statement of feminine empowerment and recasts it in Faster Pussycat's own realm of misogyny and chauvinism. Downe transforms the male antagonist of Simon's version into a victimizing and unfaithful woman who uses her sexuality only to entice her potential victims (Simon's "Your hat strategically dipped below one eye" from the first verse, for instance, becomes "Your dress strategically hiked up on one thigh").[37] We are confronted with two conflicting but simultaneous performances, each conveying its own corporeal liveness as encoded in the gendered messages of its original performance style.

As we are reminded of the apparent incompatibility of these highly gendered texts, we are also reminded of the problematics of gender performance, which is so often tied to *genre* performance. Oswald blends these genders and genres in a way that renders those of his own cyborg performer even more important, if more confused, than ever before. What coherent lyrics remain still present the woes of a jilted lover, but one that now cries foul about fast-talking womanizers and victimizing she devils. This sounding cyborg has troubled the polarizing and divisive restrictions so often imposed by conventional gender-genre distinctions in its highly charged and subversive evocations of two genders and of no gender; of two genres and of no genre. This coupling/uncoupling of gender and genre is so successful precisely because of the way in which the sounding cyborg—an embodied instantiation of virtual liveness—is unmistakably written with audible technology and, moreover, because of this cyborg's maintenance of an embodied persona even in the face of such mediatization.

Ultimately "Vane," like *Petit jardin* and many other pieces of highly mediatized music, facilitates a new perspective on bodies, technology, and liveness altogether. Although some acousmatic music completely avoids any trace of liveness, "Vane" and *Petit jardin* rely on our recognition of performed music even as they present unperformable sonic phenomena. In "Vane," Oswald relies on his listeners' familiarity with his source material and on their understandings of genre and of gender as they are invoked by this material. Virtual liveness inheres in the unique combination of Simon's acoustic folksy style with Faster Pussycat's aggressive, electric style, in the combination of the different corporeal associations carried by these styles, and in the technical manipulation toward a newly imagined, reformulated individual. The resulting virtual performance is a performance of human, of machine, of genre, of gender, and of bodies material and virtual, all recast from their usual contexts into one of subversive meaning and unsure boundaries.

With "Vane," Oswald creates a new live body that is not actually live. This cyborg demonstrates just how gendered some musical genres are by playing with these gender and genre codes in its evocation of its own hyper-gendered body. Moreover, it presents *human* and *machine* on equal footing, compelling us to eschew the technophobia so often present in discussions of technology in music. Finally, identifying the existence of this cyborg in the virtual realm resonates with a society increasingly invested in cyber realities. Social interaction is reshaped almost daily by advances in telecommunications and by the constantly changing ways users employ these technologies. Entire conversations now take place by way of "text talk" through instant messaging. For quite some time now, even dating has enjoyed its own cyber existence. Perhaps one of the most relevant widespread analogies to the sounding cyborg is the online gaming phenomenon, in which each player takes on an avatar and is known to other players only as that avatar. To look for elements of human communication in highly mediatized music—even if only simulated communication—no longer seems so unnatural in light of these other modern modes of virtual communication. In fact, it seems a vital step to take in music scholarship, particularly considering the steps already taken in this direction by other disciplines.

7 Performing Cyborgs
The Flaying of Marsyas and Turntablism

Today, the voice you speak with may not be your own.

DJ Spooky that Subliminal Kid, *Rhythm Science*

As I have demonstrated periodically throughout this book, the different categories of liveness that I present may often emerge together within a single performance context. Furthermore (and reflecting a common theme), the dividing lines between these categories are often difficult to draw, because the appreciation of one category of liveness very often depends on the simultaneous appreciation of another. I propose that such performance contexts may be thought of as establishing networks of liveness, wherein the perception and appreciation of musical performance occurs in a complex and dynamic manner as our attention is drawn to various elements of human meaning according to our own subject positions. In this chapter, I investigate two such networks of liveness, both rather complex in their makeup, within each of which are invoked multiple interdependent categories of liveness. I also invoke in both cases the category of virtual liveness, as both performance contexts take us deep into the realm of mediatized musical performance.

The figuration of the cyborg also returns to my discussions in this chapter, as I concern myself not only with the blurry lines between various categories of liveness but also those between the categories of human and machine, performer and instrument, original and copy, and several other discursive pairs. Now, however, we find ourselves in the domain of live performance, as the performance contexts I am concerned with are, first, Omar Daniel's live electronic composition, *The Flaying of Marsyas* (2002), and second, the general practice of hip-hop turntablism. As the cyborg leaves the imaginary realm within which I construct it in Chapter 6, we must be prepared to identify this figuration in the performances of fully present humans—performances that, through their extreme mediatization, invest these performers with highly technologized performing personae of their own. In this way, the figuration of the musically performing cyborg may help us understand some of the complex layers of performative meaning found in some of the more heavily mediatized examples of modern music. Ultimately, the cyborg figuration also provides a locus around which we can theorize the networks of liveness that I detect in these two performance contexts, allowing the concept of liveness itself to become a multifaceted theoretical tool with which to address complex layers of aesthetically and socially derived meaning in modern musical practices.

OMAR DANIEL'S *THE FLAYING OF MARSYAS*: A BRIEF DESCRIPTION[1]

Daniel's *The Flaying of Marsyas* is based on the mythical musical duel between Marsyas and Apollo and on the visual depiction of that myth in Titian's[2] *Flaying of Marsyas* (1575–76). According to the myth, the satyr Marsyas became such a skilled player of the pan flute that he challenged Apollo to a musical competition, with the stipulation that the winner would decide the punishment of the loser.[3] Predictably, Apollo won. As punishment, he condemned Marsyas to be hung up and flayed alive. Titian's painting (shown in Figure 7.1) depicts Marsyas in its center, hanging upside down from a tree while two Muses to his right (on the left side of the canvas) begin to cut into his skin.[4] One of these flayers kneels next to

Figure 7.1   Titian's *Flaying of Marsyas.*[5]

Marsyas, and the other stands behind the kneeling figure. Apollo, standing off to the far left (next to the standing flayer) and apparently celebrating his victory, continues to play his *lira*.[6] On the right side of the canvas, Pan brings a pail of water to help with the flaying (having sided with the winning god rather than with his fellow satyr Marsyas). Next to Pan, Midas crouches in contemplation, and a satyr child holds on to the collar of a watchful hound. A young puppy crouches directly beneath Marsyas, lapping at a pool of his blood.

Daniel's remarkable piece of sound theater for violinist and live electronic musician stages the final scene in this battle as depicted by Titian, with a focus only on the figures of Apollo and Marsyas. The suspended "Marsyas" musician (Daniel, in all performances to date)[7] hangs upside down from a metal frame, while a violinist (representing Apollo) stands for most of the piece to the left of the frame (the same position occupied by Apollo in the painting; see Figure 7.2). The violinist plays rather conventionally; her[8] sound is captured by a bridge pickup (microphone) and fed into a PCM-81 digital signal processor (DSP).[9] Daniel's own performance is highly theatrical and sonically striking, involving movements of his arms, head, and torso, which are not only dramatically important but also (to a certain extent) essential for the performance of his live electronics.[10]

Twelve different MIDI controllers are affixed to Daniel's fingers, thumbs, neck, and right wrist, all of which lead to an I-cube MIDI port affixed to his back. The MIDI port then sends control signals through a MIDI interface and then to the DSP and to a Kurzweill K2500 sampler. The controllers on his left hand are bend controllers; those on his neck and wrist are G-force controllers. All these controllers respond to his movements by sending control signals through the MIDI port to the PCM-81.[12] According to these control signals, the signal processor then effects various changes on the amplified signal it receives from the violin. Put simply, Daniel's movements control, at least in part, the sounds created by the violin (more of which below). The controllers on his right hand are touch controllers, each of which responds to touch by triggering a prerecorded sample from the sampler.

Daniel describes the premise of his composition:

> [In a performance,] Apollo, the violinist, would play and Marsyas, the suspended musician, would react. Simply put, the violin music would flay the suspended musician. There are two layers of music present: the pure, unaltered sound of the violin which exists only acoustically, and the electronic music which emanates from the loudspeakers. The electronic music is either a) a real-time manipulation [by Marsyas] of the violin sound (80% of the piece), or b) sampled sounds (triggered in real-time [again by Marsyas]) independent of the violin sound (20% of the piece). (2002b, v)

Daniel also explains the nature of these sampled sounds:

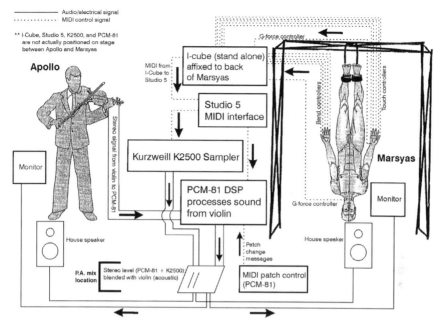

Figure 7.2 Stage setup and circuit routing for Omar Daniel's *The Flaying of Marsyas.*[11]

Samples are constructed from flute, voice, metal (excited by scratching, scraping and striking) and synthetic sounds. The premise of the sampled sounds is that it reflects Marsyas' "voice"; ie; that of a double flute, and therefore the source material has flute or voice-like qualities. (2002b, v)

In addition to the visual depiction of the musical duel's outcome (the hanging and flaying), here Daniel also reproduces sonically the dueling "voices" of violin and flute, with the violin possessing the more powerful and prominent voice. In this way, he conflates the contest and its dire consequences into one unfolding event.

Marsyas, of course, produces his "voice" through the physical manipulation of the MIDI controllers.[13] His movements, however, are far more exaggerated than is required for this purpose alone. The bend controllers respond only to finger movements (not full arm movements), and the touch controllers can be activated very subtly by touching the fingertip to any other surface (hand, leg, etc.). Only the G-force controllers, which are used far less frequently than the bend controllers, require larger movements, and even these movements are often more exaggerated than necessary in Daniel's performances. Therefore, Marsyas's movements, while corresponding to his *sonic* performance, also constitute his very important *visual* performance. The movements required to operate the MIDI controllers are incorporated into a larger choreography.[14]

Throughout the piece, Marsyas moves almost constantly. Because he is hung upside down from his ankles, his arms are much freer to move than the rest of him, but neck and torso movements also play an important part. At predetermined moments, Marsyas achieves several very deliberate and visually striking poses. Daniel (2002b, iv–v) explains that he copies these poses from woodcut illustrations (possibly by Titian) found in the anatomy treatise *De Humani Corporis Fabrica* (1545), by Andreas Vesalius.[15] Each of these illustrations (Daniel chose eleven and reproduces three in his score [2002b, ii]) depicts a body "in various stages of dissection, or flaying" (Daniel 2002b, v), as they are intended to portray the body's different muscle groups. Curiously, these illustrations all feature a carefully posed body, situated on a landscape. Brought into the context of the Marsyas narrative, these poses, when copied by Daniel, invoke the physical contortions of a man in considerable pain. In other words, these poses are mapped onto Marsyas's physical response to his torture. In all cases, Marsyas's body draws extra attention to itself by virtue of being nude from the waist up.[16] With each movement, muscles visibly flex, and tendons noticeably stretch. As I discuss below, many of these movements lend greatly to perceptions not only of corporeal liveness but also of interactive liveness and virtual liveness in a performance of *Marsyas*.

NARRATIVE STRUCTURE IN *THE FLAYING OF MARSYAS*

A performance of *Marsyas*, consisting of eight continuous sections (identified and described in Daniel 2002b, v–ix), lasts approximately eleven to thirteen minutes. Each of these sections represents a different part of Daniel's overall narrative and features a different configuration of electronic control for Marsyas. I paraphrase here in italics Daniel's descriptions of musical material, narrative context, and electronic configurations (from Daniel 2002b, v–ix), and add my own commentary in plain text.[17] My later analyses return to this narrative interpretation of the piece and to the relationships described here between the performers—and between their respective characters—through musical gestures, through physical gestures, and through Daniel's use of digital sound technologies.

Presto Possible (1st section; 0:15). *This section consists of a virtuosic passage for violin, in which Apollo demonstrates his superior musical skill. By way of a four-voice pitch-shifting algorithm controlled by left hand and right wrist, Marsyas articulates fairly regular short musical gestures, which occur in the midst of the violin's phrases.* In this section, Marsyas's sounds occur simultaneously with Apollo's sounds (he alters Apollo's sounds exactly as they take place), which is not always the case in this piece. Furthermore, the electronic processing here does not significantly alter the timbre of the violin—it just multiplies a recognizable violin sound (with subtle timbral variation) and adds a slight reverberation. As Apollo begins the piece by walking across the stage while playing, Marsyas turns his head and torso so he continually faces Apollo.[18] His arms move slowly and rather gently through this section and seem at times to reach toward Apollo. Marsyas's physical and sonic response seems like an accompanimental gesture in light of its simultaneity with and multiplication of the violin's gesture and also in light of its seemingly nonconfrontational visual attributes. Although Marsyas is already hanging upside down, this does not yet seem like a mortally dangerous battle.

Interlude (**2nd section; 2:33**). *Marsyas performs his only solo passage— his initial answer to Apollo—which is created by way of a feedback loop from the gesture just played by the violin (at the end of the first section). By applying a resonance filter (controlled again by left hand and right wrist) to this "captured" material, Marsyas performs a new melody.*[19] Significantly, due to Daniel's configuration of the resonance filter, the sounds newly created by the PCM-81 contain a timbre resembling that of a pan flute, which overwhelms the captured violin sounds. Although he uses the violin's material to create his own sound, Marsyas manages to exert his own "voice." While Marsyas performs, Apollo walks behind him. Marsyas keeps his attention focused on, and his hand pointed toward, Apollo, turning his torso to look and point backward. Marsyas's physical gestures remain rather graceful through this section, and the particularly intricate movements of his left hand seem to indicate a man still in control of his body rather than one reacting to severe torture. This impression soon changes.

Moderato, decisio (**3rd section; 3:13**). *In this section, now that Apollo and Marsyas have each made their opening gambit, the "flaying proper" begins. Apollo's brutality is heard for the first time, as her "incisive" musical figure, characterized by short chords alternating with substantial rests, cuts into Marsyas. Marsyas responds with a chorus-flange effect at the end of several violin gestures, while also controlling the placement of amplified sound in the stereo field.*[20] Marsyas's reaction is much more pronounced here than during Apollo's opening statement, as the chorus-flange effect, due to its rather long decay time, extends significantly into Apollo's rests. It also greatly alters the timbre of the violin's sound. Whereas Marsyas's reactions in the first section seem more like accompaniment than response, these musical gestures clearly stand apart from Apollo's own statements. Visually, Marsyas's physical gestures become much more exaggerated in this section. For the first time, he arches his torso and actually seems to be *contorting* his body in response to the sonic flaying he is receiving from Apollo. Marsyas's contorted movements correspond to the timing of his sonic gestures, and we thus finally get the impression that these sounds represent his cries of pain, as Daniel argues when he states that in the electronic sounds, "We hear the impact Apollo's music is having on Marsyas as he is being flayed" (2002b, v). In this, and in the simple fact that Marsyas moves and makes any sound at all, Daniel departs from Edith Wyss's interpretation of Titian's painting, in which "without contortion, without a sound,

Marsyas endures his ordeal in dignity. His body hangs freely, the bound arms are folded . . . around his head" (1996, 135). Daniel's piece thus relies as much on the entire story of Marsyas and Apollo, conflict and all, as it does on Titian's depiction of the final outcome of this conflict.

Lento I (accel. poco a poco) (4th section; 4:50). *In this section, Apollo deceptively lulls Marsyas with a calm, chantlike passage, to which Marsyas responds with a pitch-shifting algorithm similar to that heard in the first section.* Recalling the first section, Marsyas applies electronic effects to the violin sound only as Apollo plays it (rather than through Apollo's rests, as in the previous section). Marsyas, in other words, responds in the same way as he did *before* the flaying began. Apollo is toying with him—seducing him, even—and Marsyas is hopeful that the worst may be over. Apollo visually reinforces this narrative by leaning in toward Marsyas as she plays. Marsyas reaches and leans toward Apollo in response, falling for her ruse.

Presto I (5th section; 5:46). *As Apollo expands on the motivic material introduced in the previous section, Marsyas responds by triggering five different samples with the controllers on his right hand, one after the other.* As I note above, the samples represent Marsyas's own "voice." Elsewhere, Daniel (2002b, v) states that these samples represent Marsyas's fighting back. Perhaps emboldened by Apollo's less aggressive phrases from the previous section, here Marsyas makes one final attempt to save himself. Marsyas's own aggression is also mirrored in his physical gestures. Once again, he appears in control of his movements and *acts* rather than *reacts*. By pulling his torso up almost perpendicular to his legs, twisting his body, arms outstretched, first away from Apollo and then rapidly toward her in conjunction with the onset of his sampled sound, Marsyas appears to hurl his own sonic barbs at Apollo.[21] Apollo appears unfazed, however, as she continues to play through Marsyas's attack. By the end of the section, Marsyas has given up his fight and once again hangs almost immobile, while Apollo plays unaccompanied before launching a final assault.

Presto II (6th section; 7:38). *This is the first climactic passage of the piece. It features Apollo's repeating several previously stated motives in succession while Marsyas responds simultaneously with an extreme pitch shift controlled by the neck-mounted G-force controller.* Marsyas is no longer trying to fight back with his own sampled sounds, as Apollo redoubles her own aggression. As this passage progresses and as the torture intensifies, Marsyas's response also increases in intensity, leading to ever-greater distortions of the violin's sound. Marsyas's sonic gestures are highly pronounced, altering Apollo's sound more than in any previous section. Nonetheless, Apollo's lines are uninterrupted by this drastic manipulation. These sounds seem to emit from Marsyas as a continuous response to continuous torture.

In one particularly striking passage, Marsyas applies a continuously increasing pitch bend to Apollo's sound over several bars by slowly bending his torso to a ninety-degree angle with his legs (thus raising his neck and affecting the G-force controller that is attached to it). The passage finally ends when the violin climbs to *b'''*, the highest pitch yet in this section. At this moment, Marsyas falls, ending his pitch-bend manipulation; meanwhile, Apollo's violin returns to a lower register (*c#'-b'*), striking a marked contrast with the extreme contortions of body and sound that just occurred. After a brief passage of unaccompanied violin, Apollo leads into the penultimate section with several short, high, aggressive gestures, each inciting similarly abrupt and violent physical and sonic responses from Marsyas.

Lento II (7th section; 8:49). *This is the predominant climax of the piece: the mortal wounding of Marsyas. Similar to the passage of short chords that signaled the start of the flaying (third section), this passage begins with six short chords each followed by a rest of considerable duration. Marsyas responds to each of these with another four-voice pitch shifter, once again controlled by his left hand. The six chords are followed by long sustained chords, similarly modified by Marsyas's pitch shifter.* Marsyas electronically modifies the "incisive chords" in this passage more extremely than he does in the third section. His responses no longer sound like modifications of a violin's sound (even though, technically, they are exactly that) but like something else entirely. Each of the six chords prompts a drastic change in Marsyas's physical pose, as he moves violently from one twisted position to the next. During the sustained chords that follow, Apollo moves in front of Marsyas, confronting him head on for the first time in the performance. Marsyas continues to move during these chords but much more slowly and less tortuously than before. The battle appears to be over; Apollo has clearly won.

Lento III: Dirge (8th section; 10:20). *Apollo and Marsyas both realize that the end is near for Marsyas. Apollo switches to a slow melody reminiscent of the "chant" from the Lento I section (fourth section), and Marsyas answers with a subtle resonance filter. The piece ends with six "cadential" samples by Marsyas, each containing a high, flutelike timbre.* Marsyas's and Apollo's movements in this section are some of the most intriguing in the piece. As the section begins, Apollo moves back to the left of the metal frame, where she has been during most of the performance. Now, however, she kneels, in exactly the same position as the kneeling flayer in Titian's painting, who is seen by many critics, we recall, as Apollo. Here Daniel brings our attention, if only for a few moments at the end of the piece, to Apollo's other function in Titian's painting. On the one hand, the violinist continues to play here, in keeping with the musical Apollo figure in the painting. On the other hand, she kneels, seemingly imitating the kneeling Apollo figure in the painting. The dueling Apollo, at least to a certain extent, gives way to the flaying Apollo, as Daniel once again conflates the musical conflict with its resulting punishment.

Curiously, the sonic flaying seemed much more violent than anything occurring now (at the moment when the actual flayer from the painting is represented in performance). As Apollo's role shifts in this way, however, Marsyas continues his slow movements through this section, triggering six consecutive samples. Although he is clearly in his last moments, he summons a fair amount of strength with which to utter these final "words." The samples he triggers in this section are accompanied by widely stretched arms, which move deliberately, even if slowly. Furthermore, the flutelike timbres are much more apparent in these sounds than they are in those heard in the fifth section. Even in defeat and despite his imminent death, Marsyas asserts his voice. As the last of this sound fades and with Apollo finally kneeling down to the position occupied by Titian's flayer, Marsyas finally hangs exactly as we see him in the painting, with arms folded around his head, in silent dignity.[22]

A NETWORK OF LIVENESS

As I have made apparent in this narrative analysis, in his description of the piece and in the way he stages its performance, Daniel emphasizes a direct confrontation between Marsyas and Apollo. Interaction between the two performers is central not only to the practical considerations of ensemble performance but also to the dramatic narrative underlying that performance. Similarly, within the piece's narrative and its actual performance, themes of corporeality come racing to the fore in two distinct ways. First, the clash between Apollo, who is understood in modern Western culture to represent knowledge and rationality, and the satyr Marsyas, who by association with Dionysus represents passion and visceral bacchic frenzy, signals the mind/body binary invoked in my study of Glenn Gould. Recall the polarity observed by Holland in his *New York Times* piece about gesticulating pianists (as addressed in Chapter 3, n. 9), in which he classifies musicians as *either* Apollonian (with a focus on "symmetry, invention and elegance") *or* Dionysian (with a focus on "art more from the gut, more spontaneous") (*New York Times*, February 6, 2008).[23]

Second, the very blatant display of corporeality by Daniel in performance, particularly in light of his connection to digital technologies—which continue to carry broader cultural associations with disembodiment—invites an interpretation of the piece that takes corporeality as its starting point. Interactivity and corporeality are thus deeply implicated in a performance of this work, and both warrant further discussion. However, as I address below, neither interactivity nor corporeality can be fully understood in this piece without consideration of its virtual aspects, and the network of liveness I perceive at work in a performance of *Marsyas* invokes all three of these elements to great effect.

In Chapter 5, I address the emergence of an interactive quality of liveness in early live electronic music. I focus in these discussions on interactions established between performers through the mediation of various electronic sound technologies. In my final example from this tradition (Mumma's *Hornpipe*), I discuss a type of interaction established between a performer and his anthropomorphized technology: technology that is considered to take on attributes of a human performer. This is a metaphorical interaction to be sure, but, nonetheless, the *idea* of interaction in its truest sense informs that piece to a great degree.

The concept of interaction also plays a large part in recent accounts of contemporary live electronic music, which is often called *interactive computer music*. Cathy Cox (2004) argues, however, that the nature of interactivity in this music is not always fully examined by its practitioners. Thus, she calls for more thorough considerations of exactly how this interactivity is established. Pointing to the important role played by interactive relationships, she writes, "The aesthetic appreciation of a work is affected by the *type* of interactivity involved in the experience for composer, performer, and audience" (C. Cox 2004, 341; my emphasis). The broad interpretation of the concept of interactivity in this music is demonstrated by conventional definitions of the genre, in which the word *interactive* refers to *any* type of continuous real-time relationship between a musician and digital technologies. Guy E. Garnett explains, for example, that "interaction has two aspects: either the performer's actions affect the computer's output, or the computer's actions affect the performer's output" (2001, 23). According to Garnett's definition, the interaction in interactive computer music is, first, concerned mainly with relationships between performers and technologies. Second, this interaction is not necessarily *reciprocally* active, as that word seems to imply. It may simply refer, for example, to a predetermined, unchanging electronic filter that adds constant reverberation to the sound of a flute, which is hardly a fully interactive use of technology.[24]

As C. Cox (2004, 334) points out, accounts of interactive computer music that fail to query its interactivity sufficiently, settling instead for mere descriptions of the programming involved in such pieces, often also fail to identify the real aesthetic significance of the performances of this music. Although *Marsyas* clearly falls into the category of interactive computer music as defined by Garnett and others, it features far more significant interactions than those that can be identified by simply describing Daniel's particular MIDI configurations. Rather, liveness emerges in this piece from dynamic interactions between the two performers, which are mediatized by Daniel's MIDI setup. This type of "digitally enhanced" interaction is not fully recognized by the usual definitions of interaction discussed above. A more thorough look at the various layers of interactivity in *Marsyas* is therefore helpful in describing much of the vital liveness inherent in a performance of this piece.

The work of David A. Jaffe and W. Andrew Schloss (1994) may bring us closer to a concept of mediatized interaction that lends itself to a productive discussion of interactive liveness in *Marsyas*. Moreover, their term *computer-extended ensemble* hints at the type of chamber-music interactivity that is central to my earlier discussion of interactive liveness in live electronic music (see Chapter 5). Jaffe and Schloss argue that, historically, interactivity in electronic music has been conceptualized around one of two extreme models. First, they identify the "tape music model," in which performers are "slaves" to the inflexible tape part and are forced to "synchronize their tempo, dynamics, and tone quality to that of the tape." Next, they identify the "keyboard electronic music model," in which the electronics are "slaves" to the performers, because the performers control every element of sound. Neither of these models demonstrates real interaction (despite how that term has been understood in electronic music circles); rather, they demonstrate merely reaction. True interaction, which they argue has only surfaced in the past couple of decades with the emergence of musically programmable computers, only occurs on a continuum between these extremities, when neither component is fully dependent on the other (Jaffe and Schloss 1994, 78). For it is only within this space, particularly when programmable digital technologies (such as Daniel's configuration of MIDI controllers, sampler, and DSP) are used to enhance the musical relationship between two or more performers, that a model of two-way (or more) communication—interaction—in electronic music can be fully explored. In other words, it is only in these instances that a fully interactive performance network is established.

Jaffe and Schloss's model of the computer-extended ensemble focuses on "area[s] of music in which interaction between performers is central" (1994, 79) and, furthermore, in which this interaction is shaped in part by configurations of digital sound technologies. This model draws our attention once again to the potentially dialectical nature of liveness in mediatized music. In this case, a conventional model of live communication between two or more members of a performing ensemble is maintained. It is also significantly altered by the introduction of the synthetic and prerecorded (i.e., not live) sounds resulting from that interaction, leading to new understandings of mediatized performance.

A performance of Daniel's *Marsyas* presents these types of complex relationships, which seem even more complex when considered in light of the mythical narrative informing the piece. From a purely technical perspective, the following levels of interaction take place between violinist and suspended musician in a performance of *Marsyas*:

1) With the exception of the sampled material, the sounds created by the suspended musician are all manipulations of the violin's sounds. That is, the suspended musician *controls* the amplification and alteration of the sounds originally produced by the violinist.
2) These gestures by the suspended musician are all cued by the violin part. In other words, the suspended musician manipulates these controllers according to the linear unfolding of the violin line.

It would seem from this perspective, then, that two different configurations of performer agency are at work here. In the first case, as soon as the violinist surrenders her performance, via microphone, to the PCM-81 digital signal processor, she leaves it open to control by the suspended musician, who operates the DSP by moving his fingers, wrist, and neck. Contrarily, in the second case, the progression of the suspended musician's performance is highly dependent on nuances of timing performed by the violinist. As his gestures are to be performed at certain points in the violinist's phrases, and as the sound produced by these gestures (with the exception of the sampled material) is entirely reliant on the existence of violin sound in the first place, the suspended musician surrenders a certain amount of his own agency to the violinist. To fully understand this interactive dynamic, we must allow for a more nuanced approach to agency between violinist and suspended musician, which takes into account their evenly if differently calibrated power relations—power relations made possible only by Daniel's particular musician/machine configurations. Each musician surrenders something to the other, and the use of electronic technologies in this piece determines how these musical elements are surrendered and subsequently controlled. Of course, chamber-music groups regularly "share control" of a piece's performance, not only because each member is responsible for a part of the overall sound but also because these members must often take turns leading, depending on how they decide it best to bring out different voices at different times. My argument is not that a shared dynamic of control can only exist in performance if electronic technologies are used but rather that to understand this shared dynamic in *Marsyas*, we must take into account how Daniel uses these technologies to shape it.

The narrative provided to a performance of *Marsyas* by the myth of Marsyas and Apollo, however, further complicates the interactive qualities of liveness apparent in such a performance. Not only is a witness to this performance confronted with the interactive struggle for agency noted above, but he or she is also witness to the dynamic of confrontation, the "musical duel to the death" (Daniel 2002b, iv), between Marsyas and Apollo. What is more, this symbolic interaction is very complex. We see that the nature of the interaction between Apollo and Marsyas fluctuates with almost every section of the piece, including moments of gamesmanship (first and second sections), seduction (fourth section), various dynamics of outright violent conflict (third section, fifth–seventh sections), and, finally, a resolution to the conflict (eighth section). We interpret this dynamic relationship between the two characters by way of their sonic and physical interactions, both of which are informed by the mythical narrative.

Daniel further describes how he intends the narrative to influence a performance's projected interaction:

> In relation to the extra-musical theme of the piece, the suspended musician is affected by the music of the violin, and what the listener hears from the speakers in case (a) [i.e., real-time manipulations of the violin sound] is the effect of the pure violin music on the suspended musician. So, we hear the impact Apollo's music is having on Marsyas as he is

being flayed. In case (b) [i.e., sampled material], Marsyas fights back (about half way through the piece), and finally "sings" a lament at the end. (2002b, v)

According to the narrative, Daniel conceives the sounds created by Marsyas's gestures not to represent the effects of his movements on the violin sound (which, technically speaking, they are) but, conversely, to represent the torturous effects of the violin sound on Marsyas's body. In addition to the nuanced approach to agency discussed above, Daniel's conception of the interaction between Marsyas and Apollo points here to a dialogical relationship between the physical nature of that interaction (violin sounds controlled by suspended musician's gestures) and the metaphorical nature of that interaction (Marsyas responding to his sonic flaying by Apollo). Understanding these various levels of interaction clearly relies on understanding the fundamental place of corporeal experience in this piece.

In my discussion of corporeal liveness in Chapter 3, I focus on the importance of familiar physical gestures in creating meaning for listeners: I appreciate the corporeality of Gould's piano recordings, because my familiarity with the physical gestures of piano playing (and singing) allow me to identify the sounds of Gould's performing body in those recordings. In much live electronic music, familiar sound-producing actions (such as those required to play the piano) are either directed at producing unfamiliar sounds or avoided altogether. For example, an electronic keyboard can be configured so the depression of keys produces seemingly unrelated changes in an already continuous stream of sound rather than discrete notes that share a kinetic relationship with the depression of those discrete keys (as on a piano). Here, once again, we encounter the audio-visual disjunction (Corbett 1990) and its potential for liquidating corporeally informed meanings from music performance.

Many writers have remarked on this aspect of electronic art music and on its potentially detrimental effect on an audience's understanding of the music's performance. For instance, Simon Emmerson writes, "The *fact* that a specific instrumental action or human gesture (at a control desk or computer, say) causes a musical event to occur is *not a sufficient nor even a necessary* condition for a musical 'cause/effect' connection to be made in the mind of any listener" (1994, 97; original emphasis). Yet even given the rupture in perceptible action-sound relationships in much live electronic music, it remains the case that a performer's gestures, even if unconventional, may still have a significant impact on an audience's experience of the work. To that end, many argue (e.g., C. Cox 2004; Croft 2007) that when designing "interactive" performance systems, live electronic musicians should take into consideration the logic and intuitiveness of the relationship between the physical performative gestures they require and the sounds they ultimately produce.

Thus, John Croft bases his "Theses of Liveness" (2007) on a distinction between what he calls *procedural liveness* and what he calls *aesthetic liveness*. Procedural liveness is simply "defined as the material fact that live sound is being transformed in real time." Aesthetic liveness, on the other hand, is an instance of procedural liveness in which "aesthetically meaningful differences in the input sound are mapped to aesthetically meaningful differences in the output sound. . . . Thus the onus of justification of [aesthetic] liveness is shifted to the causal link between the performer's [bodily] action and the computer's response" (2007, 61). He argues that aesthetic tension in this music arises from this very interaction between live performer and electronic sounds: "A corporeal, fallible, limited human is pitted against a disembodied, 'infallible' and potentially infinite generator of sound" (2007, 63). Interactive computer music that aims to project meaningful aesthetic liveness (which amounts, ultimately, to what I have been calling *corporeal liveness*), according to Croft, must overcome this potential rupture and find a way to re-embody the electronic sound by way of appropriate performance gestures.

Following Croft's argument (while leaving his terminology behind), I posit here that although Daniel performs (at least in my perception) corporeal liveness in *Marsyas* with his mapping of electronic sound to bodily gesture, those particular sounds do not correspond, in and of themselves, to any easily identifiable physical source. Outside the context of the performance, this music (again, in my perception) does not sound particularly corporeal. Within a performance of *Marsyas*, however, corporeal qualities are central to the relationships demonstrated between these sounds and Daniel's movements. Yet simply identifying this corporeality does not tell us very much about *Marsyas*'s potential meanings. Theorizing this corporeality, on the other hand, helps demonstrate how various layers of liveness perform meaning throughout a staging of Daniel's piece.

As I mention above, the mythical opposition between Apollo and Marsyas brings the mind/body binary once again to the fore. The figure of Marsyas, a satyr, carries automatic associations with the cult of Dionysus, which is commonly opposed to that of Apollo. Apollonian behavior is usually thought to revolve around rationality and intellectualism, whereas Dionysian behavior is usually depicted as sensuous and visceral. Moreover, as Daniel reminds us, often "string instruments were considered more 'divine' by virtue of the mathematical principles that they could easily illustrate, and wind instruments were considered 'pagan.' So, the myth is . . . a parable of . . . the victory of Apollo's noble music over the rough and lascivious piping of his earthy opponent" (2002b, iv). This particular dichotomy is further played out in the staging of *Marsyas*, even though no flute is actually present. The Apollo figure plays the violin (still a symbol of "cerebral" music in Western culture), while the Marsyas figure hangs, torso bared and with nothing but his own (wired) body to use as a musical instrument.[25] Of course, his MIDI controllers and the wires attached to them are visible, but they do not ever, it seems, signify "musical instrument" in the same way that a violin does. Moreover, because they are attached directly to his body, Daniel does not perform *on* or *with* these controllers in any conventional sense. Rather, Daniel's choreography successfully incorporates all the sonically motivated physical gestures (i.e., those gestures *required* to produce electronic sound) into a larger stream of movement that portrays his narrative. Thus, the electronic sounds in this piece seem to emanate directly from the movements Marsyas makes in his interaction with Apollo and not from arbitrary "instrument control" movements that would detract from this interaction. And, of course, because Apollo's attack on Marsyas's body and Marsyas's physical responses are at the heart of this relationship, corporeality and interactivity become intertwined.

For instance, as Apollo lulls Marsyas in the fourth section with a plaintive chant (4:50), Marsyas responds by reaching toward Apollo (for mercy, perhaps?). In the act of reaching, he generates the subtle pitch shift reminiscent of the opening section, referencing sounds from before the brutal torture began. Similarly, Marsyas's hurling gestures in the following section (5:46) clearly represent his own attack on Apollo. The true weapon in this battle, however, is sound: As Marsyas hurls it, the samples representing his own "voice" emanate abruptly and loudly from the speakers. In short, thanks to Daniel's marriage of choreography with MIDI control and electronic sound, Marsyas appears to emit his sonic attack directly from within his own body. What is more, because Marsyas's gestures are so blatantly "of the body," both visibly and with respect to their narrative significance, they bring corporeal meaning to their associated sounds that, in many cases, would not otherwise exist. Of course, the pitch bending that Marsyas imposes on the violin sound at various moments in the piece often corresponds quite logically to his bending body. The long (and quite severe) pitch bend that results when Marsyas slowly raises his head in the sixth section (8:10) provides an excellent example.

Many other electronic sounds in the piece, however, do not feature necessarily "corporeal" qualities—or if these qualities do exist, they do not seem to share a kinetic or physical logic with the performative gestures that cause them. Yet the logic of the Apollo-Marsyas confrontation seems to maintain for these sounds a meaningful connection to Marsyas's physical movements. The "hurled" samples in the fifth section of the piece, for example (5:46–7:38), feature a mixture of harsh metallic and high sustained ringing timbres, all of which develop over the span of a couple of seconds. None of these sounds seems to connect logically, at least in any kinetic sense, to the quick thrusting and hurling motions of Marsyas's arms, yet they do not seem at all out of place in the larger theatrical and narrative context of the performance. They still seem connected to Marsyas's body, because we understand them, if only within the context of this piece, to be generated from his physical movements—his electronically wired physical movements—in response to the physical torture inflicted upon him by

Apollo. Because these connections between gesture and sound are formed in the technosphere rather than in the material world according to its physical laws, I turn finally to a discussion of *Marsyas*'s virtual qualities to explore even more deeply these perceived instances of liveness.

Virtuality does not exist for me in a performance of *Marsyas* in the same way it exists when I listen to John Oswald's "Vane." That is, the sounds I hear do not prompt me to engage with a virtual performing persona that does not physically exist. Indeed, the personae of the Marsyas myth *do* exist before my eyes, and their concrete reality bestows its own presence upon the performance. Yet the musician/machine relationships I discuss in this chapter, which inspire my perception of corporeal and interactive qualities of liveness, are invested with their own virtualities nonetheless. After all, as I have already argued, all liveness has the potential for virtuality. The perception of liveness in music is the perception of that which reminds us of music's basis in performance. Thus the value of liveness is not located in what is *actually* happening but in what we *perceive* as happening. This perception may result more from a person's cognitive functions than from any concrete reality lying outside that person's body. Some of *Marsyas*'s qualities of interactivity and corporeality depend on such qualities of virtuality.

For instance, I argue above that many of the relationships between Marsyas's gestures and sounds are not grounded in the conventional kinetic relationships we usually witness in the performance of acoustic music: those of musically vibrating bodies set in motion by human bodily gestures. Yet Marsyas's sonic gestures still connect perceptibly with his physical gestures in the context of the performance. This connection, in other words, only exists virtually and is only made possible by Daniel's configuration of MIDI technology. This virtuality is in effect an inversion of that described in my discussion of "Vane." In that case, electronic sounds, by virtue of their grounding in a perceptible corporeality (the imagined physical performance gestures of Carly Simon and Faster Pussycat), generate a virtual performing cyborg—an imagined man/woman/machine hybrid absent from the listener's view but embedded nonetheless in his or her imagination.

In the case of *Marsyas*, it is the very corporeal presence of the performers (particularly Daniel/Marsyas) and the narrative of interaction between those performers that provide a context within which otherwise nonlive electronic sounds are invested with their own traces of interactivity and corporeality. These traces do not result from any qualities of interactivity or corporeality that exist within the sounds themselves. Rather, they exist only virtually—that is, they exist only within the perceived metaphoric relationships that Daniel establishes between Marsyas and Apollo and between Marsyas's movements and sounds. Moreover, they are part of the technosphere—a virtual construction itself—that constitutes an essential part of an audience's reception of this work.

Although this account of virtual liveness differs somewhat from that provided in my discussion of "Vane," these two analyses nonetheless both

hinge on the implication of the cyborg as a central figure. In "Vane," I
identify a virtual sounding cyborg. In *Marsyas*, I point to a cyborg that
performs visually as well as sonically. As Marsyas thrashes around, we see
the wires running from his neck and hands to his back. As I suggest above,
these wires do not seem to constitute the category *musical instrument* in
any conventional sense. They seem instead to be closely integrated parts
of Marsyas's own body, which clearly signals "human" in its display of
physicality and "machine" in its display of wires and electronic sensors.
Moreover, we hear the electronic nature of the sounds produced by these
movements—the *wired body*, in effect, acts as the site of electronic sound,
thus producing another kind of dialectically performing cyborg. The (Post)
modern nature of this figure is made even more apparent when we consider
the contrastingly ancient story on which the entire performance is based.

If Oswald's cyborg performs a commentary on the binary nature of
gender construction in rock music, what does Daniel's cyborg perform?
After all, the true theoretical value of the cyborg figuration is its ability
to trouble such dualistic boundaries. In *Marsyas*, challenged boundaries
abound. First, mind (Apollo) confronts body (Marsyas); but this is not a
clash between polar opposites. Rather, the conflict is played out in dialectical mergings of Apollo's sounds with Marsyas's movements, and of concrete entities with their virtual interactions. Furthermore, although Apollo
dominates the duel, Marsyas actually exercises sonic control over Apollo's
expressions. Second, recorded (dead) sound exists only as performed (live)
sound, as Marsyas's samples are caused by his physical gestures. Third, and
central to the cyborg figuration itself, human merges with machine when
Daniel affixes MIDI controllers to his partially nude body and so skillfully
navigates this intimate interface between flesh and circuitry.

THE HIP-HOP TURNTABLIST AS PERFORMING CYBORG

I wish here, as we near the end of this book, to return to the musical territory that I briefly invoke at its beginning. The musical practices of hip-hop,
it seems to me, perhaps more than any other widespread contemporary
musical practice evoke entirely new and incredibly complex understandings
of liveness (and many familiar ones, too). Much of this complexity arises
from the central reliance of much of hip-hop music, since its beginnings in
the 1970s, on the sampled records of others, and on the importation of those
recordings into the realm of live performance by turntablists.[26] In fact, even
a cursory glance at hip-hop's various musical practices reveals constant
ambiguity in the division between the conventional roles, and associated
values and ideologies, of live performance and ("not-live") studio practice.
For instance, within much contemporary studio-based hip-hop, the use of
prerecorded and subsequently sampled sounds is often greatly valued over
those recorded "live" in the studio, thus reversing the evaluative ideologies

of a traditional live/recorded binary. In addition, the extremely performative art of turntablism, in addition to its live reappropriation of "dead" recordings, has also enjoyed an equally vital existence as a recorded medium itself, in the form of mixtapes. The implications of liveness within hip-hop music are indeed extensive enough to warrant a book-length study rather than the brief attention that I pay them here. Nonetheless, I wish to suggest here some directions in which such a study may proceed, with a particular focus on the role played by reconfigured recordings within the broad range of hip-hop practices. As I mention above, the central, even iconic, figure within any discussion of hip-hop and sampling is the turntablist, whom I wish to present here as another configuration of the performing cyborg, as I discuss below.

As argued by Aram Sinnreich (2010), contemporary developments in audio technologies and their uses have led to the rapid rise within modern music of an aesthetic of reconfiguration (he identifies a broad category of "configurable music") to which turntablism and much studio-based hip-hop subscribe—one in which, especially with the aid of digital technologies, fragments of recorded sound (of all sizes) are freely reconstituted, completely apart from their original contexts, in the creation of newly formed musical experiences. Realized in many of these new musical contexts— be they recorded mashups, live club mixes by a DJ, hip-hop recordings, hip-hop turntablist performances, or any number of other contexts—are challenges to several long-standing binary divisions, along with the resulting dialectical tensions between these elements that were once viewed in complete opposition to one another. It is here, of course, that we enter the domain of the cyborg.

For example, by sampling previously recorded music and reconstituting it in the context of a new performance or recording, the configurable musician merges the consumption of music (i.e., listening to recordings) with its production (presenting a new musical experience for a potential audience). In addition, music of the past becomes music of the present, as familiar sounds are offered within new musical frameworks. Similarly, the distinction between *copying* those familiar sounds and creating *original* music is also challenged. This particular dissolved binary has clear ramifications within discussions of intellectual property and copyright inside the music industry, but it also raises aesthetic questions about the value of creation and what are considered legitimate "raw materials" for such creation. When the line between copy and original becomes difficult, if not impossible, to distinguish, as it does in so much sample-based music, a musicker's experiences of musical agency, authenticity, and compositional and performative voice become highly complex and dynamic, depending especially on their relationship to the music being sampled and on the precise articulation of those samples within their newly configured musical contexts.

Sinnreich, for instance, demonstrates that for some producers and DJs, sample-based music is often perceived as more authentic—because it is "more original"—if it incorporates "larger, more recognizable samples" rather than samples that are smaller and less obviously indebted to their original contexts (2010, 131). Moreover, as Cutler (2004, 146–148) reminds us, when an art form such as turntablism relies in its very essence on previously recorded material—*any* previously recorded material, so long as it is accessible on phonograph disc[27]—the distinctions between popular music and art music (and any other tradition of recorded music you could care to name) may break down very quickly: Inasmuch as it all provides material to be sampled, all recorded music is equal. Hip-hop turntablists regularly draw from any number of musical genres in constructing their mixes. Cut Chemist and Z-Trip offer one notable example at the Future Primitive Sound Session in San Francisco, as captured in the final scene of Doug Pray's turntablism documentary *Scratch* (Pray 2002). Just before the end credits begin to roll, we witness Cut Chemist scratching virtuosically over a recording of Apollo 100's pop-inspired arrangement of Edvard Grieg's *In the Hall of the Mountain King.* This particular performance pushes further genre boundaries, as hip-hop painter Doze Green paints a scene on a wall next to Cut Chemist and Z-Trip, and film of skateboarders and surfers, among other things, projects onto a screen behind them.[28]

The dialectical tensions just described may be witnessed in many types of sample-based music. Turntablists, however—perhaps the most clearly articulated examples of the performing cyborg, providing a human locus for the expression and exploration, through technological means, of the dissolved binaries discussed above—enact these tensions in such a way as to have a direct bearing on the perception of liveness. Most obviously, in bringing recorded sound into the domain of live performance, a turntablist adopts as his or her "live instrument" an electronic reproduction technology, one that in a broader modern cultural context still carries the label of "machine" in a way that pianos and saxophones, for instance, do not. In this, of course, the turntablist shares her cyborg nature with other live electronic musicians, so recognition of a broader history of sample-based performance is in order.

The real-time manipulation of recorded music in performance, as is addressed in Chapter 5, predates the development of hip-hop by almost forty years. Between the time of Cage's *Imaginary Landscape No. 1* (1939) and the spread of scratching techniques in hip-hop in the late 1970s and early 1980s,[29] such artists as Mauricio Kagel, Christian Marclay, and Laurie Anderson all developed methods for the real-time manipulation of recorded media.[30] Yet it is clearly within the art of the hip-hop turntablist that the technological appropriation of past recorded performances into new live performances has taken place on the largest scale. The various sampling and sample-manipulation techniques first developed by turntablists have in turn informed the widespread use of digital samples in studio-produced hip-hop, making the sample a ubiquitous element of hip-hop musical aesthetics (the significance of which is further explored below).

The hip-hop turntablist-as-cyborg is a particularly suitable theoretical trope to employ in the consideration of one common element of the turntablism found particularly at DJ battles: the practice of "speaking" not with one's own voice but with the sampled voices of others. DJ battles are, quite simply, turntablism competitions. Individual turntablists, or groups (crews) of turntablists, each take turns performing their well-rehearsed routines, and at the end of each event, a winner is declared.[31] A typical element of these routines is the "message," a sampled fragment of speech or song that typically declares something about the turntablist's superiority or his opponents' inferiority (Katz 2004, 123–125). Usually, the turntablist mouths the sampled words along with the recording and often adds appropriate physical gestures for emphasis. At the 1997 DMC DJ Championship World Final, for instance, DJ A-Trak began his winning routine with the composite message (the first phrase from one recording, and the last two from another), "All you other DJs are a bunch of jerks. . . . You wanna test me, you're stupid. . . . You gotta be outta your fuckin' mind." A-Trak mouthed each word as it was heard, and a couple of times when he repeated the words "fuckin' mind," he tapped his fingers to his temple.[32] The routine ended with a similarly confident send-off, which sounds as though it were likely sampled from the soundtrack of an overdubbed kung fu movie: "Well I've beaten most of the people here. . . . Who do you have who could possibly beat me?"[33]

In this scenario, then, the turntablist's performative voice does not emanate from his own vocal apparatus but from those of others, captured on a recording and spun out again at a later time in the context of the DJ battle: cut, scratched, rearranged, and potentially combined with other recorded voices (as in the case of A-Trak's routine) to speak not as originally intended but on behalf of the turntablist. Although it is not uncommon to speak of an acoustic instrument as the source of its performer's "voice," what makes the turntablist's battle message unique—*and thrusts it into the realm of virtual liveness, located in the actions of a performing cyborg*—is its technological appropriation of another person's voice, its substitution of what are, effectively, *machine sounds* for the actual organic voice of the turntablist such that, for the audience, the former is perceived as equivalent to—or perhaps even, as I suggest below, more authentic than—the latter.

In its performance, turntablism also relies for its full effect on the appreciation of several categories of liveness in addition to the specific invocation of virtual liveness that I have just identified. Inasmuch as turntablism is witnessed in a traditional live performance setting, temporal and spatial liveness clearly play a part in constructing meaning. Corporeal liveness also seems to carry a great deal of importance for many practitioners and fans. For instance, battle routines (particularly before the early 1990s) often feature what are known as "body tricks," wherein a routine is made more difficult by the imposition of physical stunts that are otherwise unnecessary for the production of the routine's purely sonic content. Cutmaster Swift, for example, in a routine that won him the DMC Championship World Final in 1989, ended with a series of body tricks that included spinning in place, passing one hand under his raised leg repeatedly to backspin one of his records, and operating one of the faders on his mixer with his cheek (see Cutmaster Swift 1989). Furthermore, Rob Swift emphasizes that battle routines are meant to communicate spontaneity, even though they are highly rehearsed and involve very little, if any, improvisation (Katz 2004, 127). In *Scratch* (Pray 2002), Z-Trip also speaks about the importance of improvisation in reading a crowd (outside the battle scene) and ensuring that he is playing records that keep them involved in the performance—in other words, he identifies the need for spontaneity in preserving a desired interaction between turntablist and audience. Thus, temporality, spatial proximity, corporeality, spontaneity, and interaction, all understood in rather straightforward terms, are valued elements of turntablism in performance.

Complications to a straightforward understanding of liveness arise, however, in the ambiguous relationship that has always existed between the performance of hip-hop music more generally and its recording—a relationship made even more complex by the involvement of previously recorded music on stage and in the recording studio. Peter Shapiro emphasizes this ambiguous relationship when he writes of Grandmaster Flash's seminal mix, "The Adventures of Grandmaster Flash on the Wheels of Steel" (1981; on Grandmaster Flash & the Furious Five 2005): "In the studio, Flash recorded the track live on the decks; if he messed up, he erased everything and started again from scratch. He nailed it on the fourth or fifth take" (2009, 104). The complex ambiguity to which I am referring (complex and ambiguous, that is, at least in reference to other instances of liveness with which I have been concerned in this book) is that a type of musicking so aware of—indeed, so utterly dependent on—the malleability of recorded music will still find value in the "take one-ness" (to reconfigure Gould's phrase) of the live performance, *even in the studio*. In an apparent appeal to corporeal liveness, Paul D. Miller, aka DJ Spooky that Subliminal Kid, transfers this value of the performing DJ's art to his assessment of sample-based music in general, found in the liner notes to his *Songs of a Dead Dreamer*. Even as he presents on this CD music produced by digital means in a studio (not "live on the decks," as in Grandmaster Flash's case), he makes reference to sampled sounds that are "triggered by the sensuous touch of the DJ's hands guiding the mix" (2004a, 350).

At the same time, we should also consider that Grandmaster Flash's "Wheels of Steel" was in fact a recorded product itself, one in a long line of hip-hop mixtapes that were central to the spread of hip-hop turntablism, especially in the 1980s.[34] The art of turntablism, which relies so heavily on the particularities of live performance—such as the spontaneity, interactions, and physical demonstrations of skill discussed above—for its effectiveness, has also relied for its very popularity and dissemination on an audio format that has the potential to severely mask (if not negate altogether) all those qualities. As Shapiro further writes, "While turntablism was meant to be heard (and seen) live, it probably works best in the mixtape format, where the DJ's propensity for indulgent scientifical madness is reined in by the high 'thrills per minute' ratio that is crucial to the medium" (2009, 108). Keeping in mind, then, the importance of previously recorded music in a turntablist's performance, the importance of liveness (of many types) in the communication of meaning in such performance, and, finally, the importance of recorded mixes in disseminating this style of performance, one can see a pattern emerging in which *the live act of turntablism is in fact a mediation* between the original recordings on which the live act is based and the creation of the mixtape or any other recording on which the turntablist is featured.

It would seem that, within this particular construction at least, the authenticity of liveness afforded to some hip-hop recordings involves a circular logic similar to that discussed in the context of rock music in Chapter 4—one in which live and recorded are appreciated in constant reference to one another. Yet liveness for the sake of liveness may not be the endgame in this hip-hop scenario. Joseph Schloss demonstrates that for many modern hip-hop producers, who rely almost entirely on digital samplers rather than on the performance of turntables for their musical borrowing, a connection to the authenticity of the performing DJ is still central to their aesthetic. This authenticity (for these producers, at least) is not to be found in the turntablist's liveness, however, but in the foundational role the turntablist played in the establishment of hip-hop culture and in the emphasis on exact audio quotation played out by the turntablist and the sampling studio producer.

This connection to the recorded sample, in fact, was demonstrated to be so important to many of Schloss's inverviewees (a collection of sample-based hip-hop producers), that for them samples carry far more authenticity than sounds recorded "live" in the studio (Schloss 2004, esp. Ch. 2 and 3). One producer (DJ Kool Akiem) even explained that the practice employed in the late 1970s and early 1980s by the Sugar Hill label of *imitating* recorded samples with live instruments on their recordings was an inauthentic blip on the radar, only to be corrected when the invention of the digital sampler allowed for an authentic connection to the foundational art of the turntablist to be restored. He argues, "Hip-hop is about the turntables. And cats was rhymin' on turntables. And when they started makin' records . . . they had no choice but to get a band . . . but as soon as there was a sampler, they went back to the root. How it originally was, you know what I mean?" (DJ Kool Akiem, quoted in Schloss 2004, 51).

In this scenario, then, the valuation of liveness is flipped on its head. Authenticity is to be found in a sense of history and in a connection to the perceived roots of hip-hop culture, in a similar manner to the authenticity sought in the "salvation moments" of rock that are discussed in Chapter 4. Whereas those appeals to historical authenticity in rock are also appeals to liveness, however, it would seem in hip-hop—at least in some cases—that perhaps the focus is not so much on the live as it is on the revivification of the dead, as turntablists and other DJs breathe new life into long-forgotten recordings. The importance of, and the *authenticity* located in, the use of obscure and unknown samples (see Schloss 2004, esp. Ch. 4), makes the distance between the "death" of the record and its revivification by the DJ seem even more vast. With this in mind, if we return our focus once more to the battle DJ, we might say that the authenticity in his virtual voice comes from just this configuration of values—as this musically performing cyborg, emphasizing once again the dialectical nature of mediatized liveness, conjures the sounds of records past and coaxes them to speak anew, he is actually allowing his own authentic voice to be heard.

8   Conclusion

Liveness is a dynamic and versatile concept. As performance practices in any cultural form change, shared understandings of what makes those performances *live* or *not live* will also change. Similarly, as the technologies against which the concept of liveness is measured are brought into performances once considered incompatible with technological mediation, relationships between liveness and mediatization must be reconsidered. In innumerable different regions of modern musicking, electronic technologies have become important parts of everyday practice. Musicological scholarship, however, has not yet developed to the point where these technologies are fully understood as significant contributors to many experiences of musical liveness. In fact, the use of electronic technologies is often seen as a threat to conventional values of music performance. I attempt to demonstrate in this volume that mediatization may also be construed as a productive way to project new and necessary understandings of performative meaning in music. By theorizing various qualities of liveness emerging from relationships between musickers and electronic technologies, we may begin to understand how performance has become mediatized while still maintaining many of the qualities that make it performative, revealing the ever-changing social values reflected in the presentation and reception of musical performance.

In any given musical performance context, liveness can emerge in a variety of ways. We may experience liveness as a condition of temporality or of spatial proximity. We may consider musical sound to be live in its fidelity to an original or ideal "true" utterance. We may interpret liveness as a quality of spontaneity, thought to reside especially in the uniqueness of individual performances. We may encounter liveness as a trace of corporeality, as an indication of musical interactivity, or as a condition of some other perceptual category not explored in this book. Our perceptions of liveness may also be virtual, and it is within this domain that mediatization may have its most significant impact. Electronic sound technologies allow for the modification of some of the most recognizable qualities of musical performance; they also allow for the creation and perception of sounds that project these qualities even when the performance we hear never actually took place in a traditional sense.

These different valences of liveness exist as fluid perceptions, sometimes giving way to one another, sometimes acting in complex relationships with one another. No particular single understanding of liveness exists for all performance contexts. Moreover, each performance context, especially when involving some form of mediatization, may present its own unique network of liveness. I offer here a theoretical apparatus to assist in navigating these networks, so that some conclusions may begin to be drawn about exactly how the use of electronic technologies has affected traditional values of performance in music and, perhaps more importantly, how these same technologies have assisted in the formation of entirely new values associated with the performance of music.

I have presented five individual case studies as examples of how such investigations into liveness in mediatized performance might be carried out. Each one has demonstrated how important the concept of liveness can be to understanding performative meaning; each one has accomplished this task with reference to a different area or areas of modern musicking. Glenn Gould's recordings of canonical piano repertoire, the discourse of rock authenticity surrounding the White Stripes, examples from the emerging genre of live electronic music in the late 1950s and 1960s, John Oswald's plunderphonics, Omar Daniel's recent piece of interactive computer music, and hip-hop turntablism practices (along with various other examples raised more briefly throughout this book) all present mediatized performance contexts in which electronically influenced instantiations of liveness forge new relationships between performance as it is traditionally understood and electronic technologies as they have recently been incorporated into music. In each of these discussions, important performative meanings, with respect to musical practice and wider cultural and social contexts, were located within human/machine relationships—within the mediatization of performance.

Underlying all my arguments is a concern with precisely how the tensions between *live* and *mediated* are understood. Not only live/mediated but also other related conceptual pairs, such as human/machine, natural/artificial, production/reproduction, and authentic/inauthentic, have long been understood in musical discourse as constructions of binary opposition. Recent musical practice, however, as demonstrated throughout this book, presents situations in which these static binaries no longer seem appropriate. I chose instead to focus on tensions that exist in creative instability within each of these pairings. Liveness in mediatized performance emerges from more dialogic interactions such as these—that is, liveness in mediatized performance results from a *synthesis* of liveness conventionally understood on the one hand and the processes of electronic mediation once thought to threaten this liveness on the other. Nowhere is this dialectical construction of meaning more apparent than in the conditions of virtual liveness I propose in Chapters 6 and 7. The figuration of the musically performing cyborg exemplifies the synthesis of musician and machine so central to my overall concept of liveness and, especially, to that of virtual liveness—a liveness in which musician and machine perform meaning in equal measure.

In the course of presenting these arguments, however, I leave many important questions unanswered, all of which I hope to see addressed in the near future as the vital issue of liveness finds its way into increasingly more musicological discourse. Most pressing among these would be a deeper investigation into categories of liveness not thoroughly addressed, or perhaps not even introduced, in this document. Despite the rather straight-forward descriptions I offer of temporal liveness and spatial liveness, each of these conditions of liveness begs much further scrutiny, not least because of the extent to which they have already been invoked in the literature without much recourse to in-depth, analytical discussion. I make reference in Chapter 5 to instances where the presentation of prerecorded material alongside live material complicates the issue of performative temporality. The use of multiple loudspeakers to project sound to different locations within a performance space (not to mention the broadcasting of perfor-mance over the radio or the use of the Internet to connect musickers over great distances) presents similar complications to the issue of performative spatiality. Both of these situations are found frequently in art-music and popular-music practices and as such present numerous opportunities for future investigation.

The importance of spontaneity to many understandings of performance and the extent to which mediatized performance contexts play with this sense of spontaneity also warrant deeper inquiry. For instance, although a typical performance of mixed music presents a prerecorded fixed-media element lacking in any type of spontaneity, a liveness of spontaneity may still be found in the ways an instrumentalist responds to these prerecorded sounds. Certainly, a sense of spontaneity is also an important part of any inter-musician interactions in ensemble performance; an investigation into how electronic mediation alters this particular sense of liveness in various performance contexts might reveal much about how the idea of spontane-ity informs our various understandings of performance. Finally, although I often refer to notions of performer skill and to the uniqueness of a live per-formance event in discussions of my seven categories of liveness, it seems to me that these concepts could very well warrant consideration as individual categories themselves. Again, drawing lines between these different catego-ries is often a difficult thing to do, and a slight shift in perspective can easily cause a redrawing of lines. One such redrawing might lead to discussions of a liveness of virtuosity or a liveness of uniqueness/individuality.

In addition to these underexplored conditions of liveness in contem-porary musical practice, I leave many avenues regarding specific musical styles and genres uninvestigated. For example, my discussions of hip-hop practices in the previous chapter are cursory, at best. But as I hope to demonstrate even within those brief discussions, there is much still to address in hip-hop music with respect to new understandings of liveness— certainly much more than I begin to suggest within these pages. I also do not address (with the possible exception of Oswald's rather unique and highly mediatized *plunderphonics*) the implications of common studio practices in the creation of much modern pop music. Although I offer brief nods to the potentially dehumanizing uses of Auto-Tune technologies, for instance, I do not address the potential for liveness in music that features such high levels of mediatization through these technologies (the music of Imogen Heap comes to mind here). Within art-music practices, several genres of mediatized performance not discussed here also have much to offer an investigation into the construction and reception of liveness. Chief among these may very well be the practices of *interactive composition* to which I allude in Chapter 5. I very briefly recognize the role that Internet technologies are currently playing in the reconfiguration of the concept of liveness, but a more extensive discussion of this topic would teach us much about the place of music within a modern cyberculture. Laptop performance (whether networked or un-networked) and the construction of musically performing robots also offer rich examples of newly configured conditions of liveness.

In all these suggested areas of future research, as in each of my own case studies within this book, I propose the study of liveness with very particular goals in mind, for liveness is more than a means by which to identify or describe music ("That performance is live, whereas this recording is not."). Liveness, at least as presented here, is a means by which to *understand* music: how it is made, how it is heard, and how it creates particular meanings for both those creating it and those hearing it. The concept of liveness has always been invoked in reference to electronic mediation in music, although this has often been done in a clumsy or simplistic fashion, calling only on the binary *live/recorded* to fully explain its meaning. I argue here for a more sophisticated model of analysis that allows for more precise and nuanced understandings of the often subtly differentiated musician/ machine relationships explored in mediatized music.

My offering of a new analytical approach to liveness in music is not meant to suggest, however, that *all* music ought to be understood as somehow live. For instance, much acousmatic music (particularly music composed by some of the high-Modernist composers discussed in Chapter 5) would prove rather resistant to an analysis directed at qualities of liveness. If everything were considered live, in fact, one might ask what utility the whole trope of liveness has to offer. I do, however, suggest that the idea of liveness can and ought to be deployed more regularly within analyses of mediatized music and, moreover, that liveness still warrants continued rigorous theorizing within the musicological discipline more broadly. As an important step toward these goals, I offer here several interrogations of liveness where liveness may not previously have been considered. There is still much work to be done before we exhaust the analytical possibilities of this concept. As musicology progresses through the twenty-first century— a century whose cultural practices promise to be characterized, even more than those of the twentieth, by their relationships with electronic technologies—we would do well to adopt a vocabulary and a means of analysis appropriate to the task of understanding these relationships. I offer some of the constituents of such a vocabulary here.

Notes

NOTES TO CHAPTER 1

1. As has been argued by Auslander (2008), Gracyck (1996), and others, many recordings of popular music have assumed the status of "primary text" (Moore 2001) against which most fans judge any subsequent live performances.
2. Auslander (2008), Couldry (2004), Emmerson (2007), and Wurtzler (1992), among others, all argue that if it is to reflect the complexities of contemporary performance environments, the discourse of liveness must move beyond the binary construction of live/mediated to a more nuanced and flexible concept. Although not all scholars focus exclusively (or at all, in some cases) on liveness in *music*, the foundational opposition between live and recorded (or otherwise "artificial") performance remains consistent throughout the literature.
3. For instance, see John Philip Sousa's 1906 polemic, "The Menace of Mechanical Music" (reprinted in Sousa 1993). Although it predates the emergence of the term *live*, it is typical of later liveness discourse in its attack on recorded music. Sousa argues that "these talking and playing machines [will] reduce the expression of music to a mathematical system of megaphones, wheels, cogs, disks, cylinders, and all manner of revolving things, which are as like real art as the marble statue of Eve is like her beautiful, living, breathing daughters" (1993, 14). His invocation of "living, breathing" humans in contrast with the artificial is also telling.
4. For a thorough explanation of the terms *musicking* and *musickers*, see Small (1998), as discussed more briefly below.
5. Musicological literature of the last few decades has featured prominent debates about other concepts through which broader musical and cultural meaning is understood. For instance, Historically Informed Performance scholars have paid much attention to the concept of *authenticity* (see Leech-Wilkinson [1984] and Taruskin [1995] for a small sampling of this literature). Similarly, the concept of the musical work has given rise to important scholarship by Ashby (2010), Cook (2003), Goehr (1992), and others. Central to both of these debates has been much discussion about exactly what these concepts or terms represent and how best to define them—concerns that feature prominently throughout this book.
6. The extent to which this last statement is true depends on the broadcast practices of the particular program on which the performance takes place. Many nightly talk shows film much earlier in the day, for instance, while other programs employ a short time delay (even of only a few seconds). Nevertheless, many audiences still attach a temporal sense of liveness to any television broadcast of an original (as opposed to rerun) program, regardless of when

(and how) that program was actually recorded. For more in-depth discussions of televisual liveness, see Couldry (2004) and Feuer (1983).

7. This phrase is Glenn Gould's (see Gould and McClure 1968). Gould frequently remarked that he preferred the environment of the recording studio to that of the concert hall, in part because the studio offers the option of beginning again if one is unhappy with how the performance has begun or of trying a few different interpretations and then working with those during the production process, outside the pressures of the performance moment. This type of practice, obviously, is completely unwelcome within the conventions of live performance, at least of traditional art music.

8. I am well aware of Auslander's argument (2008) that liveness in fact *has* lost all cultural currency and present here an alternate reading. My reasons for this difference of opinion are fully explained below.

9. I often use the term *performance* in a broad sense to include actual performances *and* other representations or conceptualizations of them.

10. I, however, confine my discussions of liveness primarily to Western musical contexts, acknowledging where possible related issues in theatrical, televisual, online, and other relevant experiences (and, as we have already seen, these different cultural fields often intersect). One of the regrettable characteristics of much liveness scholarship has been a tendency to define theories only as they apply to a limited field of cultural activity (e.g., contemporary electronic art music, television broadcasts, etc.), to the extent that these theories are often similarly limited in their ability to help us understand liveness in other fields (and shared experiences between fields). I attempt here to avoid this trap as much as possible—all the while cognizant of my primary concern with, and bias toward, musical contexts—recognizing liveness as a shared cultural concept that draws its significance in part from the ubiquity of electronic technologies across modern Western culture and not just from activity confined to one particular medium or cultural discipline.

11. As he hints here, Auslander essentially limits his discussion of mediatization (and, by extension, liveness) to culture in which *reproduction* (i.e., recording) is the primary technological process at work. More specifically, his concern is mostly with the social and economic implications of *mass reproduction*. Although reproduction is always part of the mediatization I discuss (even the simple act of amplification is technically a reproduction), I often consider mediatized performance that exists largely outside, or at least partially subverts, the economies of mass circulation (i.e., popular culture) so prominently explored in Auslander's (and Baudrillard's) usage.

12. Auslander's account of the ideology of rock (2008, Ch. 3), as based on the common impression of rock as a performing art (despite its ontological foundation in recordings), is more nuanced and creates a certain tension against his theoretical explanation of what liveness "is," as discussed here. I return to a discussion of rock's ideology in Chapter 4.

13. The emphasis on music's broad social context has been an essential part of developments in musicological study over the past three decades or so, as demonstrated especially in the work of Born (1995), Cook (2001, 2003, 2007), Cottrell (2004), Kerman (1985), Kingsbury (1988), Leppert (1993, 2007), and McClary (1991, 1992, 2004), among many others. The value of considering music as a socially *performed* art rather than as a collection of reified objects (i.e., works manifest in the form of scores) has been argued particularly convincingly by Cook (2001, 2003) and Small (1998; as discussed above). My approach to liveness owes much to this perspective, because liveness finds its greatest significance within this arena of social performance. The significance of the individual subject in the creation of

musical meaning has also been emphasized in recent musicological work. For instance, Cumming's *The Sonic Self: Musical Subjectivity and Significa-tion* (2000), as its title implies, argues for the importance of listening and performing subjects; Emmerson (2007, 29–31) asks what any given musi-cal experience means "to me"; Norman (2004, 8–11) describes an indirect communication and a kind of secondhand performance that she enacts as she listens to a particular piece of electroacoustic music rich in recognisable sound sources. As to understanding liveness as a musical element worthy of musicological analysis, important steps in this direction have already been taken by Emmerson (2007). I discuss Emmerson's work in greater detail in the following chapters.

Compared to the musicological traditions represented above, popular-music studies have become much more comfortable, much more quickly, with the idea that recognizing music's social contexts and roles and identifying a listening subject offers crucial insight into the determination of the potential communicative meanings of any given piece of music (demonstrating in this instance, perhaps, much more of a debt to precursors in the fields of folk-lore study, ethnomusicology, sociology, and media and cultural studies, than to any Western-musicological model). Among the many major foundational studies to emphasise the importance of listener subjectivity, for instance, are Frith (1981, esp. Pt. III) and Middleton (1990, esp. Ch. 5 and 7).

14. In addition to its ability to signify complex relationships between multiple contributing elements, the analogy of the network is also useful in a discus-sion of modern mediatized music for the way it suggests that such relation-ships are electronically enabled.

15. I do not deny that very real distinctions exist between these different cat-egories, nor that recognizing these distinctions is often important in the academic discussion of music (for all that clarifying these distinctions has proven to be a very difficult task, as demonstrated by Ashby [2010], Bowen [1993], Cook [2001, 2003], Goehr [1992], and many others). I argue, how-ever, that a productive discussion of liveness must often recognize ways in which these categories overlap and meld.

NOTES TO CHAPTER 2

1. Crisell (2012) offers a slightly different perspective on the introduction of liveness in his account of liveness in radio and television broadcasting. He argues that radio, from its inception, introduced liveness to mass commu-nications, which had previously relied on media that had to record infor-mation for later dissemination (newspapers, audio recordings, etc.). Crisell's approach to liveness is somewhat different than that of Auslander, Thornton, or myself, however, in that he discusses it narrowly as an ontological cat-egory based in its temporal dimension (i.e., live broadcasts convey to their audiences something that is happening "right now") rather than as a concept attached to ontologically varied experiences.

2. Perhaps the most enthusiastic statement of a technological Modernism in music from the early twentieth century, and certainly the most colorful in its rhetoric, is the Italian Futurist Luigi Russolo's 1913 manifesto "The Art of Noises" (Russolo 1986), in which he describes newly invented instruments designed to imitate, among other things, the noises of modern civilization. I discuss Russolo and Futurist music more thoroughly in Chapter 5.

3. See also Derrida (1976), in which his deconstruction of the speech/writ-ing binary at work in various linguistic theories is central to his critique of

logocentrism: the privileging of thought, reason, or logic over the signs or acts in which that thought or reason is made materially manifest.

4. For instance, Ashby links a suspicion of the recording in art-music discourse to a fear of the "marauding machine" (2010, 13) in Western culture more broadly. He contends that classical musicologists have historically been unwilling to address the significance of recordings because of a misplaced and somewhat superstitious belief that they distract the listener's attention from the transcendental work and focus it instead on a frozen (and infinitely repeated/repeatable) interpretation of that work.

5. Les Paul identifies his 1948 hit "Lover" (on Paul 1991, CD 1) as the first recording in which he was able to combine all the recording techniques he had been developing over the previous decade or so in one recording. Most notably, the track features eight simultaneous guitar parts, all played by Paul, several of which were recorded at different speeds so they sound faster and higher or slower and lower on the final record than as they were originally performed in his home recording studio (see Cunningham 1998, 23–34; Shaughnessy 1993, 124–43; Waksman 2010, 272). I elaborate further on Schaeffer's *musique concrète* and German *elektronische Musik* in Chapter 5.

6. Early radio crooners (or microphone singers, as Lockheart [2003] calls them) included Rudy Vallee, Kate Smith, and, most famously, Bing Crosby. Billie Holiday and Frank Sinatra were among the crooners to develop their microphone singing styles primarily in front of big bands (although these performances took place usually for the purpose of radio broadcast as well). Lockheart (2003) offers a good account of the historical emergence of the microphone singing style. Like Lockheart, Chanan (1995) and Frith (1986) also emphasize that the central aesthetic of this style was based on the capabilities of the electric microphone. Perhaps reflecting a difference in the reception of crooning between British and North American audiences, Frith (1986, 264–265) relates that many of these singers were actually perceived as somehow perverse, or *un*natural, by some British critics.

7. Despite early experiments by Cage and a few other composers and performers, widespread performance of electronic art music did not occur until the 1960s. See Manning (2004, 157–167) for a brief discussion of these developments.

8. *Synchronisms No. 6, for Piano and Electronic Sounds* (1970) remains a standard example of this genre. See Davidovsky (1972) for a score of this work; it can be heard on Petrowska Quilico (2003).

9. Gould was one of the first writers to address these concerns about electronic technology in art-music practice. See, for example, Gould (1966) and (1999a).

10. Heard on Varèse (1998a, CD 2).

11. Although the term *acousmatic* technically refers to any music heard over loudspeakers or headphones, I use it in reference to recorded (i.e., nonperformed) electronic art music—what has sometimes been called *tape music* or *fixed-media music*—in keeping with the term's normal use in art music (see Smalley 1992, 552 n. 1).

12. Frampton's "Do You Feel Like We Do" and "Show Me the Way" from his seminal 1976 album *Frampton Comes Alive!* (Frampton 2003) feature extensive use of the Talk Box. Roger Troutman of soul/funk band Zapp was another prolific Talk Box user; Zapp's "More Bounce to the Ounce" (1980; on Zapp 1989a) and "Computer Love" (1985; on Zapp 1989b) provide excellent examples of Troutman's synthesizer-based (rather than guitar-based) Talk Box vocals. See Frampton ("Tutorial") for more on controlling the device in performance. Tomkins (2010, 131–145) gives an excellent account of Talk Box performances by Frampton, Troutman, and others.

13. Arguments to this effect are expressed throughout two recent collections of essays on the study of recorded music published by Cambridge University Press: *Recorded Music: Performance, Culture and Technology* (Bayley 2010) and *The Cambridge Companion to Recorded Music* (Cook et al. 2009).

14. A substantial amount of literature is dedicated specifically to the study of electronic art music. A portion of this literature deals with performance and, as would be expected, with the implications of using electronic technology in the performance of music. Consideration of this literature is reserved for my focused discussions of liveness, in this and other chapters, as much of it addresses one type of liveness or another rather directly.

15. In opera, the historically changing performance of gender has played out with particular significance in the case of the castrato. Along these lines, J. Q. Davies (2005) argues that the demise of the castrato in the early nineteenth century corresponds to changing values regarding the normative performance of masculinity and gender differentiation in Western European culture. Beginning in the 1970s, glam-rock artists, such as David Bowie (and many since then who have felt Bowie's enormous influence), have deliberately performed varied and ambiguous representations of gender and sexuality in an open embrace of the performative power of popular music—its identity as "show business" (see Auslander 2006b).

16. Foremost among these warnings are Ellul's *The Technological Society* (1964), Heilbroner's "Do Machines Make History?" (1967), and Mumford's "Authoritarian and Democratic Technics" (1964). For a similar (and more recent) critique of technological "progress" at Boulez's IRCAM, see Born's *Rationalizing Culture: IRCAM, Boulez, and the Institutionalization of the Musical Avant-Garde* (1995).

17. A more welcoming stance toward the use of modern technologies in performance art can be found in two recent collections of essays edited by Broadhurst and Machon (2006, 2010).

18. Within theater studies, Barker (2003) and Reason (2006) present excellent examples of empirical audience-based research into various understandings of liveness.

19. Finally, for an articulated approach to *authenticity* similar to my approach to liveness, see Taylor (1997).

20. "To an ever greater degree the work of art reproduced becomes the work of art designed for reproducibility. From a photographic negative, for example, one can make any number of prints; to ask for the 'authentic' print makes no sense" (Benjamin 1968, 226).

21. Ashby (2010) also invokes Benjamin's concept of aura throughout his account of the place of recordings in the contemporary consumption of absolute art music.

22. Auslander's references, for example, to repeated identical performances all over the world of the Ronald McDonald character (1999, 49–50) seem appropriate to an account of auratically deficient performances.

23. Auslander's account of the authenticity of rock records (2008, Ch. 3) differs slightly from that of Gracyck, who argues that this authenticity stems not from the record's relationship with a live performance but from its primary position within the "history of production" of rock songs (1996, 32): First comes the master tape, then the recorded copies, then the live performances. For Gracyck, the key defining feature of rock is that it is created in a recording studio—everything else, including performance, is incidental. My own sympathies lie more with Auslander than with Gracyck, as I agree with Auslander's assessment that the aura associated with live performance (temporal

liveness and spatial liveness) is as essential to rock ideology as are the sounds of the record. I discuss this perception more thoroughly in Chapter 4.

24. Individual sounds can be treated with reverberation to give the aural impression that they exist within specific spatial limitations. Manipulation of the stereo field can give the impression of sounds moving along a left-right axis.

25. Auslander likewise adopts this temporally oriented concept of liveness in his recent accounts of liveness in an Internet environment (2002, 2005), where he argues that because of the commonality of live broadcasts, "Our current conception of liveness emphasizes a temporal relationship of simultaneity more than a physical relationship of co-presence" (2005, 8). Although I agree with his connection of temporal liveness to the prevalence of Internet use, his generalized statement about "our current conception of liveness" leaves little room for the kinds of elaborations on liveness that I undertake here.

26. In preparing his essay, Gould interviewed several leading musical figures of the day, such as composers, performers, artists' managers, and record-company executives, including Mohr. In its original version (Gould 1966), the essay includes selections from these interviews along the margins of the text, which creates a wonderful dialogue between Gould's own arguments and the often-opposing views of others. Unfortunately, these inserts (including Mohr's comment) are not included in the 1990 reprint edition with which most readers are familiar, somewhat diminishing the essay's original power. All subsequent references to this essay are thus to the original edition. For an online version of Gould's text that includes the marginal inserts, see www.collectionscanada. gc.ca/glenngould/028010–4020.01-e.html (accessed May 1, 2012).

27. See also Auslander's account of the Milli Vanilli lip-synching scandal of 1990 and its aftermath within the popular music industry and of a similar incident in 2004 when Ashlee Simpson was caught lip-synching during a performance on *Saturday Night Live* (2008, Ch. 3). The broad implications of an industry's ideology of performance, based in large part on what I describe as liveness of fidelity, are thoroughly discussed in Auslander's work.

28. Paradoxically, the disdain for technology that imposes itself *audibly* (i.e., "sound[s] like a radio or phonograph") was not matched by a disdain for technology that imposes itself *visibly*. Indeed, the fetishization of large, visible, tactile machines is demonstrated by Keightley (1996, 151) to have been a very important part of the male cult of hi-fi in the late 1940s and 1950s. In this case, the negative valuation of technology only extends as far as its imposition on the "true" sound of music. As Keightley argues, many aspects of the hi-fi culture were not related to music at all but rather to an effort on the part of men to reclaim domestic space in the face of increased feminine values in the post-WWII American home.

Schafer (1994) presents another use of the term *hi-fi* in his discussion of hi-fi and lo-fi soundscapes. Although it has very little, if anything, to do with liveness as I present it here, Schafer's perspective similarly presents the term *hi-fi* with all the positive valuation one would expect, because he uses it to describe soundscapes that are free of "interference": "The hi-fi soundscape is one in which discrete sounds can be heard clearly because of the low ambient noise level. The country is generally more hi-fi than the city; night more than day; ancient times more than modern" (1994, 43).

29. On the other hand, recorded studio performances regularly achieve a much more consistent level of excellence than do live performances, due largely to the opportunity to rerecord unsuccessful attempts. Despite the lack of chance/spontaneity involved, some listeners and performers (such as Gould) prefer the assured standard of performance offered by the recording process.

30. Gould famously retired from the concert stage in 1964, at the unprecedented age of thirty-one. He continued to record, write, and produce radio and television programs until the year of his death, 1982.

31. Several music scholars have recently argued (explicitly or implicitly) for the same shift in discourse I observe here: from discussions of music as a collection of notes and abstract musical structures to discussions of music as physical/embodied expression and reception. This emphasis is especially reflected in the titles of much of this work: "The Operatic Scandal of the Singing Body: Voice, Presence, Performativity" (Duncan 2004), "Analyzing from the Body" (Fisher and Lochhead 2002), *Boccherini's Body: An Essay in Carnal Musicology* (Le Guin 2006), and "Bodily Hearing: Physiological Metaphors and Musical Understanding" (Mead 1999) are just a few examples, let alone the large body of work from the past two decades by music psychology scholars dedicated to the empirical study of the perception of bodily expression in music or the empathetic bodily perception of motion in music. See, for example, A. Cox (2001), Davidson (1991, 1993), Shove and Repp (1995), and Todd (1995). Cusick (1994) argues that when musicology (as it has traditionally been practiced) focuses only on the composer's texts and intentions, it denies the presence of bodies in making music, thus exercising a gendered preference for masculine thought (the composers' and analysts' minds) over feminine presence (as *body* is typically cast as the feminine, and thus subordinate, half of the mind/body binary). Similar arguments can be found in Cumming (2000).

32. I maintain that all *perception*, even of acousmatic music, is embodied—hence the centrality of corporeality to my account of liveness.

33. I would argue that a music scholarship similarly based solely on the perspective of the performer or listener would also lack this very important social orientation.

34. McMullen defines a similar concept, *intercorporeality*, as referring to "face-to-face embodied collaborations" (2006, 64). As many of the relationships explored in this book occur not face-to-face but "through the technosphere," as it were, *intercorporeity* remains a more suitable term for my use than *intercorporeality* (except, of course, for discussions of particularly nonmediatized interaction). I should note that these terms are not intrinsically different from a strictly linguistic perspective—both denote a relationship between or among material (in our case, human) bodies. In the interest of maintaining (or helping establish) consistent scholarly usage, however, I observe this difference between the two terms.

35. This includes "exterior" movements, such as walking and descending, and "interior" movements, such as the beating of a heart.

36. Here, the relationship between Conant's subversive performances and Butler's description of the performativity of gender is impossible to ignore, although Butler—in fact, any discussion of performativity—is curiously absent from McMullen's arguments.

37. See my discussion of performance networks in Chapter 5.

NOTES TO CHAPTER 3

1. As Lydia Goehr (1992) suggests, since circa 1800, works of Western art music have generally been considered to be unique (and entirely reified) objects representative of a specialized genius labor (composition). The usual existence of these works in written scores reiterates this reification.

2. Hoffmann's views are particularly significant to my account of this historically consistent perspective on music and mind, due to the extent to which
his writings served as models for a developing style of Germanic music criticism in the nineteenth century (see Strunk's introduction to Hoffmann [1998,
1193]). Twentieth-century musicology, and evidently Gould's own approach
to the evaluation of music, grew out of this very tradition.

3. For a further discussion of phallogocentrism, see especially Derrida (1979).

4. Jacques Attali links this concept further to relationships of power as they
are carried out in the social practice of music, particularly focusing on the
increasing commodification of music through history. Although I do not
engage with Attali's economic discussions, I believe that his poetic use of the
word *noise* (*bruit*, in the original French) fits well in the context of a mind/
body discussion of musical value.

5. The reference here is to the so-called Second Viennese School, usually considered to comprise Arnold Schoenberg and his pupils, Anton Webern and
Alban Berg. Gould was about to publish a short monograph about Schoenberg (Gould 1964) and had also given several talks on the topic of twelve-
tone music.

6. Indeed, as I discuss below, this is how Gould often described his relationship
with the piano and with the music he played.

7. A further glance at the Gould bibliography reveals several more titles
announcing a similar focus on Gould's intellect and its products. See, for
example, *Philosopher at the Keyboard* (Angilette 1992), *The Idea of Gould*
(Bergman 1999), and "The Zany Genius of Glenn Gould" (Gould and Bester
1964). Significantly, the book that deals more than any other with Gould's
physiological issues still maintains the "mind" bias: Peter Ostwald's *Glenn
Gould: The Ecstasy and Tragedy of Genius* (1997). Georges Leroux (2010)
also offers serious consideration of Gould's body (see esp. Ch. 3, "The Hands
of Gould, the Body of Glenn") but ultimately establishes the same bias to
which I am referring here: one in which Gould's body is depicted as an
unwilling (because imperfect) servant to his unique genius.

8. Late in his career, Gould struggled to maintain complete control over his
left hand. Roberts's comments on this struggle present a clear image of a
mind under attack by a body: "Gould's effort to control every function of
his performing mechanism made superhuman demands on his mind and it
seems that, at times, when he relaxed these demands and concentrated on the
music, he achieved better results" (1999, 25).

9. A *New York Times* article by Bernard Holland presents a scathing criticism of pianists (including Gould) whose physical "histrionics" apparently
"undermine the music." Holland offers two categories of musicians: the
Apollonian, which refers to "symmetry, invention and elegance," and the
Dionysian, which refers "to art more from the gut, more spontaneous." He
concludes, "Dionysian pianists care about Dionysian pianists, whereas Apollonian pianists care about music" (*New York Times*, February 6, 2008).
Clearly, the mind/body problem is hard at work in this piece. Curiously, Holland lumps Gould in solely with the Dionysians in this particular context.

10. Gould worked very hard to promote a particular image of himself. My own
impression is that some of his mannerisms and pronouncements were as
much adopted (or at least exaggerated) for the sake of this image as they were
reflections of his true thoughts and feelings. Nevertheless, the persona Gould
crafted for himself *was* accepted by a vast public. As I am concerned here
with the Gould discourse more than with the conditions of Gould's private
reality (whatever they may have been), I relate his professed beliefs without
questioning their veracity.

11. Elsewhere (Gould and Braithwaite 1999, 41), Gould explains that one of the reasons he avoids so much Romantic piano repertoire is that it requires more arm strength in *fortissimo* passages than he can generate given his low seating position.

12. As discussed above, Roberts relates that in 1977, Gould actually did suffer from a loss of manual control. He explains to Roberts that "his hands were 'out of sync' with his mind" (Roberts 1999, 24).

13. See Bazzana (2003, 194–197) for further explanation. During the ensuing legal discussions, Gould argued that he was of a particularly frail disposition and that he had previously warned the people at Steinway that they should accordingly avoid unnecessary physical contact with him.

14. *Audio imaging* is the term often applied to the practice of creating a spatially visualizable sound field on a recording, through stereo placement, careful use of reverberation (to create the aural impression of distance), and other techniques.

15. In this, parallels with Merleau-Ponty's foundational arguments (as discussed in Chapter 2) are evident. For instance, Merleau-Ponty writes, "The perceiving subject is not [an] absolute thinker; rather, it functions according to a natal pact between our body and the world, between ourselves and our body" (1964, 6). More recently, neuroscientists have provided empirical evidence to support the assertion that "a disembodied mind as such does not exist" (Leman 2008, 13). See, for example, Damasio (2000) and Jeannerod (2002).

16. See also Fisher and Lochhead (2002, 47), who do not offer a new label but argue that listeners "engage musical sounds with their bodies in the creative and improvisatory process of understanding. Although listeners' embodied experience may involve little or no visible movement, their performative enaction of musical meaning has an intercorporeal dimension."

17. See, for example, Gould and McClure (1968).

18. As Bazzana (1997, 240, 247) discusses, Gould's usual microphone placement, particularly for the contrapuntal works he favored, was about five feet from the piano, which provided a closer, "dryer" perspective than that demonstrated in most classical piano recordings by his contemporaries.

19. It is widely accepted that art-music recordings, particularly in Gould's time, embrace a "documentary" aesthetic (Toynbee 2000, 70) in an effort to replicate the concert situation as closely as possible.

20. In an essay on jazz pianist Keith Jarrett's "extraneous" singing and gesticulating that has many parallels with the current chapter, Jairo Moreno links the types of criticisms aimed at Jarrett and Gould (and, I would suggest, Gould's own criticisms of his singing) with an abiding system of discipline within Western musical practice and discourse that "seeks . . . to control movement and gesture. These elements are controlled because there is in place a conventional belief in the role of the performer; thus the articulations and gesticulations of the body are part of the mechanics of reproduction, but not, perversely enough, of the articulation of meaning" (1999, 81). My thanks to Alan Stanbridge for bringing this article to my attention.

21. Regarding my choice of recorded sources, I ought to point out that I have sought recordings in which Gould's corporeal liveness is most perceptible, regardless of format. In some cases, the original vinyl issues have proven better sources in this regard, and in others, CD reissues seem to portray these elements more clearly. Further, I have listened to these materials in front of a conventional stereo-speaker array and through headphones (although in most cases, headphone listening reveals more detail than "open-air" listening). I have also listened to each recording with a variety of equalization

settings, experimenting until these traces of Gould's body are most audible. I have adopted this varied approach to these sources, rather than observing a strict listening methodology, to reflect as much as possible the variety of contexts in which any group of Gould listeners may encounter these recordings. As what I propose in this chapter is a strategy for hearing corporeal liveness in recordings, it is important to emphasize that listeners may employ their recording playback technology in whatever way necessary to make that corporeal liveness most evident. It is significant, however, that often listeners must indeed work very hard to hear even faint traces of corporeality in recordings. This is because, in many cases, recording technicians work very hard themselves to scrub these sounds from recordings, precisely for the reasons outlined by Corbett above: The people making these recordings subscribe to a "fantasy of absolutely independent music." As Corbett further suggests, and as Burston (1998) clearly argues, this fantasy of independent music and its resulting erasure of the sounds of performing bodies often align with the financial interests influencing the commercial production of music.

22. Particularly audible breaths occur at 0:07, 0:26, 1:18, 4:30, 4:45, and 5:16 (timings refer to the progression of the individual variation, separately tracked on Gould [2002, CD 2], rather than to the progression of the entire work).

23. Gould (2002, CD 2). The piano score is reproduced from Bach (1943, 54).

24. I often refer to timings in recordings and to measure numbers in written scores. I include measure numbers as a convenience to readers but with a very particular goal in mind: Elements of liveness in a performance are not necessarily encoded in a *work* as it is represented in a score, but their perception may very well derive—as in my interpretations of Gould's recordings—from a performer's physical efforts to represent that score in performance. The score, then (to appropriate Cook's [2001, 2003] arguments about scores and performances), is a potential *script for liveness*.

25. Gould (2002, CD 2). The piano score is reproduced from Bach (1943, 5), with a slight alteration to the thirty-second-note rhythm to reflect Gould's performance.

26. At 0:09 in Variation 5 (Gould 2002, CD 2), a similar vocal swell allows us momentarily to hear Gould's voice clearly over a rather busy piano part, which obscures his vocalizations throughout the rest of the variation. This increase in vocal energy indicates an embodied voice asserting itself over and above the sounds of what Gould would have considered the "music" (i.e., the pitches of the composition as played on the piano).

27. Of course, I can only hazard a guess, but the inclusion of this noise on the recording seems to me an inadvertent result of allowing the microphones to capture the last of the piano's decay, and of Gould's releasing the pedal before the decay had naturally ended, rather than a deliberate attempt to end the piece with a bit of piano noise.

28. Both examples from Bach ([1731] n.d., 22).

29. Lyrics are provided in the liner notes to Lerche (2004) and can also be accessed online at www.metrolyrics.com/two-way-monologue-lyrics-sondre-lerche.html (accessed May 1, 2012).

NOTES TO CHAPTER 4

1. *Shorter Oxford English Dictionary*, 6th ed., s.v. "fidelity."

2. Throughout this chapter, I frequently use the phrase *liveness of fidelity* and the phrase *fidelity to liveness*, depending on context. When I wish to emphasize a perceived quality of liveness, I use *liveness of fidelity*, in keeping with

the way in which I have been indicating such categories of liveness throughout the book. When I wish to emphasize The White Stripes' perceived *commitment* to a live aesthetic, I use *fidelity to liveness*. Despite these subtle differences, I believe the two concepts are very closely related, particularly in the context of the discussions I undertake here, and work together in the construction of The White Stripes' perceived authenticity.

3. Jack White is a musical figure who has much in common with Glenn Gould: Both have expressed very carefully constructed ideologies regarding their musicking, and both have likewise shared very carefully constructed images of themselves—images that are closely intertwined with these ideologies. As in my discussions of Gould in Chapter 3, I am here concerned primarily with The White Stripes' (and thus Jack White's) professed and accepted ideological values and activities rather than with their veracity. Although closer scrutiny of many of these ideological values, as expressed here, may very well bear interesting and informative results, such concerns are not within the purview of the current chapter.

4. Although the duo officially disbanded in February 2011, they maintain an active presence, particularly for fans, by way of a still-functioning official website (www.whitestripes.com; accessed May 1, 2012), continued releases of previously unreleased material via Jack White's Third Man Records label, and continued circulation of The White Stripes mythology by fans on such websites as YouTube.com. In other words, although the band no longer performs or records together, they still seem (at least at the time of publication) to exist for many fans "in the present." Therefore, I find it appropriate to adopt the present tense in this chapter in reference to their perceived image and ideologies.

5. The first three studio albums of The White Stripes—*The White Stripes*, *De Stijl*, and *White Blood Cells*, from 1999, 2000, and 2001, respectively—were all released by the independent label Sympathy for the Record Industry. All three were reissued by Third Man Records/V2 Records in 2002. Thus, for *The White Stripes*, see The White Stripes (2002c); for *De Stijl*, see The White Stripes (2002a); for *White Blood Cells*, see The White Stripes (2002b).

6. I draw here especially from Simon Frith (1981), who treats this topic from a wide variety of perspectives; Lawrence Grossberg (1992, esp. Ch. 8), who offers an understanding of rock authenticity in the context of the emergence of postmodernity; and Keir Keightley (2001), who offers a broad perspective on the concept of authenticity in rock and other forms of popular music. Other useful contributions to the discussion of authenticity include Auslander (2008, Ch. 3), Frith (1986, 1996, 2007), Gracyck (1996), and Grossberg (1994).

7. Joe Hagan of *The New York Times*, for instance, writes, "They have made rock rock again by returning to its origins as a simple, primitive sound full of unfettered zeal" (*The New York Times*, August 12, 2001). Christopher Scapelliti (2004) of *Guitar World* introduces his piece with the claim, "In two meteoric years, Jack White has resurrected rock-and-roll and reclaimed its place in popular music." Will Welch of *Fader* magazine casts them as would-be saviors not just of rock music but of all American culture, although in an admittedly losing cause: "The White Stripes want truth, romance and beauty for a fallen America. That's impossible and they know it. There's no home for you here" (2005, 97–98).

8. For more extensive discussions of these and other inherent contradictions of rock ideology, see Frith (2007) and Keightley (2001).

9. See Grossberg (1992, 131–135). With the term *rock formation*, Grossberg is referring to the broad range of social and cultural practices within which the more specifically musical practices of rock musicians and their fans take

place. Thorough consideration of such a formation, then, must include not only the music but also the activities of production and reception involving producers, agents, labels, rock critics, publicists, and others, along with musicians and fans.

In discussing the authenticity of The White Stripes, I am primarily concerned with this authenticity *as it is promoted and commonly received* within the modern rock formation; I am not here weighing in on the debate myself, nor am I claiming that the authenticity that I discuss holds any absolute value. It should also be noted that The White Stripes (like most successful popular-music acts) have detractors as well as devoted fans. Common criticisms among these detractors, in fact, take the form of attacks on The White Stripes' authenticity.

10. Keightley (2001) also discusses the importance of the recurring (largely mistaken) perception throughout rock's history (and that of some earlier styles of popular music, as well) that it has been born outside the commercial mainstream.
11. This account very closely mirrors one offered by interviewer Andrew Perry of *Blender* magazine in 2003, presumably based on information provided by Jack (2003, 108). In a *Guitar World* interview, Jack also provides a similar description of his teenage years (Scapelliti 2004, 151).
12. Brian Wilson (like Jack White) has often acted as songwriter, performer, and producer on his recordings. Although Spector was also a songwriter, he usually shared the songwriting credits with others or left the songwriting to others entirely.
13. *Auteur* was a label first applied to film directors, such as Jean Renoir and Alfred Hitchcock, who were seen to create films that reflected, first and foremost, their own personal visions. See Wexman (2003) for a thorough treatment of this concept in film. It should be noted here how closely related this concept of auteurism, so important to ideologies of authenticity in rock and in film, is to the Romantic concept of artistic genius, as discussed in Chapter 3.
14. As addressed in Chapter 2, this interpretation of rock authenticity runs counter to Gracyck's (1996) assertions that in rock (which for Gracyck often seems to stand for most popular music in general), authenticity for consumers resides wholly in the recorded product.
15. My use of the male pronoun here is deliberate, as hi-fi technologies were marketed to, and consumed by, an overwhelmingly large male majority. For discussion of the gendered terms of hi-fi discourse, see Keightley (1996) and Taylor (2001, Ch. 4).
16. For instance, see Katz (2004, 18–19) and Symes (2004, 67) for descriptions of the "realism tests" conducted by the Edison company in the 1910s and 1920s to demonstrate the fidelity of its phonograph system, in which audiences (blindfolded or with their eyes closed) purportedly could not distinguish between live performance and recorded sound issuing from the same stage.
17. Broesche (2012) and personal communication. As Broesche puts it, "The poison becomes the cure, as that which is seen to have destroyed the aura of the art work—mechanical reproduction and mediation—becomes the very same means by which its revivification is attempted" (2012, 3). As may be evident in his choice of language, Broesche is here working in rather Benjaminian terms; I believe the concept translates equally well to discussions of liveness and fidelity that exceed Benjamin's more restrictive definition of aura (as discussed in Chapter 2). Further elaborations on the concept will be included in Broesche's forthcoming PhD dissertation from the University of Wisconsin-Madison.

18. "1969" can be heard on The Stooges (2010). "96 Tears" can be heard on ? and the Mysterians (2005).
19. Exactly which songs by The Who and Led Zeppelin Bangs had in mind can only be guessed. However, The Who had very recently (in 1969) released their "rock opera," *Tommy* (The Who 2000), which announced its artistic pretensions in its overall concept and framing as an "opera." By the time this article was published in *Creem* (November–December 1970), Led Zeppelin had just released their third studio album, and all three of their offerings to that time include examples of the complexity and artiness that Bangs seems to target: lyrical references to fantasy and mythology, as in "Immigrant Song" (on Led Zeppelin 2005c) and "Ramble On" (on Led Zeppelin 2005b), for instance; complex song forms involving multiple changes in tempo and texture in the course of a single song, as in "Dazed and Confused" (on Led Zeppelin 2005a) and "What Is and What Never Should Be" (on Led Zeppelin 2005b); and, very significantly in light of the comments quoted above, the consistently virtuosic musicianship of the band, especially guitarist Jimmy Page and drummer John Bonham.
20. See Gendron (2002, 227–247) for a discussion of aesthetic links between the writings of Lester Bangs and the emergence of punk.
21. In a piece for *Blender* magazine, "All Hail the New King and Queen of Rock," Andrew Perry explicitly places The White Stripes within this lineage of rock's saviors: "The duo is the greatest rock-and-roll band in the world. Like Nirvana, The Sex Pistols, and even The Rolling Stones before them, their music is a desperate, furious return to the basics of rock & roll" (2003, 106).
22. In *Retromania: Pop Culture's Addiction to Its Own Past* (2011), Simon Reynolds identifies an obsession with invoking past styles as a defining characteristic of popular culture in the first decade of the twenty-first century, which he labels "the 're' decade" (2011, xi). This perspective offers an alternative to my reading of the White Stripes' historicism as a recurring part of an ongoing cycle in rock music.
23. Much has also been made of Jack's refusal to use a cell phone, as is demonstrated in the epigraph at the beginning of this chapter.
24. The August 2012 issue of *Electronic Musician* magazine features Jack White on its cover, with the headline, "Preserving the Craft of Analog Recording." Because I became aware of this issue only days before sending this book to press, I was unable to consult the featured article itself. It seems, at least on the surface, however, to propagate the same image of White as a keeper of rock authenticity through his commitment to lo-fi technologies. My thanks to Garreth Broesche for bringing this to my attention.
25. This phrase is from a brief description of the lo-fi popular-music genre, found on the homepage of an online community dedicated to lo-fi music (see "Lo-Fi Music"). I quote it here as a representation of one common ideological argument for the value of lo-fi music, which is clearly in line with the broader conceptualization of technology as a mark of inauthenticity discussed above.
26. See Auner (2000) and Taylor (2001, 107–111) for comparable accounts of digital-era popular musicians associating analog technologies with an authenticity perceived to be lacking in digital technologies.
27. Jack explains that on some occasions, they deliberately break free of the constrictions of a two-piece band in the studio "to see what happens. And when we *do* break the rules, like, 'What if we do 16 tracks of vocals on this?', it's something we obviously can't do live. And people notice that, because of the structure of the band" (Murray 2007).
28. See, for instance, *Guitar World* (2006), Perry (2003, 109), and Scapelliti (2004).

29. See Théberge (1997, Ch. 9) for a discussion of attempts in some digitally produced music to capture the "feel" of liveness by employing so-called humanizing features on digital sequencers, which ultimately amount to the introduction of subtle random adjustments in timing so as to escape the otherwise "inhuman" perfection of digital technologies.

30. Also witness the difference, between the 1970s and the 1990s, in the reception of analog synthesizers, as discussed above.

NOTES TO CHAPTER 5

1. Many live electronic music groups that emerged in the 1960s functioned primarily as improvising ensembles, thus producing music that was never "composed" in the sense usually understood in Western art music. These groups include Musica Elettronica Viva (Rome), Gruppo di Improvvisazione Nuova Consonanza (Rome), and AMM (Britain). Peter Manning (2004, 161–162) provides a brief introduction to these groups.

2. See, for instance, Mumma (1975), Schrader (1982, 160–176), and Schwartz (1975, 102–127).

3. For example, Emmerson and Smalley ("Electro-Acoustic Music") and Manning (2004, 157–167).

4. The labeling of electronic music and its subgenres is a complex task, due to the vast array of terminology that has been used in different contexts to name these various musical practices and products. For instance, although some practitioners have altered the basic definition of live electronic music from its early use, others have stopped using it altogether. Some have replaced this label with "real-time electronic music" (see Emmerson 1994), while many others have begun using "music for/with live electronics." Similarly, many refer to the typical combination of acoustic instrument with prerecorded tape/CD/sound file as *mixed music*, while others use the more specifically descriptive "music for instrument(s)/voice(s) with fixed media." Because my perspective in this chapter is largely historical, I opt to observe the terminologies for musical practices that were in use during the historical periods in question, wherever possible. In instances where some confusion might arise, I attempt to clarify my chosen terminologies and their meanings. My thanks go to D. Andrew Stewart for offering his perspective on this matter.

5. As discussed in Chapter 2, Théberge (1989) laments the loss of interaction within rock groups that is often caused by multi-track recording practices. In my own experience as a flutist and choral singer, this type of interactivity also extends to performance in large groups (orchestras, choirs), even if guided by a conductor.

6. See, for example, Croft (2007) and Garnett (2001).

7. Attali especially attacks the rejection of tonal harmony and deliberate attempts to create a new dominant musical language demonstrated by composers of this music. The compositional styles of Pierre Boulez and Iannis Xenakis are particularly targeted in this criticism.

8. Jonathan Sterne (2003) similarly characterizes the Modernist approach to listening by its reification of sound: Sound became a "thing" that could be captured, measured, transformed, and rationalized. He writes, "In modern life, sound becomes a problem: an object to be contemplated, reconstructed, and manipulated, something that can be fragmented, industrialized, and bought and sold" (2003, 9).

9. Attali was working within a tradition of social theory that is particularly critical of French technocratic control. For example, Jacques Ellul levels

similar critiques (although not specific to music) in *The Technological Society* (1964; originally published in 1954).

10. See, for example, discussions by Chadabe (1997, 2) and Manning (2004, 5–7).

11. All the *Intonarumori* were mechanical devices encased in wooden boxes. As Russolo left very little description of the mechanisms themselves, all of which are believed to have been destroyed in WWII, many details about the construction of the *Intonarumori* are unknown. It is clear, however, that most of the instruments relied on various means of exciting some form of diaphragm with wire springs, metal balls, and other devices. Some models employed a small electric motor to cause the medium of excitation to vibrate. Mechanisms were activated by means of levers and switches that protruded from the boxes (including one that controlled pitch), and the sound was amplified by way of large acoustic horns. See Brown (1982) for further details.

12. Adapted from Russolo (1986, 28).

13. Futurist Balla, for example, designed a necktie that held a small electric lightbulb, which could be switched on and off by the wearer (Temkin 1983, 36).

14. Balla claimed that his painting inspired Marinetti's poem. He states, "I wanted to show that romantic 'moonlight' had been defeated by the light of the modern electric lamp. In other words, it was the end of romanticism in art: the phrase 'Let's kill off the moonlight' came from my painting" (in Marinetti 2006a, 431 n. 8).

15. Born (1995, 107–111) identifies similarly frightening connections between warfare and musical developments of technology at *Institut de Recherche et Coordination Acoustique/Musique* (IRCAM) in the mid-1980s. Rather than making it available to a larger musical community, IRCAM sold the design of its 4X synthesizer to a military organization that wanted to use it in its flight simulators.

16. In light of discussions in Chapter 3, we can also detect in Varèse's comment— that these new instruments should be "obedient to [his] thought"—another instantiation of the mind/body problem at work: Varèse's body is nowhere to be found. This divisive strategy for understanding music is often made even more apparent in acousmatic music, particularly in cases where sounds of bodies are neither recorded nor imitated electronically.

17. Cahill actually preferred to call his instrument the *dynamophone*, but telharmonium has always been the name more commonly used by others (Weidenaar 1995, 79).

18. The telharmonium generated its various timbres by way of additive synthesis: Magnetic tone wheels were each tuned to produce an individual sine tone, and several sine tones were combined at prescribed amplitudes to create the desired timbre. This method of synthesis, in addition to the telharmonium's touch-sensitive keyboard, envelope control, dynamic control, and filtering and mixing features, would form the technological basis for analog performance synthesizers in the second half of the twentieth century. Reynold Weidenaar (1995, esp. Ch. 3) provides an extensive discussion of the instrument's design.

19. Bohuslav Martinu's *Fantaisie pour theremin (ou ondes martenot), hautbois, piano, et quatuor à cordes* from 1944 (see Martinu 1973) and André Jolivet's *Concerto pour ondes martenot et orchestre* from 1952 (see Jolivet 1978), for instance, feature such use of these electronic instruments.

20. Thomas Edison patented his cylinder phonograph in 1877, while Emile Berliner patented his disc phonograph in 1887. Berliner's discs proved more durable and more popular than the tinfoil-and-wax cylinders used on the Edison model. It took another nine years, however, for Berliner's model (now

called the gramophone) to reach a state of reliability sufficient for the mass market. Pekka Gronow and Ilpo Saunio (1998) offer an excellent history of these early recording technologies.

21. "Mais le phonographe, jusqu'à présent, ne sort pas de son rôle d'archives" (Milhaud 1924). Milhaud goes on to state that the use of the phonograph had not yet developed to the same state as that of the player piano. He praises Stravinsky's use of the player piano to realize scores that could not possibly be performed on a conventional piano (by a conventional pianist).

22. Schaeffer's studio at RF began as *Studio d'Essai* in 1942 and was renamed *Club d'Essai* in 1946. Although his research into sound began in earnest with the studio's establishment, Schaeffer did not actually produce any compositions until 1948. In 1951, the studio was equipped with new tape recorders (to replace the phonographs) and renamed again as *Groupe de Recherche de Musique Concrète*. The addition of more new composers and another name change, this time to *Groupe de Recherches Musicales*, occurred in 1958 (Chadabe 1997, 26–34). As the studio is now known by this latter name, I refer to it as such in my text.

23. The studio at WDR was constructed in 1951–52 under the initial direction of Eimert. Other early studios for the composition of electronic art music included the *Studio Fonologia Musicale* established in 1955 at *Radio Audizioni Italiane* in Milan; the NHK studio established in 1953 in Tokyo; and Louis and Bebe Barron's private tape music studio in New York City, which ran from 1948–53 (Chadabe 1997, 42–51; Manning 2004, 70–75).

24. As explained in the next chapter, these associations proved more difficult to eliminate than Schaeffer had initially thought.

25. *Sinus tone* is a less commonly used term for *sine tone*.

26. A potentiometer is a common device used to adjust an assigned aspect of the signal being passed through it. The most common pots are used simply to adjust a signal's amplitude, but others may also be found, such as the pan pot, which adjusts the mix of a signal between two stereo speakers.

27. It has also been called *potentiometer d'espace* (Manning 2004, 26).

28. All the musicians at the RF studio at this time were men.

29. Adapted from Jacques Poullin, "L'apport des techniques d'enregistrement dans la fabrication de matières et de formes musicales nouvelles. Applications a la musique concrète," *L'Onde Électrique* 34/3 (March): 289. Used with permission of *Société d'Electricité, de l'Electronique et des Technologies de l'Information et de la Communication*.

30. Stockhausen and other composers at the WDR studio also employed multiple loudspeakers to localize sound throughout the performance hall. The original presentation of Stockhausen's *Gesang der Jünglinge* (1956), in which sound was distributed among five groups of loudspeakers, provides an example (see Stockhausen 1961, 68). In their approach to sound localization, however, composers working at WDR made no attempt to "perform" in the same way as the composers of *musique concrète*. The distribution of sound among various channels (and thus to various speakers) was realized during the construction of the master recordings and was in fact integrated into the total formal organization of many of the compositions (Stockhausen 1961; Théberge 1993, 170).

31. Corporeal liveness in the performance of live electronic music is explored further in Chapter 7.

32. Here I refer to the usual configuration of a solo performer with accompanimental fixed media, as I discuss in the introduction to this chapter. Of course, some mixed music has been composed for numerous performers with fixed media, in which case conventional notions of ensemble interaction may

apply between those performers. To the extent that the prerecorded material remains fixed, however, it also remains noninteractive.

33. Heard on Kagel (2003). For a score to *Transición II*, see Kagel (1963).
34. All musical instruments are machines. However, as is central to my discussion in the previous chapter, there is a long tradition of resistance to new technologies in music making, in which the traditional, established instruments are somehow seen as more organic or "natural" than the "machinelike" new instruments, which carry with them associations with an increasingly industrialized, and now electrified and digitized, society. See Pinch and Trocco (2002, 306–308).
35. Heard on Stockhausen (1995a). For a score of *Mikrophonie II*, see Stockhausen (1974).
36. *Gesang der Jünglinge* can be heard on Stockhausen (1991); *Carré* on Stockhausen (2000); and *Momente* on Stockhausen (1992).
37. The passage heard on tracks 39–48 of Stockhausen (1995a)—corresponding to Moments 6–15 in Stockhausen's score (1974)—demonstrates a range of mixes between amplified, acoustic, unmodified, and modified sounds, along with some prerecorded material (*Momente*, track 41/Moment 8; *Gesang der Jünglinge*, track 44/Moment 11).
38. Tracks 61–62/Moments 28–29 of Stockhausen (1995a) present a passage in which nonmodulated voices contrast with obviously ring-modulated voice-and-organ combinations.
39. Heard on Mumma (2002).
40. I also address the concept of interaction with respect to one *specific* example of contemporary live electronic music, Omar Daniel's *The Flaying of Marsyas*, in Chapter 7.
41. See also Oliveros (1984).
42. MAX/MSP is one of the leading programming languages used in the creation of interactive digital audio (and video) synthesis environments for music with live electronics.
43. For a more thorough description of recent activities of the Avatar Orchestra Metaverse, visit its blog, http://avatarorchestra.blogspot.ca (accessed May 1, 2012).

NOTES TO CHAPTER 6

1. According to Rosi Braidotti, a *figuration* is "a figurative style of thinking . . . a style of thought that evokes or expresses ways out of the phallocentric vision of the subject. A figuration is a politically informed account of an alternative subjectivity." She describes the cyborg figuration as "a high-tech imaginary, where electronic circuits evoke new patterns of interconnectedness and affinity" (Braidotti 1994, 1, 3). Alternatives to phallocentrism, alternative subjectivities, and interconnectedness between humans and electronic circuits all play important roles in my account of the virtual sounding cyborg.
2. Unless otherwise noted, each plunderphonic piece I discuss can be found on Oswald's retrospective collection of plunderphonics, *Plunderphonics 69/96* (Oswald 2001a). In each case, I specify the piece's original date of composition/realization as identified by Oswald, even though some of these pieces were slightly revised for inclusion on the box set.
3. Schaeffer constructed his first *musique concrète* composition, *Étude aux chemins de fer* (1948), from railway sounds. See Manning (2004, 20) for a description of the piece. See Thoresen and Hedman (2007, 132) for a succinct description of Schaeffer's concept of reduced listening, including bracketing.

4. For instance, Luc Ferrari's *Presque rien No. 1 (Le lever du jour au bord de la mer)* (1970; heard on Ferrari 1995) and Hildegard Westerkamp's *Talking Rain* (on Westerkamp 1998) both invite the listener to draw significance, and even narrative interest, from recognizable sounds of children, birds, and the seaside (in Ferrari's piece) or rain falling in natural environments (in Westerkamp's piece).

5. In some instances, this interplay occurs between what Emmerson terms *mimetic* sounds—those that are "imitative of, and referential to some aspect of the world not 'normally' found in music"—and what he terms *aural* sounds—those that are "abstract and not obviously source-referential" (2007, 14). See Emmerson (1986) for an extensive discussion of the distinctions between *mimetic* and *aural* sounds. Other useful accounts of source recognition in acousmatic music are provided in Smalley (1986, 1992) and Windsor (2000).

6. See Chapter 1, n. 13 for a brief summary of various studies of subjectivity in music.

7. A low-pass filter attenuates parts of a sound signal's frequency spectrum above a certain cut-off point. A rising low-pass filter would raise this cut-off point over time, thus increasing a sound's high-end frequencies over its duration.

8. As Sterne (2003) points out, however, listening to recordings at the turn of the twentieth century was often a more public event, as several listeners could gather around a gramophone, each with his or her own set of headphones. They could thus gather to listen "alone together" (Kenney 1999, 4), which may have seemed like a less anonymous event than a private listening situation. (My thanks to Sandra Mangsen for bringing this passage by Kenney to my attention.) The current ubiquity of MP3 players seems to have given rise to a new form of listening alone together: a bus or subway car full of people each listening to their own private audio streams, even while groups of these listeners may still be talking among themselves, is an increasingly common sight. Significantly, the *sound* of a subway ride, at least to a rider *not* plugged into a private audio stream, has not been largely altered by this development.

9. Of course, each listening space and each set of speakers will make their own sonic imprints on the music as it is heard, so no two sounding instantiations of any recording are identical. Nevertheless, the myth of identical repetition propels the dissemination of music recordings. Thus, most listeners think of listening to one copy of a CD or audio file, regardless of when or where they hear it, as being identical to listening to another.

10. Both Corbett (1990) and Burston (1998) examine listening situations in popular music—Corbett with the typical popular music recording (if such a thing exists) and Burston with the highly technologized megamusical—in which sonic illusion may also represent the not-so-innocent cleaning up of a musical surface for the purposes of creating a more profitable sound. In these cases, recorded sounds are "scrubbed" of their noisier elements, which carry with them traces of individual performing bodies (corporeal liveness), to achieve the "studio sound" expected by mass audiences (Burston 1998, 207).

11. *Shorter Oxford English Dictionary*, 6th ed., s.v. "personality."

12. Ibid., s.v. "persona."

13. Comparisons here could be drawn between personae (and liveness more generally, for that matter) and Roland Barthes's concept of writerly texts: those texts that are "rewritten" with new meaning by each individual reader. Readerly texts, by contrast, locate the reader only as a receiver of an unchanging

and essential reading. For Barthes's most cogent description of readerly and writerly texts, see *S/Z* (1974). As is demonstrated below, our writerly interpretations of a particular musically performing persona may be, at least in part, influenced by the composer's own interpretation of that persona, where such an interpretation is known.

14. Knowing this, however, has not prevented the popular imagination's long fascination with the prospect of autonomous technologies; moreover, the field of artificial intelligence continues to investigate these possibilities.

15. Although there is nothing essentially feminist about the interface between humans and machines, many writers see this potential transgression of boundaries lending itself to a model for a social politics that would productively reconfigure the gender and, to a lesser extent, racial boundaries that define our current society. See, for instance, Balsamo (1997), Braidotti (1994), and Haraway (1991).

16. Particularly Haraway (1991).

17. See Shields (2003, 12–13) and Turner (1974).

18. It has long been accepted that most popular music cannot be *exactly* duplicated in performance as it is realized on recording. As discussed in Chapter 4, many popular-music styles strive for a certain degree of correspondence between performances and recordings, so that performance remains an important part of these styles. Oswald's music is closer ontologically to popular-music styles (such as many forms of electronica) that exist primarily in recorded format and do *not* lend themselves easily to any further instantiations in live performance.

19. In addition to the discussion I offer here, see Cutler (2004) for further contextualization of plunderphonics among various other styles of performed and recorded music that rely on the reinterpretation of other recordings—what Aram Sinnreich (2010) has recently dubbed *configurable music*.

20. The plunderphonic in question here is "White" (1989).

21. Here I refer to mashups as they were originally conceived and practiced—as an entirely sample-based genre featuring the simultaneous mixture of two or more distinct recorded sources—rather than the current *Glee*-inspired understanding of mashups as arranged (and performed) medleys.

22. In addition to Oswald, Jones discusses the music of Chris Cutler, Fred Frith (both of whom were central members of the avant-rock group Henry Cow through the 1970s), John Zorn, Zeena Parkins, and several others.

23. Of significant interest within the context of the present chapter, mashups also very much invoke the virtual dimension, as the mashup community exists largely online. For more on the creative and aesthetic impetus behind mashup creation and consumption, see McGranahan (2010), Shiga (2007), and Sinnreich (2010).

24. See, for instance, "Pretender" (1988), in which Oswald applies various tempo modifications to Parton's recording of "The Great Pretender" (1984), revealing a "slightly slurring but beautiful tenor" (2001b) as the piece reaches the slower end of its tempo continuum.

25. Of his extended pop-music plunderphonic piece *Plexure* (1993), for instance, Oswald explains that he attempts to keep his "electroquotations near a tip-of-your-tongue state of recall" rather than making them too obvious (Oswald and Igma 2001, 14).

26. This is not to argue that rhythmic regularity is absent from the doo-wop style, but rather that other important features of that style are eradicated in this piece and that a new rhythmic impulse of Oswald's own creation now dominates the recording in such a way as to distance it significantly from its original doo-wop context.

27. Oswald and Igma (2001), for some unspecified but obviously deliberate reason, avoid capitalizing the personal pronoun "I" and some other proper nouns that are normally capitalized. In the interest of accuracy, I have observed this idiosyncrasy in my quotations from this source.

28. Oswald plundered several Doors tracks for "O'hell" (1990) and several Metallica tracks for "2net" (1990).

29. We now have access to "Vane" on *Plunderphonics 69/96*.

30. Better-known, similar groups from this era, also sometimes referred to as hair-metal bands, include Mötley Crüe, Poison, and Cinderella.

31. Auslander (2006a) emphasizes the important factor that genre can play in the identification and definition of individual musical personae.

32. Lyrics to Simon's recording can be found on her official website, www.carlysimon.com/vain/vain.html. A reliable transcription of lyrics to Faster Pussycat's recording can be found at www.lyricstime.com/faster-pussycat-you-re-so-vain-lyrics.html (both sites accessed May 1, 2012).

33. On the construction of gender in metal, see especially Walser (1993, Ch. 4). Despite their androgynous appearance (like that of many other glam-metal bands), Faster Pussycat has consistently projected a highly misogynistic image. Their lead singer's stage name (Taime Downe = Tie Me Down), their group name (lifted from sexploitation filmmaker Russ Meyer's 1965 film, *Faster Pussycat! Kill! Kill!* [Meyer 2005]), and many of their album covers and titles, song titles, and song lyrics work explicitly to achieve the sexual objectification of women. More specific to my discussion here, their video for "You're So Vain" also demonstrates the phallic guitar-playing gestures found in much rock (especially metal) performance, in addition to a sequence during which Downe humps a bed frame while watching the silhouette of an exotic dancer through a bedroom curtain (Faster Pussycat, "You're So Vain" video).

34. Lyrics reproduced with the permission of the composer.

35. Oswald explains that for this phrase, he clipped a short bit from each phoneme in Simon's recording so it would progress at the same tempo as Faster Pussycat's (Oswald and Igma 2001, 8).

36. Oswald reproduces the entire image in Oswald and Igma (2001, 8–9), but he states that Elektra censored Simon's breast on the *Rubaiyat* EP cover. Ironically, Elektra had previously allowed the image to be printed, as it originally appeared on the cover to an album it released.

37. In casting the (male) singer as the victim of women's sexuality, Faster Pussycat's "You're So Vain" conforms to one of metal's generic constructions of gender roles (Walser 1993, 117–120).

NOTES TO CHAPTER 7

1. The reader may wish to consult the video of a performance of this piece, provided on my website (www.paulsanden.com). Timings indicated in the text refer to this video.

2. Italian painter Tiziano Vecellio (1485–1576).

3. Although Titian has painted a pan flute into his depiction, many accounts have Marsyas playing the double flute, or aulos. For a discussion of various accounts, see Piers Rawson (1987), who describes numerous visual depictions of the myth in ancient Greek and Roman art. Similarly, Wyss (1996) addresses several different interpretations of the myth throughout history, with a particular focus on visual depictions from the Italian Renaissance.

4. I repeat here Daniel's interpretation of the painting (2002b, iv).

5. Titian (1575–76). Image used with the permission of the Bridgeman Art Library, London.

6. Apollo was known for his performance on the lyre, but Titian took some historic license and painted a *lira da braccio*, a Renaissance instrument with a strong resemblance to the violin. Different critics have read Titian's painting in various ways, however, throwing doubt on the identity of the *lira* player. In many accounts, the kneeling figure that Daniel identifies as a Muse is taken to be Apollo himself. The musician in the painting, then, is interpreted as a second manifestation of Apollo (Neumann 1962, n.p.; cited in Wyss 1996, 167 n. 17), Apollo's son Orpheus (Rapp 1987, 75–89), or an anonymous musician representing harmony and musical inspiration (Wyss 1996, 138–139, 167 n. 17). Even in Wyss's account, the musician has close ties to Apollo, as the seven strings of his *lira* parallel the seven strings of the lyre with which Apollo was said to control "the seven planets and their heavenly music" (Wyss 1996, 138). Because all these accounts associate the musician with Apollonian interests and because my primary concern is the role this myth plays in Daniel's piece, I maintain Daniel's interpretation (that the musician is Apollo) throughout my discussion (with one slight twist, explained below).

7. In preparing this chapter, I have consulted archival audio and video recordings of *Marsyas* (Daniel 2002a, 2003, 2004). I also draw on my impressions from a performance I attended in London, Ontario, February 10, 2002 (Daniel, Miyagawa, and Stanford 2002). In addition, I have spoken with Daniel in person on numerous occasions about this piece and his various performances of it. The score for *The Flaying of Marsyas* (Daniel 2002b) is available for loan at the Canadian Music Centre.

8. All performances to date have featured a woman in the role of Apollo. My subsequent references to Apollo are, when appropriate, likewise to these female performers.

9. A digital signal processor carries out various electronic manipulations of digital sound signals. Live, synthesized, or prerecorded sounds are fed into the DSP, which, according to preset or constructed algorithms, effects changes to those sounds. Common effects include chorusing (multiplying a voice at preset or dynamic pitch intervals), reverberation, and delay (repetitions of a voice at preset or dynamic time intervals).

10. Adapted from Daniel (2002b, iii). Used with the permission of the composer.

11. The term *live electronics*, as in my discussion of live electronic music, indicates the real-time (in-performance) manipulation of electronic sound technologies. As I discuss below, this relationship between electronics and performer is often also called *interactive*.

12. MIDI (Musical Instrument Digital Interface) is a standardized electronic instrument protocol that was initially developed for use with commercial keyboard synthesizers and allows for control signals to flow from any device designed to send MIDI data to any electronic sound-producing device designed to respond to that data. In its most basic application, MIDI can be used simply to turn a sound on when a key or button is depressed and to turn it off when that key or button is released. On a typical MIDI keyboard, each key corresponds to a different preset sound event, often a single note. The velocity at which a key is pressed often corresponds to the amplitude at which that sound event is produced, although velocity may also be mapped to other parameters.

    More complex applications of the MIDI protocol, such as those performed in *Marsyas*, can be performed by way of innovative controllers and sophisticated sound-producing devices. Daniel's bend controllers send instruction to the PCM-81 signal processor according to the degree to which he bends his fingers. His G-force controllers send similar signals according to acceleration and to gravity—in other words, according to how quickly he moves them and to whether they are turned upside down or right-side up. Daniel maps each of these controllers to different control parameters, which change throughout the piece. At times, for instance, the movement of the controller on his left ring finger corresponds to the degree to which the PCM-81 bends the pitch of the signal from the violin, while the movement of the controller on his right wrist sometimes corresponds to the movement of all amplified sound within a stereo spectrum spread across the stage. See Pellman (1994, Ch. 5, Ch. 6, and Appendix C) for a thorough introduction to MIDI technology and its potential musical applications.

A sampler is a sophisticated recording and playback device. In performances, it can be used to record sounds that are being produced in real time by other means and play them back with or without variation. It can also be used simply to play back prerecorded/precompiled sound samples. Daniel uses the machine in its playback function only, having compiled the samples in advance.

13. Where appropriate, I refer to the performers of the piece by the names of their respective characters. This is to emphasize the importance of the piece's narrative context, which is explained further below.

14. According to Daniel (private communication), large movements doubly serve to stimulate blood flow throughout his body. If he were to hang upside down for the amount of time required for this performance *without* making such movements, the increased flow of blood to his head would likely cause him to lose consciousness. On one occasion, it actually caused a blood vessel to burst near his eye.

15. These illustrations can be seen in Saunders and O'Malley (1950, 85–119).

16. Daniel's spandex shorts also draw attention to the shape of his body.

17. I rely for my own commentary on Daniel's written score, the piece's underlying mythical narrative, archival audio and video recordings of performances, and my own remembered impressions of a performance of *Marsyas*. Although Daniel's particular configurations of MIDI controllers and DSP (not to mention decisions made in each performance by both performers) can and do result in variations from one performance to the next, the performance elements I discuss throughout this chapter, unless otherwise noted, are features of all the performances under review.

18. In the London, Ontario, performance (Daniel, Miyagawa, and Stanford 2002), the violinist performed from a score rather than from memory (as in other performances). As such, she remained on stage in a stationary position, to the left of the metal structure, throughout the performance. Subsequent references to Apollo's onstage movements do not apply to this performance.

19. The feedback loop records the violin gesture as it is played and stores it for use by Marsyas in this section. A resonance filter amplifies selected frequencies within a given sound signal, effectively providing those frequencies with extra "resonance" within the overall signal. Daniel's configuration requires the selection of resonant frequencies by way of a bend controller on his left index finger.

20. *Flanging* is a time-based effect that results from mixing two identical sound signals, one of these signals being slightly time-delayed by a constantly changing amount. Extra resonance and attenuation are produced within the frequency spectrum, sweeping through the spectrum as a result of the changes to the time delay.

21. Daniel actually triggers these sounds by briefly touching the corresponding finger of his right hand to his torso. As these subtle motions are incorporated into the larger hurling gestures, they do not interrupt the flow of the physical narrative in any way and can indeed be easily overlooked.
22. As characterized by Wyss (1996, 135).
23. Wyss (1996, 27) reminds us that the Apollonian/Dionysian dichotomy is actually a construct of nineteenth- and twentieth-century writers and that earlier interpreters of myth celebrated the Apollonian and Dionysian states of mind as "harmoniously complementing each other, even at times as two manifestations of one and the same deity." However, the flute and lyre (the two instruments most often associated with Marsyas and Apollo, respectively) have long been considered incompatible instruments (Wyss 1996, 26).
24. Croft gives a similar definition of interaction: "By 'interaction' here I refer to any causal connection between a performing body . . . and a sound-producing system whose observable physical characteristics do not determine the characteristics of the sound produced—for instance, a computer. I am *not* here considering the notion of the computer as a kind of improvising partner, where the interaction extends to the human performer's response to novel output from the computer" (Croft 2007, 60; original emphasis). Neither does Croft focus on any type of inter-performer interaction. I return to Croft in my discussion of corporeality, as his primary concern is really with the corporeal significance of musician/machine interaction.
25. I return to the significance of the *wired* body below.
26. Two clarifications of terminology are in order. First, although the term *sample*, especially in hip-hop usage, very often refers specifically to a digital file representing a portion of a previously recorded track, accessed by a sampler or other computer and usually in a studio setting, I use it here in reference to any borrowed (or *plundered*, to use Oswald's terminology) segment of recorded music, whether in studio or on stage, from digital file or from vinyl disc. In other words, I am recognizing with this word simply the act of musical borrowing via recording technologies, regardless of precise medium or musical context.

    Second, the term *turntablist* is often used to signify a DJ whose musicianship is based on advanced scratching techniques and other extensive methods of record manipulation, as distinct from one who does not approach the turntables as instruments to be "played" to nearly the same extent. Use of the term is rather inconsistent, however, and often *DJ* or *scratch DJ* are used in reference to the very same musicians. As I am primarily concerned in this section with instances in which the active and extensive real-time manipulation of recordings is carried out in performance, I use the terms *turntablist* and *turntablism* throughout, except in instances when I am referring to a broader DJ practice. For a succinct account of the development of turntablism as it relates to the broader category of DJing and to hip-hop culture in general, see Katz (2004, 114–117). Chapter 6 of Katz's volume deals specifically with the culture of the DJ battle, which is perhaps the most highly specialized venue for the performance of turntablism.
27. My wording here reflects traditional turntablism practice, which uses analog turntables to access the soundforms physically etched in the grooves of a vinyl disc. The arguments I make about turntablism in this section, however, could just as easily apply to recent applications of digital technologies, such as digital turntables by Pioneer, Technics, and other companies, that simulate the physical manipulation requirements of a traditional, vinyl-playing turntable while actually accessing databases of digitally stored media.

28. In fact, the example Cutler presents in the context of this discussion is not a hip-hop turntablist but electronic art-music composer James Tenney, whose *Blue Suede* (1961) plunders Elvis Presley's version of "Blue Suede Shoes," and whose *Viet Flakes* (1967) mixes samples of popular music, art music, and Asian traditional music.
29. Grand Wizard Theodore is usually credited with introducing the scratch (see, for instance, Pray 2002), which involves manually spinning a record back and forth in deliberate rhythms beneath the stylus. Scratching earned widespread mainstream attention after Grand Mixer DST added his scratching skills to Herbie Hancock's 1983 hit, "Rockit" (on Hancock 2007).
30. Cutler (2004), H. Davies (1996), and Shapiro (2009) all offer useful histories of these practices. Cutler offers a consideration of some of the aesthetic, ethical, and legal implications of what he calls *plundered music*, with a focus mostly on non-hip-hop practices. Davies offers a history of musical sampling by various technological means, with a focus mainly on art-music practices. Shapiro focuses directly on turntablism, dividing his attention between hip-hop turntablists and those more easily classified among the avant-garde in art music.
31. As mentioned above, see Katz (2004, Ch. 6) for an in-depth discussion of the culture of DJ battles.
32. Repetitions are typically achieved by way of a technique known as the *backspin*, wherein the turntablist spins the record backward beneath the stylus to the point at which he or she wishes to begin the sample again.
33. This performance circulates periodically on blogs dedicated to turntablism and sample-based music and is (as of summer 2012) also the recipient of frequent hits on YouTube.com. See, for instance, DJ A-Trak (1997). Although it is currently under reconstruction, the DMC World DJ Championships organization hosts an online archive of past DMC performances (www.dmc-world.com/dmctv). Once it is relaunched (likely by the time this book is published), this website will be an invaluable resource for anyone with an interest in the DJ battle.
34. Beginning in the late 1970s, it became common to circulate cassette tapes of independently recorded DJ sets, often compiled in a home-studio environment, either to gain a following (if a DJ were relatively unknown) or to "advertise" upcoming releases (if the DJ were more established). Similar compilations on other media (CD or online digital files, for instance) are often still called *mixtapes*. For instance, www.hotnewhiphop.com/mixtapes (accessed May 1, 2012) is one of several current online venues for accessing such recordings.

References

PUBLIC EVENT

Daniel, Omar, Aya Miyagawa, and Jason Stanford. 2002. *The Flaying of Marsyas*. Première performance, part of "The Music of Omar Daniel" concert. Von Kuster Recital Hall, the University of Western Ontario. London, ON, Canada (February 10).

SOUND AND VIDEO RECORDINGS

? and the Mysterians. 2005. "96 Tears." On *Cameo Parkway 1957–1967* (various artists), CD 4. ABKCO Records 9223 (4 CDs).

The Beatles. 2009. *Sgt. Pepper's Lonely Hearts Club Band*. Capitol/Apple Corps 82419 (CD). Reissue of original release by Parlophone (1967).

Babin, Magali. 2002. *Chemin de fer*. No Type IMNT 0203 (CD).

Cher. 1998. *Believe*. Warner Bros. 47121 (CD).

Cutmaster Swift. 1989. Winning routine at DMC World DJ Championships. http://www.youtube.com/watch?v=TB0-qCASEaA (accessed May 1, 2012).

Daniel, Omar. 2002a. *The Flaying of Marsyas*. NUMUS Concert in Kitchener-Waterloo, ON, Canada (November 18). Archival video (VHS).

———. 2003. *The Flaying of Marsyas*. Regina New Music Festival, Regina, SK, Canada (April 24). Copy of Canadian Broadcasting Corporation archival audio recording (CD).

———. 2004. *The Flaying of Marsyas*. Winnipeg New Music Festival, Winnipeg, MB, Canada (January 27). Archival video (DV).

DJ A-Trak. 1997. Winning routine at DMC World DJ Championships. http://www.youtube.com/watch?v=5cYRgzeTUe8 (accessed June 28, 2012).

Faster Pussycat. "You're So Vain" video. http://www.youtube.com/watch?v=41zKVmk4z8Q (accessed May 1, 2012).

Ferrari, Luc. 1995. *Presque Rien*. INA/GRM-MUSIDISC 254172 (CD).

Frampton, Peter. 2003. *Frampton Comes Alive!* (25th Anniversary Deluxe Edition). A&M AAB-000101726 (2 CDs). Reissue of original release by A&M/Polygram Records (1976).

Furtwängler, Wilhelm. 1986. *Richard Wagner: Tristan und Isolde*. EMI Classics 7473228 (4 CDs).

Gould, Glenn. 1956. *Bach: The Goldberg Variations*. Columbia Masterworks ML 5060 (LP).

———. 1963. *Bach: Partitas Nos. 3 & 4/Toccata No. 7*. Columbia Masterworks MS 6498 (LP).

———. 1965. *Glenn Gould Plays Beethoven Piano Sonatas, Opus 10 Complete.* Columbia Masterworks MS 6686 (LP).

———. 1982. *Goldberg Variations: BWV 988.* CBS Masterworks IM 37779 (LP).

———. 2002. *Glenn Gould: A State of Wonder: The Complete Goldberg Variations 1955 & 1981.* Sony Classical/Legacy S3K 87703 (3 CDs).

Gould, Glenn, and John McClure. 1968. *Glenn Gould: Concert Dropout, in Conversation with John McClure.* Recorded interview. Columbia Masterworks BS 15 (LP).

Grandmaster Flash and the Furious Five. 2005. *The Message.* DBK Works 513 (CD). Reissue of original release by Sugar Hill (1982).

Guggenheim, Davis. 2009. *It Might Get Loud.* Sony Pictures Classics 31515 (DVD).

Hancock, Herbie. 2007. *Future Shock.* Sony Music Distribution 10074 (CD). Reissue of original release by Columbia (1983).

The Hives. 2000. *Veni Vidi Vicious.* Epitaph 82005 (CD).

Jacskon, Michael. 1991. *Bad.* Epic 40600 (CD). Reissue of original release by Epic (1987).

Kagel, Mauricio. 2003. *Transición II; Phonophonie.* Mode Records 127 (CD).

Lang, Fritz. 2002. *Metropolis.* Restored authorized ed. Kino on Video K275 (DVD).

Led Zeppelin. 2005a. *Led Zeppelin.* Warner Music WPCR 75001 (CD). Reissue of original release by Atlantic (1969).

———. 2005b. *Led Zeppelin II.* Warner Music WPCR 75002 (CD). Reissue of original release by Atlantic (1969).

———. 2005c. *Led Zeppelin III.* Warner Music WPCR 75003 (CD). Reissue of original release by Atlantic (1970).

Lee, Curtis. 1996. *Pretty Little Angel Eyes.* Collectables 9152 (CD).

Lerche, Sondre. 2004. *Two-Way Monologue.* Astralwerks ASW 98027 (CD).

Meyer, Russ. 2005. *Faster, Pussycat! Kill! . . . Kill!* Fremantle (DVD).

Mumma, Gordon. 2002. *Live Electronic Music.* Tzadik TZ-7074 (CD).

Oswald, John. 1993. *Plexure.* Avan 016 (CD).

———. 2001a. *Plunderphonics 69/96.* Pfony 069/96 (2 CDs).

Outkast. 2003. *Speakerboxxx/The Love Below.* Arista 50133 (2 CDs).

Parton, Dolly. 2001. *Dolly Parton Gold: Greatest Hits.* RCA 74321840202 (CD).

Paul, Les. 1991. *Les Paul: The Legend and the Legacy.* Capitol C2–97654 (4 CDs).

Petrowska Quilico, Christina. 2003. *Gems with an Edge.* Welspringe Productions WEL0007 (CD).

Pray, Doug. 2002. *Scratch.* Palm DVD 3046–2 (DVD).

Rubaiyat: Elektra's 40th Anniversary. 1990. Elektra 960940–2 (2 CDs).

Simon, Carly. 1990. *No Secrets.* Elektra 75049–2 (CD). Reissue of original release by Elektra (1972).

Stockhausen, Karlheinz. 1991. *Elektronische Musik 1952–1960.* Stockhausen Complete Edition 3 (CD).

———. 1992. *Momente.* Stockhausen Complete Edition 7 (CD).

———. 1995a. *Mikrophonie I and Mikrophonie II; Telemusik.* Stockhausen Complete Edition 9 (CD).

———. 2000. *Gruppen; Carré.* Stockhausen Complete Edition 5 (CD).

The Stooges. 2010. *The Stooges.* Elektra/Warner Music 79796 (CD). Reissue of original release by Elektra (1969).

The Strokes. 2001. *Is This It.* RCA 68101 (CD).

Varèse, Edgard. 1998a. *The Complete Works.* Decca 289460208–2 (2 CDs).

West, Kanye. 2008. *808s & Heartbreak.* Roc-A-Fella Records 1787279 (CD).

Westerkamp, Hildegard. 1998. *Harangue I.* Earsay ES98001 (CD).

The White Stripes. 2002a. *De Stijl.* Third Man Records/V2 Records 27132 (CD). Reissue of original release by Sympathy for the Record Industry (2000).
———. 2002b. *White Blood Cells.* Third Man Records/V2 Records 27124 (CD). Reissue of original release by Sympathy for the Record Industry (2001).
———. 2002c. *The White Stripes.* Third Man Records/V2 Records 27131 (CD). Reissue of original release by Sympathy for the Record Industry (1999).
———. 2003. *Elephant.* Third Man Records/V2 Records 27148 (CD).
———. 2005. *Get Behind Me Satan.* Third Man Records/V2 Records 27256 (CD).
———. 2007. *Icky Thump.* Third Man Records/Warner Bros. Records 162940 (CD).
The Who. 2000. *Tommy.* Polydor 5310432 (CD). Reissue of original release by Polydor (1969).
Yeah Yeah Yeahs. 2003. *Fever To Tell.* Interscope 34902 (CD).
Zapp. 1989a. *Zapp.* Warner Bros. 3463 (CD). Reissue of original release by Warner Bros. (1980).
Zapp. 1989b. *The New Zapp IV U.* Warner Bros. 7599253272 (CD). Reissue of original release by Warner Bros. (1985).

PAINTINGS

Balla, Giacomo. c. 1910–11. *Lampada ad arco.* Oil on canvas, 174.7 x 114.7 cm. New York: The Museum of Modern Art. http://www.moma.org/collection/provenance/provenance_object.php?object_id=78382 (accessed May 1, 2012).
Titian (Tiziano Vecellio). 1575–76. *Flaying of Marsyas.* Oil on canvas, 212 x 207 cm. Kromeriz, Czech Republic: Archbishop's Gallery. http://www.the-athenaeum.org/art/detail.php?ID=37049 (accessed May 1, 2012).

SCORES

Bach, Johann Sebastian. [1731] n.d. *Partita Nr. 4 D-dur, BWV 828.* In *Partiten Nr. 4–6, BWV 828–830.* Wiesbaden, Germany: Breitkopf und Härtel.
———. 1943. *Aria mit 30 Veränderungen (Goldberg-Variationen), BWV 988.* Wiesbaden, Germany: Breitkopf und Härtel.
Cage, John. 1960. *Imaginary Landscape No. 1, for Records of Constant and Variable Frequency, Large Chinese Cymbal, String Piano.* New York: Henmar Press.
Daniel, Omar. 2002b. *The Flaying of Marsyas: For Violin and Suspended Musician with Live Electronics.* Unpublished score. Canadian Music Centre.
Davidovsky, Mario. 1972. *Synchronisms No. 6, for Piano and Electronic Sounds.* New York: E. B. Marks Music Company.
Jolivet, André. 1978. *Concerto pour ondes martenot et orchestre.* Paris: Heugel.
Kagel, Mauricio. 1963. *Transición II: Für Klavier, Schlagzeug und 2 Tonbänder, 1958/59.* London: Universal Edition.
Martinu, Bohuslav. 1973. *Fantaisie pour theremin (ou ondes martenot), hautbois, piano, et quatuor à cordes.* Paris: Éditions Max Eschig.
Stockhausen, Karlheinz. 1974. *Mikrophonie II.* London: Universal Edition.

BOOKS AND ARTICLES

Angilette, Elizabeth. 1992. *Philosopher at the Keyboard: Glenn Gould.* Metuchen, NJ: Scarecrow Press.

Ashby, Arved. 2010. *Absolute Music, Mechanical Reproduction*. Berkeley: University of California Press.

Ashley, Robert. 2000. *Music with Roots in the Aether: Interviews and Essays about Seven American Composers*. Cologne, Germany: MusikTexte.

Attali, Jacques. 1985. *Noise: The Political Economy of Music*. Trans. Brian Massumi. Minneapolis: University of Minnesota Press.

Auner, Joseph. 2000. "Making Old Machines Speak: Images of Technology in Recent Music." *Echo* 2, no. 2 (Fall). http://www.echo.ucla.edu/Volume2-Issue2/auner/aunerframe.html (accessed May 1, 2012).

Auslander, Philip. 1999. *Liveness: Performance in a Mediatized Culture*. London: Routledge.

———. 2002. "Live from Cyberspace: Or, I Was Sitting at My Computer This Guy Appeared He Thought I Was a Bot." *PAJ: A Journal of Performance and Art* 24, no. 1 (January): 16–21.

———. 2004. "Performance Analysis and Popular Music: A Manifesto." *Contemporary Theatre Review* 14, no. 1: 1–13.

———. 2005. "At the *Listening Post*, or, Do Machines Perform?" *International Journal of Performance Arts and Digital Media* 1, no. 1: 5–10.

———. 2006a. "Musical Personae." *Drama Review* 50, no. 1 (Spring): 100–119.

———. 2006b. "Watch That Man: David Bowie: Hammersmith Odeon, London, July 3, 1973." In *Performance and Popular Music: History, Place and Time*, ed. Ian Inglis, 70–80. Aldershot: Ashgate.

———. 2008. *Liveness: Performance in a Mediatized Culture*, 2nd ed. London: Routledge.

Balsamo, Anne. 1997. *Technologies of the Gendered Body: Reading Cyborg Women*. Durham, NC: Duke University Press.

Bangs, Lester. 2003. "Of Pop and Pies and Fun: A Program for Mass Liberation in the Form of a Stooges Review, or, Who's the Fool? (1970)." In *Psychotic Reactions and Carburetor Dung*, ed. Greil Marcus, 31–52. New York: Anchor Books.

Barker, Martin. 2003. "*Crash*, Theatre Audiences, and the Idea of 'Liveness.'" *Studies in Theatre and Performance* 23, no. 1: 21–39.

Barthes, Roland. 1974. *S/Z*. Trans. Richard Miller. New York: Hill and Wang.

———. 1989. "The Grain of the Voice." In *Image-Music-Text*, trans. and ed. Stephen Heath, 179–189. New York: Noonday Press.

Baudrillard, Jean. 1981. *For a Critique of the Political Economy of the Sign*. Trans. Charles Levin. St. Louis: Telos Press.

Bayley, Amanda, ed. 2010. *Recorded Music: Performance, Culture, and Technology*. Cambridge, UK: Cambridge University Press.

Bazzana, Kevin. 1997. *Glenn Gould: The Performer in the Work*. Oxford: Clarendon Press.

———. 2003. *Wondrous Strange: The Life and Art of Glenn Gould*. Toronto: McClelland and Stewart.

Benjamin, Walter. 1968. "The Work of Art in the Age of Mechanical Reproduction." Trans. Harry Zohn. In *Illuminations*, ed. Hannah Arendt, 217–251. New York: Schocken Books.

Berghaus, Günter, ed. 2006. *F. T. Marinetti: Critical Writings*. Trans. Doug Thompson. New York: Farrar, Straus, and Giroux.

Bergman, Rhona. 1999. *The Idea of Gould*. Philadelphia: Lev.

Born, Georgina. 1995. *Rationalizing Culture: IRCAM, Boulez, and the Institutionalization of the Avant-Garde*. Berkeley: University of California Press.

Bowen, José A. 1993. "The History of Remembered Innovation: Tradition and Its Role in the Relationship between Musical Works and Their Performances." *Journal of Musicology* 11, no. 2 (Spring): 139–173.

————. 1996. "Performance Practice versus Performance Analysis: Why Should Performers Study Performance?" *Performance Practice Review* 9, no. 1 (Spring): 16–35.

Braidotti, Rosi. 1994. *Nomadic Subjects: Embodiment and Sexual Difference in Contemporary Feminist Theory.* New York: Columbia University Press.

Broadhurst, Susan, and Josephine Machon, eds. 2006. *Performance and Technology: Practices of Virtual Embodiment and Interactivity.* Basingstoke, UK: Palgrave Macmillan.

————. 2010. *Sensualities/Textualities and Technologies: Writings of the Body in 21st-Century Performance.* Basingstoke, UK: Palgrave Macmillan.

Broesche, Garreth. 2012. "The Intimacy of Distance: Glenn Gould and the Poetics of the Recording Studio." Unpublished paper, delivered at the Midwest Graduate Music Consortium, Northwestern University, March 2–3.

Brown, Barclay. 1982. "The Noise Instruments of Luigi Russolo." *Perspectives of New Music* 20:31–48.

Burston, Jonathan. 1998. "Theatre Space as Virtual Place: Audio Technology, the Reconfigured Singing Body, and the Megamusical." *Popular Music* 17, no. 2: 205–218.

Busoni, Ferrucio. 1999. "Sketch of a New Aesthetic of Music." Trans. Theodore Baker. In *Composers on Modern Musical Culture: An Anthology of Readings on Twentieth-Century Music,* ed. Bryan R. Simms, 11–30. New York: MacMillan.

Butler, Judith. 1990a. *Gender Trouble: Feminism and the Subversion of Identity.* New York: Routledge.

————. 1990b. "Performative Acts and Gender Constitution: An Essay in Phenomenology and Feminist Theory." In *Performing Feminisms: Feminist Critical Theory and Theatre,* ed. Sue-Ellen Case, 270–282. Baltimore: Johns Hopkins University Press.

————. 1993. *Bodies That Matter: On the Discursive Limits of "Sex."* New York: Routledge.

Carlson, Marvin. 2004. *Performance: A Critical Introduction,* 2nd ed. New York: Routledge.

Chadabe, Joel. 1997. *Electric Sound: The Past and Promise of Electronic Music.* Upper Saddle River, NJ: Prentice Hall.

Chanan, Michael. 1995. *Repeated Takes: A Short History of Recording and Its Effects on Music.* London: Verso.

Columbia Masterworks. 1956. Press release issued with the release of Gould's 1956 *Goldberg Variations* recording. Quoted in Page 2002, 8–9.

————. 1963. Promotional description of Glenn Gould. Part of liner notes accompanying Gould (1963).

Cook, Nicholas. 2001. "Between Process and Product: Music and/as Performance." *Music Theory Online* 7, no. 2 (April). http://www.societymusictheory.org/mto/issues/mto.01.7.2/mto.01.7.2.cook.html (accessed May 1, 2012).

————. 2003. "Music as Performance." In *The Cultural Study of Music: A Critical Introduction,* ed. Martin Clayton, Trevor Herbert, and Richard Middleton, 204–214. London: Routledge.

————. 2007. *Music, Performance, Meaning: Selected Essays.* Aldershot, UK: Ashgate.

Cook, Nicholas, Eric Clarke, Daniel Leech-Wilkinson, and John Rink, eds. 2009. *The Cambridge Companion to Recorded Music.* Cambridge, UK: Cambridge University Press.

Corbett, John. 1990. "Free, Single, and Disengaged: Listening Pleasure and the Popular Music Object." *October* 54 (Autumn): 79–101.

Cottrell, Stephen. 2004. *Professional Music-Making in London.* Aldershot, UK: Ashgate.

Couldry, Nick. 2004. "Liveness, 'Reality,' and the Mediated Habitus from Television to the Mobile Phone." *Communication Review* 7, no. 4: 353–361.

Cox, Arnie. 2001. "The Mimetic Hypothesis and Embodied Musical Meaning." *Musicae Scientae* 5, no. 2 (Fall): 195–212.

Cox, Cathy. 2004. "Interactive Technologies in Music Composition: Towards a Theory of Interactivity." In *Music Research: New Directions for a New Century*, ed. Michael Ewans, Rosalind Halton, and John A. Phillips, 333–342. London: Cambridge Scholars Press.

Cox, Christoph, and Daniel Warner, ed. 2004. *Audio Culture: Readings in Modern Music*. New York: Continuum.

Crisell, Andrew. 2012. *Liveness and Recording in the Media*. Basingstoke, UK: Palgrave Macmillan.

Croft, John. 2007. "Theses on Liveness." *Organised Sound* 12, no. 1: 59–66.

Cumming, Naomi. 2000. *The Sonic Self: Musical Subjectivity and Signification*. Bloomington: Indiana University Press.

Cunningham, Mark. 1998. *Good Vibrations: A History of Record Production*, 2nd ed. London: Sanctuary Publishing.

Cusick, Suzanne. 1994. "Feminist Theory, Music Theory, and the Mind/Body Problem." *Perspectives of New Music* 32, no. 1 (Winter): 8–27.

Cutler, Chris. 1993. *File under Popular: Theoretical and Critical Writings on Music*. Brooklyn: Autonomedia.

———. 2004. "Plunderphonia." In *Audio Culture: Readings in Modern Music*, ed. Christoph Cox and Daniel Warner, 138–156. New York: Continuum.

Damasio, Antonio R. 2000. *The Feeling of What Happens: Body and Emotion in the Making of Consciousness*. New York: Harcourt Brace.

Davidson, Jane W. 1991. "The Role of the Body in the Production and Perception of Solo Vocal Performance: A Case Study of Annie Lennox." *Musicae Scientae* 5, no. 2 (Fall): 235–256.

———. 1993. "Visual Perception of Performance Manner in the Movements of Solo Musicians." *Psychology of Music* 21, no. 2: 103–113.

Davidson, Jane W., and Jorge Salgado Correia. 2002. "Body Movement." In *The Science and Psychology of Music Performance: Creative Strategies for Teaching and Learning*, ed. Richard Parncutt and Gary E. McPherson, 237–250. Oxford: Oxford University Press.

Davies, Hugh. 1996. "A History of Sampling." *Organised Sound* 1, no. 1: 3–11.

Davies, J. Q. 2005. "'Veluti in Speculum': The Twilight of the Castrato." *Cambridge Opera Journal* 17, no. 3 (November): 271–301.

Day, Timothy. 2000. *A Century of Recorded Music: Listening to Musical History*. New Haven, CT: Yale University Press.

Derrida, Jacques. 1976. *Of Grammatology*. Trans. Gayatri Chakravorty Spivak. Baltimore: Johns Hopkins University Press.

———. 1979. *Spurs: Nietzsche's Styles*. Trans. Barbara Harlow. Chicago: University of Chicago Press.

———. 1981. *Positions*. Trans. Alan Bass. Chicago: University of Chicago Press.

Di Perna, Alan. 2007. "Jack the Ripper." Includes interview with Jack White. *Guitar World*, August. http://www.whitestripes.com/lo-fi/PDFs/070801_Guitarworld.pdf (accessed May 1, 2012).

Dolan, Jon. 2007. "New Jack City." Includes interview with the White Stripes. *Blender*, July. http://www.whitestripes.com/lo-fi/PDFs/070701_Blender.pdf (accessed May 1, 2012).

Duncan, Michelle. 2004. "The Operatic Scandal of the Singing Body: Voice, Presence, Performativity." *Cambridge Opera Journal* 16, no. 3 (November): 283–306.

Echard, William. 2006. "Sensible Virtual Selves: Bodies, Instruments, and the Becoming-Concrete of Music." *Contemporary Music Review* 25, no. 1 (February): 7–16.

Eimert, Herbert. 1958. "What Is Electronic Music?" *Die Reihe* 1 (English edition only): 1–10.

Eisenberg, Evan. 1987. *The Recording Angel: Explorations in Phonography*. New York: McGraw-Hill.

Ellul, Jacques. [1954] 1964. *The Technological Society*. Trans. John Wilkinson. New York: Vintage Books.

Emmerson, Simon. 1986. "The Relation of Language to Materials." In *The Language of Electracoustic Music*, 17–39. Basingstoke, UK: Macmillan.

———. 1994. "'Live' versus 'Real-Time.'" *Contemporary Music Review* 10, no. 2: 95–101.

———, ed. 2000. "'Losing Touch?': The Human Performer and Electronics." In *Music, Electronic Media and Culture*, 194–216. Aldershot, UK: Ashgate.

———. 2007. *Living Electronic Music*. Aldershot, UK: Ashgate.

Emmerson, Simon, and Dennis Smalley. "Electro-Acoustic Music." In *Grove Music Online. Oxford Music Online*. http://www.oxfordmusiconline.com (accessed May 1, 2012).

Feuer, Jane. 1983. "The Concept of Live Television: Ontology as Ideology." In *Regarding Television: Critical Approaches—An Anthology*, ed. E. Ann Kaplan, 12–22. Los Angeles: American Film Institute.

Fisher, George, and Judy Lochhead. 2002. "Analyzing from the Body." *Theory and Practice* 27:37–67.

Frampton, Peter. "Tutorial." *Peter Frampton*. http://www.frampton.com/tutorial.html (accessed May 1, 2012).

Frith, Simon. 1981. *Sound Effects: Youth, Leisure, and the Politics of Rock'n'Roll*. New York: Pantheon Books.

———. 1986. "Art versus Technology: The Strange Case of Popular Music." *Media, Culture and Society* 8, no. 3: 263–279.

———. 1996. *Performing Rites: On the Value of Popular Music*. Cambridge, MA: Harvard University Press.

———. 2007. "The Industrialization of Popular Music." In *Taking Popular Music Seriously: Selected Essays*, 93–118. Aldershot, UK: Ashgate.

Frost, Thomas. 1965. Inset text explaining sounds of Glenn Gould's creaking chair on the record. Part of liner notes accompanying Glenn Gould, *Glenn Gould Plays Beethoven Piano Sonatas, Opus 10 Complete* (1965).

Garnett, Guy E. 2001. "The Aesthetics of Interactive Computer Music." *Computer Music Journal* 25, no. 1 (Spring): 21–33.

Gendron, Bernard. 2002. *Between Montmartre and the Mudd Club: Popular Music and the Avant-Garde*. Chicago: University of Chicago Press.

Gershwin, George. 2004. "The Composer in the Machine Age." In *Modernism and Music: An Anthology of Sources*, ed. Daniel Albright, 385–389. Chicago: University of Chicago Press.

Godlovitch, Stan. 1998. *Musical Performance: A Philosophical Study*. London: Routledge.

Goehr, Lydia. 1992. *The Imaginary Museum of Musical Works: An Essay in the Philosophy of Music*. Oxford: Oxford University Press.

Goodwin, Andrew. 1990. "Sample and Hold: Pop Music in the Digital Age of Reproduction." In *On Record: Rock, Pop, and the Written Word*, ed. Simon Frith and Andrew Goodwin, 258–273. London: Routledge.

———. 1964. *Arnold Schoenberg: A Perspective*. Cincinnati: University of Cincinnati Press.

———. 1966. "The Prospects of Recording." *High Fidelity Magazine* (April): 46–63. Partially reprinted in *The Glenn Gould Reader*, ed. Tim Page, 331–353 (Toronto: Key Porter, 1990). Also available online at http://www.collection-scanada.gc.ca/glenngould/028010–4020.01-e.html (accessed May 1, 2012).

———. 1967. Liner notes accompanying *Canadian Music in the 20th Century* (Columbia Masterworks 32110046, LP).

———. 1992. *Glenn Gould: Selected Letters.* Ed. John P. L. Roberts and Ghyslaine Guertin. Toronto: Oxford University Press.

———. 1999a. "Forgery and Imitation in the Creative Process." In *The Art of Glenn Gould: Reflections of a Musical Genius*, ed. John P. L. Roberts, 205–221. Toronto: Malcolm Lester Books.

———. 1999b. "Sviatoslav Richter." In *The Art of Glenn Gould: Reflections of a Musical Genius*, ed. John P. L. Roberts, 50–54. Toronto: Malcolm Lester Books.

Gould, Glenn, and Jim Aikin. 1999. "Provocative Insights from a Controversial Pianist: Gould in Conversation with Jim Aikin." In *The Art of Glenn Gould: Reflections of a Musical Genius*, ed. John P. L. Roberts, 259–278. Toronto: Malcolm Lester Books.

Gould, Glenn, and Bernard Asbell. 1999. "The Artist Speaks for Himself." In *The Art of Glenn Gould: Reflections of a Musical Genius*, ed. John P. L. Roberts, 185–195. Toronto: Malcolm Lester Books.

Gould, Glenn, and Alfred Bester. 1964. "The Zany Genius of Glenn Gould." *Holiday*, April: 149–156.

Gould, Glenn, and Dennis Braithwaite. 1999. "'I'm a Child of Nature': Gould in Conversation with Dennis Braithwaite." In *The Art of Glenn Gould: Reflections of a Musical Genius*, ed. John P. L. Roberts, 38–46. Toronto: Malcolm Lester Books.

Gould, Glenn, and Tim Page. 1990. "Glenn Gould in Conversation with Tim Page." In *The Art of Glenn Gould: Reflections of a Musical Genius*, ed. John P. L. Roberts, 451–461. Toronto: Malcolm Lester Books.

Gould, Glenn, and Alan Rich. 1999. "The Composing Career That Eluded Gould and the Performing Career That Did Not: Gould in Conversation with Alan Rich." In *The Art of Glenn Gould: Reflections of a Musical Genius*, ed. John P. L. Roberts, 132–152. Toronto: Malcolm Lester Books.

Gould, Glenn, and Vincent Tovell. 1999. "At Home with Glenn Gould: Gould in Conversation with Vincent Tovell." In *The Art of Glenn Gould: Reflections of a Musical Genius*, ed. John P. L. Roberts, 66–88. Toronto: Malcolm Lester Books.

Gracyck, Theodore. 1996. *Rhythm and Noise: An Aesthetics of Rock.* Durham, NC: Duke University Press.

Gronow, Pekka, and Ilpo Saunio. 1998. *An International History of the Recording Industry.* Trans. Christopher Moseley. London: Cassell.

Grossberg, Lawrence. 1992. *We Gotta Get Out of This Place: Popular Conservatism and Postmodern Culture.* New York: Routledge.

———. 1994. "Is Anybody Listening? Does Anybody Care? On Talking about 'The State of Rock.'" In *Microphone Fiends: Youth Music, Youth Culture*, ed. Andrew Ross and Tricia Rose, 41–58. New York: Routledge.

Guberman, Daniel. 2011. "Post-Fidelity: A New Age of Music Consumption and Technological Innovation." *Journal of Popular Music Studies* 23, no. 4: 431–454.

Guitar World. 2006. "Jimmy Page and Jack White." Includes interview with Page and White. February. http://www.whitestripes.com/lo-fi/PDFs/GuitarWorld_Feb2006.pdf (accessed May 1, 2012).

Hagan, Joe. 2001. "Hurling Your Basic Rock at the Arty Crowd." *New York Times*, August 12.

Haraway, Donna. 1991. "A Cyborg Manifesto: Science, Technology, and Socialist-Feminism in the Late Twentietch Century." In *Simians, Cyborgs, and Women: The Reinvention of Nature*. London: Free Association Books.

Harvey, David. 1990. *The Condition of Postmodernity: An Enquiry into the Origins of Cultural Change*. Cambridge, MA: Blackwell.

Harvith, John, and Susan Harvith, eds. 1987. *Edison, Musicians, and the Phonograph: A Century in Retrospect*. New York: Greenwood Press.

Hayles, N. Katherine. 1999. *How We Became Posthuman: Virtual Bodies in Cybernetics, Literature, and Informatics*. Chicago: University of Chicago Press.

Heilbroner, Robert. 1967. "Do Machines Make History?" *Technology and Culture* 8, no. 3 (July): 335–345.

Hoffman, E. T. A. 1998. "Beethoven's Instrumental Music." Trans. Oliver Strunk. In *Source Readings in Music History*, rev. ed., ed. Oliver Strunk and Leo Treitler, 1193–1198. New York: Norton.

Holland, Patrick. 2008. "When Histrionics Undermine the Music and the Pianist." *New York Times*, February 6.

Holm-Hudson, Kevin. 1996. "John Oswald's *Rubaiyat (Elektrax)* and the Politics of Recombinant Do-Re-Mi." *Popular Music and Society* 20, no. 3 (Fall): 19–36.

———. 1997. "Quotation and Context: Sampling and John Oswald's Plunderphonics." *Leonardo Music Journal* 7:17–25.

Jaffe, David A., and W. Andrew Schloss. 1994. "The Computer-Extended Ensemble." *Computer Music Journal* 18, no. 2 (Summer): 78–86.

Jarmusch, Jim. 2003. "The White Stripes: Getting to Know the Most Interesting Band in Music Today." Interview with the White Stripes. *Interview*, May: 89–91.

Jeannerod, Marc. 2002. *La Nature de l'esprit: Sciences cognitives et cerveau*. Paris: Jacob.

Jones, Andrew. 1995. *Plunderphonics, 'Pataphysics and Pop Mechanics: An Introduction to Musique Actuelle*. Wembley, UK: SAF.

Jones, Steven. 1993. "A Sense of Space: Virtual Reality, Authenticity and the Aural." *Critical Studies in Mass Communication* 10:238–252.

Jordà, Sergi. 2007. "Interactivity and Live Computer Music." In *The Cambridge Companion to Electronic Music*, ed. Nick Collins and Julio d'Escriván, 89–106. Cambridge, UK: Cambridge University Press.

Katz, Mark. 2004. *Capturing Sound: How Technology Has Changed Music*. Berkeley: University of California Press.

Keightley, Keir. 1996. "'Turn It Down!' She Shrieked: Gender, Domestic Space, and High Fidelity, 1948–59." *Popular Music* 15, no. 2 (May): 149–177.

———. 2001. "Reconsidering Rock." In *The Cambridge Companion to Pop and Rock*, ed. Simon Frith, Will Straw, and John Street, 109–142. Cambridge, UK: Cambridge University Press.

Kenney, William Howland. 1999. *Recorded Music in American Life: The Phonograph and Popular Memory, 1890–1945*. New York: Oxford University Press.

Kerman, Joseph. 1985. *Contemplating Music: Challenges to Musicology*. Cambridge, MA: Harvard University Press.

———. 1994. *Write All These Down: Essays on Music*. Berkeley: University of California Press.

Key, Susan. 2002. "John Cage's *Imaginary Landscape No. 1*: Through the Looking Glass." In *John Cage: Music, Philosophy, and Intention, 1933–1950*, ed. David W. Patterson, 105–133. New York: Routledge.

Kingsbury, Henry. 1988. *Music, Talent, and Performance: A Conservatory Cultural System*. Philadelphia: Temple University Press.

Lacasse, Serge. 2000. "'Listen to My Voice': The Evocative Power of Vocal Staging in Recorded Rock Music and Other Forms of Vocal Expression." PhD diss., University of Liverpool.

Le Guin, Elisabeth. 2006. *Boccherini's Body: An Essay in Carnal Musicology*. Berkeley: University of California Press.

Leech-Wilkinson, Daniel. 1984. "What We Are Doing with Early Music Is Genuinely Authentic to Such a Small Degree That the Word Loses Most of Its Intended Meaning." *Early Music* 12:13–15.

Leman, Marc. 2008. *Embodied Music Cognition and Mediation Technology*. Cambridge, MA: MIT Press.

Leppert, Richard. 1993. *The Sight of Sound: Music, Representation, and the History of the Body*. Berkeley: University of California Press.

———. 2007. "The Musician of the Imagination." In *Sound Judgment: Selected Essays*, 143–176. Aldershot, UK: Ashgate.

Leroux, Georges. 2010. *Partita for Glenn Gould: An Inquiry into the Nature of Genius*. Trans. Donald Winkler. Montreal: McGill-Queen's University Press.

Lidov, David. 2005. *Is Language a Music? Writings on Musical Form and Signification*. Bloomington: Indiana University Press.

Lloyd, Llewelyn S., and Richard Rastall. "Pitch Nomenclature." In *Grove Music Online. Oxford Music Online*. http://www.oxfordmusiconline.com (accessed May 1, 2012).

Lockheart, Paula. 2003. "A History of Early Microphone Singing, 1925–1939: American Mainstream Popular Singing at the Advent of Electronic Microphone Amplification." *Popular Music and Society* 26, no. 3: 367–385.

"Lo-Fi Music." Online discussion group at *Last.fm*. http://www.last.fm/group/Lo-Fi+music (accessed May 1, 2012).

Male, Andrew. 2002. "Basic Instinct." Includes interview with the White Stripes. *MOJO*, September. http://www.whitestripes.com/links/PDFs/Mojo_Sept2002.pdf (accessed May 1, 2012).

Manning, Peter. 2004. *Electronic and Computer Music*, 2nd ed. Oxford: Oxford University Press.

Marinetti, Filippo Tommaso. 2006a. "Electric War: A Futurist Visionary Hypothesis." In *F. T. Marinetti: Critical Writings*, trans. Doug Thompson, ed. Günter Berghaus, 221–225. New York: Farrar, Straus, and Giroux.

———. 2006b. "The Foundation and Manifesto of Futurism." In *F. T. Marinetti: Critical Writings*, trans. Doug Thompson, ed. Günter Berghaus, 11–17. New York: Farrar, Straus, and Giroux.

———. 2006c. "Second Futurist Proclamation: Let's Kill Off the Moonlight." In *F. T. Marinetti: Critical Writings*, trans. Doug Thompson, ed. Günter Berghaus, 22–31. New York: Farrar, Straus, and Giroux.

Mauceri, Frank X. 1997. "From Experimental Music to Musical Experiment." *Perspectives of New Music* 35, no. 1 (Winter): 187–204.

McClary, Susan. 1991. *Feminine Endings: Music, Gender, and Sexuality*. Minneapolis: University of Minnesota Press.

———. 1992. *George Bizet: Carmen*. Cambridge, UK: Cambridge University Press.

———. 2004. *Modal Subjectivities: Self-Fashioning in the Italian Madrigal*. Berkeley: University of California Press.

McGranahan, Liam. 2010. "Mashnography: Creativity, Consumption, and Copyright in the Mashup Community." PhD diss., Brown University.

McKenzie, Jon. 2001. *Perform or Else: From Disciple to Performance*. New York: Routledge.

McMullen, Tracy. 2006. "Corpo-Realities: Keepin' It Real in 'Music and Embodiment' Scholarship." *Current Musicology* 82 (Fall): 61–80.

Mead, Andrew. 1999. "Bodily Hearing: Physiological Metaphors and Musical Understanding." *Journal of Music Theory* 43, no. 1 (Spring): 1–19.

Merleau-Ponty, Maurice. 1964. "An Unpublished Text by Maurice Merleau-Ponty: A Prospectus of His Work." Trans. Arleen B. Dallery. In *The Primacy of Perception and Other Essays on Phenomenological Psychology, the Philosophy of Art, History and Politics*, ed. James M. Edie, 3–11. Evanston, IL: Northwestern University Press.

Middleton, Richard. 1990. *Studying Popular Music.* Buckingham, UK: Open University Press.

Milhaud, Darius. 1924. "Les ressources nouvelles de la musique." *L'esprit nouveau* 25 (n.p.).

Miller, Paul D., aka DJ Spooky that Subliminal Kid. 2004a. "Algorithms: Erasures and the Art of Memory." In *Audio Culture: Readings in Modern Music*, ed. Christoph Cox and Daniel Warner, 348–354. New York: Continuum.

———. 2004b. *Rhythm Science.* Cambridge, MA: MIT Press.

Mills, Roger. 2010. "Dislocated Sound: A Survey of Improvisation in Networked Audio Platforms." *Proceedings of the 2010 Conference on New Interfaces for Musical Expression (NIME 2010)*, Sydney, Australia. http://www.educ.dab.uts.edu.au/nime/PROCEEDINGS/papers/Paper%20J1-J5/P186_Mills.pdf (accessed May 1, 2012).

Moore, Allan F. 2001. *Rock, the Primary Text: Developing a Musicology of Rock.* Aldershot, UK: Ashgate.

Moreno, Jairo. 1999. "Body'n'Soul? Voice and Movement in Keith Jarrett's Pianism." *Musical Quarterly* 83, no. 1 (Spring): 75–92.

Morse, Margaret. 1998. *Virtualities: Television, Media Art, and Cyberculture.* Bloomington: Indiana University Press.

Mumford, Lewis. 1964. "Authoritarian and Democratic Technics." *Technology and Culture* 5, no. 1 (Winter): 1–8.

Mumma, Gordon. 1972. Liner notes for "Hornpipe." On *Electric Sound*, by Sonic Arts Union (Mainstream Records MS 5010, LP).

———. 1975. "Live-Electronic Music." In *The Development and Practice of Electronic Music*, ed. Jon Appleton and Ronald Perera, 286–335. Englewood Cliffs, NJ: Prentice-Hall.

Murray, Noel. 2007. Interview with Jack White. *A.V. Club.* http://www.avclub.com/articles/jack-white,14117 (accessed May 1, 2012).

Neumann, Jaromir. 1962. *Titian, the Flaying of Marsyas.* London: Spring Books.

Norman, Katharine. 2004. *Sounding Art: Eight Literary Excursions through Electronic Music.* Aldershot, UK: Ashgate.

Oliveros, Pauline. 1984. "Tape Delay Techniques for Electronic Music Composers." In *Software for People: Collected Writings 1963–80*, 36–46. Baltimore: Smith Publications.

———. n.d. "Expanded Instrument System." *Deep Listening Institute.* http://deep-listening.org/site/content/expandedmusicalinstruments (accessed May 1, 2012).

———. n.d. "Telematic Circle." *Pauline Oliveros.* http://www.paulineoliveros.us/telematic-circle.html (accessed May 1, 2012).

Ostwald, Peter. 1997. *Glenn Gould: The Ecstasy and Tragedy of Genius.* New York: Norton.

Oswald, John. 2001b. "Revolutions and Mister Dolly Parton: A Vortex of Androgyny." Reproduction of article in Oswald and Igma (2001), 15.

Oswald, John, and Norman Igma. 2001. Untitled interview. Liner notes accompanying *Plunderphonics 69/96* (Pfony 069/96, 2 CDs).

Page, Tim. 2002. "Glenn Gould: A State of Wonder." Liner notes accompanying Gould (2002).

Pauli, Hansjörg. 1971. *Für wen komponieren Sie eigentlich?* Frankfurt: Fischer.

Parmenter, Ross. 1956. "Concert Is Given at Canadian Fete: Glenn Gould Is Piano Soloist, Conductor and Annotator of Program at Stratford." *New York Times*, July 10.

Payzant, Geoffrey. 1978. *Glenn Gould: Music and Mind.* Toronto: Van Nostrand Reinhold.

Pellman, Samuel. 1994. *Introduction to the Creation of Electroacoustic Music.* Belmont, CA: Wadsworth.

Perry, Andrew. 2003. "All Hail the New King and Queen of Rock!" Includes interview with the White Stripes. *Blender*, May: 104–109.

Phelan, Peggy. 1993. "The Ontology of Performance: Representation without Reproduction." In *Unmarked: The Politics of Performance*, 146–166. London: Routledge.

Philip, Robert. 2004. *Performing Music in the Age of Recording.* New Haven, CT: Yale University Press.

Pinch, Trevor, and Frank Trocco. 2002. *Analog Days: The Invention and Impact of the Moog Synthesizer.* Cambridge, MA: Harvard University Press.

Potter, Tully. 1996. Concert review of Midori and Joshua Bell. *Strad*, July: 734–735.

Poullin, Jacques. 1954. "L'apport des techniques d'enregistrement dans la fabrication de matières et de formes musicales nouvelles. Applications a la musique concrète." *L'Onde Électrique* 34/3 (March): 282–291.

———. 1957. "Son et espace." *La Revue Musicale* 236 ("Vers une musique expérimentale sous la direction de Pierre Schaeffer"): 105–114.

Rapp, Jürgen. 1987. "Tizians *Marsyas* in Kremsier." *Pantheon* 45: 70–89.

Rawson, Piers B. 1987. *The Myth of Marsyas in the Roman Visual Arts: An Iconographic Study.* Oxford: BAR International Series.

Read, Oliver, and Walter Welch. 1976. *From Tin Foil to Stereo: Evolution of the Phonograph*, 2nd ed. Indianapolis: Howard W. Sams and Bobbs-Merrill.

Reason, Matthew. 2006. "Young Audiences and Live Theatre, Part 2: Perceptions of Liveness in Performance." *Studies in Theatre and Performance* 26, no. 3: 221–241.

Reynolds, Simon. 2011. *Retromania: Pop Culture's Addiction to Its Own Past.* London: Faber and Faber.

Roberts, John P. L., ed. 1999. *The Art of Glenn Gould: Reflections of a Musical Genius.* Toronto: Malcolm Lester Books.

Russolo, Luigi. 1986. "The Art of Noises: Futurist Manifesto." In *The Art of Noises*, trans. and ed. Barclay Brown, 23–30. New York: Pendragon Press.

Saunders, J. B. de C. M., and Charles D. O'Malley. 1950. *The Illustrations from the Works of Andreas Vesalius of Brussels.* New York: Dover Publications.

Scapelliti, Christopher. 2004. "The House That Jack Built." Includes interview with Jack White. *Guitar World*, May. http://www.whitestripes.com/lo-fi/PDFs/GuitarWorld_May2004.pdf (accessed May 1, 2012).

Schafer, R. Murray. 1994. *The Soundscape: Our Sonic Environment and the Tuning of the World.* Rochester, VT: Destiny Books.

Schloss, Joseph. 2004. *Making Beats: The Art of Sample-Based Hip-Hop.* Middletown, CT: Wesleyan University Press.

Schonberg, Harold. 1959. "Colorful Canadian: Glenn Gould, Pianist, Presents Program." *New York Times*, February 14.

Schrader, Barry. 1982. *Introduction to Electro-Acoustic Music.* Englewood Cliffs, NJ: Prentice-Hall.

Schwartz, Elliot. 1975. *Electronic Music: A Listener's Guide*, rev. ed. New York: Praeger.

Shapiro, Peter. 2009. "Turntablism." In *The Wire Primers: A Guide to Modern Music*, ed. Rob Young, 103–109. London: Verso.

Shaughnessy, Mary Alice. 1993. *Les Paul: An American Original*. New York: William Morrow.

Shields, Rob. 2003. *The Virtual*. London: Routledge.

Shiga, John. 2007. "Copy-and-Persist: The Logic of Mash-Up Culture." *Critical Studies in Media Communication* 24, no. 2 (June): 93–114.

Shove, Patrick, and Bruno Repp. 1995. "Musical Motion and Performance: Theoretical and Empirical Perspectives." In *The Practice of Performance: Studies in Musical Interpretation*, ed. John Rink, 55–83. Cambridge: Cambridge University Press.

Sinnreich, Aram. 2010. *Mashed Up: Music, Technology, and the Rise of Configurable Culture*. Amherst: University of Massachusetts Press.

Small, Christopher. 1998. *Musicking: The Meanings of Performing and Listening*. Middletown, CT: Wesleyan University Press.

Smalley, Denis. 1986. "Spectro-morphology and Structuring Processes." In *The Language of Electroacoustic Music*, ed. Simon Emmerson, 61–93. Basingstoke, UK: Macmillan.

———. 1992. "The Listening Imagination: Listening in the Electroacoustic Era." In *Companion to Contemporary Musical Thought*, vol. 1, ed. John Paynter, Tim Howell, Richard Orton, and Peter Seymour, 514–554. London: Routledge.

Sonami, Laetitia. "Lady's Glove." http://www.sonami.net/lady_glove2.htm (accessed May 1, 2012).

Sousa, John Philip. 1993. "The Menace of Mechanical Music." *Computer Music Journal* 17, no. 1 (Spring): 14–18.

Sterne, Jonathan. 2003. *The Audible Past: Cultural Origins of Sound Reproduction*. Durham, NC: Duke University Press.

Stockhausen, Karlheinz. 1961. "Music in Space." Trans. Ruth Koenig. *Die Reihe 5* (English edition): 67–82.

———. 1995b. "Mikrophonie II (1965)." In liner notes accompanying Stockhausen 1995a, 73–97.

Strunk, Oliver. 1998. Introduction to "Beethoven's Instrumental Music," by E. T. A. Hoffmann. In *Source Readings in Music History*, rev. ed., ed. Oliver Strunk and Leo Treitler, 1193. New York: Norton.

Symes, Colin. 2004. *Setting the Record Straight: A Material History of Classical Recording*. Middletown, CT: Wesleyan University Press.

Taruskin, Richard. 1995. "On Letting the Music Speak for Itself." In *Text and Act*, 51–66. Oxford: Oxford University Press.

Tatnall, Edward. 1951. "Liveness in the Listening." *Saturday Review of Recordings*, June. Quoted in *From Tin Foil to Stereo: Evolution of the Phonograph*, 2nd ed., ed. Oliver Read and Walter Welch, 378. Indianapolis: Howard W. Sams and Bobbs-Merrill.

Taylor, Timothy. 1997. *Global Pop: World Music, World Markets*. London: Routledge.

———. 2001. *Strange Sounds: Music, Technology and Culture*. London: Routledge.

Temkin, Ann. 1983. "*Luce futurista*: Art for an Electric Age." In *The Futurist Imagination: Word + Image in Italian Futurist Painting, Drawing, Collage and Free-Word Poetry*, ed. Anne Coffin Hanson, 30–39. Exhibition catalogue, Yale University Art Gallery.

Théberge, Paul. 1989. "The 'Sound' of Music: Technological Rationalization and the Production of Popular Music." *New Formations* 8:99–111.

———. 1993. "Random Access: Music, Technology, Postmodernism." In *The Last Post: Music After Modernism*, ed. Simon Miller, 150–182. Manchester: Manchester University Press.

———. 1997. *Any Sound You Can Imagine: Making Music/Consuming Technology*. Hanover, NH: Wesleyan University Press and University Press of New England.

Thoresen, Lasse, and Andreas Hedman. 2007. "Spectromorphological Analysis of Sound Objects: An Adaptation of Pierre Schaeffer's Typomorphology." *Organised Sound* 12, no. 2 (August): 129–141.

Thornton, Sarah. 1995. *Club Cultures: Music, Media and Subcultural Capital.* London: Routledge.

Todd, Neil P. McAngus. 1995. "The Kinematics of Musical Expression." *Journal of the Acoustical Society of America* 97, no. 3 (March): 1940–1949.

Tomkins, Dave. 2010. *How to Wreck a Nice Beach: The Vocoder from World War II to Hip-Hop.* New York: Melville House.

Toop, David. 2004. *Haunted Weather: Music, Silence and Memory.* London: Serpent's Tail.

Toynbee, Jason. 2000. *Making Popular Music: Musicians, Creativity and Institutions.* London: Arnold.

Turner, Victor. 1974. *Dramas Fields and Metaphors.* Ithaca, NY: Cornell University Press.

Varèse, Edgard. 1998b. "The Liberation of Sound." In *Contemporary Composers on Contemporary Music*, expanded ed., ed. Elliot Schwartz and Barney Childs, 196–208. New York: Da Capo Press.

Waksman, Steve. 2010. "Les Paul: In Memoriam." *Popular Music and Society* 33, no. 2 (May): 269–273.

Walser, Robert. 1993. *Running with the Devil: Power, Gender, and Madness in Heavy Metal Music.* Hanover, NH: Wesleyan University Press.

Weidenaar, Reynold. 1995. *Magic Music from the Telharmonium.* Metuchen, NJ: Scarecrow Press.

Welch, Will. 2005. "The White Stripes." Includes interview with the White Stripes. *Fader*, July/August: 100–105.

Wexman, Virginia Wright, ed. 2003. *Film and Authorship.* New Brunswick, NJ: Rutgers University Press.

Windsor, Luke. 2000. "Through and Around the Acousmatic: The Interpretation of Electroacoustic Sounds." In *Music, Electronic Media and Culture*, ed. Simon Emmerson, 7–35. Aldershot, UK: Ashgate.

Wurtzler, Steve. 1992. "She Sang Live, but the Microphone Was Turned Off: The Live, the Recorded, and the *Subject* of Representation." In *Sound Theory Sound Practice*, ed. Rick Altman, 87–103. New York: Routledge.

Wyss, Edith. 1996. *The Myth of Apollo and Marsyas in the Art of the Italian Renaissance: An Inquiry into the Meaning of Images.* Newark: University of Delaware Press.

Index